© Copyright Clayton Goodwin 1986

All rights reserved. No reproduction, copy or transmission
of this publication may be made without written permission.
No paragraph of this publication may be reproduced, copied
or transmitted save with written permission or in accordance
with the provisions of the Copyright Act 1956 (as amended).
Any person who does any unauthorised act in relation to
this publication may be liable to criminal prosecution and
civil claims for damages.

First published 1986

Published by *Macmillan Publishers Ltd*
London and Basingstoke
*Associated companies and representatives in Accra,
Auckland, Delhi, Dublin, Gaborone, Hamburg, Harare,
Hong Kong, Kuala Lumpur, Lagos, Manzini, Melbourne,
Mexico City, Nairobi, New York, Singapore, Tokyo*

ISBN 0–333–40256–1

Printed in Hong Kong

British Library Cataloguing in Publication Data
Goodwin, Clayton
    West Indians at the wicket.
    1. Cricket — West Indians — History
    I. Title
    796.35'8'09729   GV928.W/

ISBN 0–333–40256–1

Photograph acknowledgements
The authors and publishers wish to acknowledge, with thanks, the
following photographic sources.
Y. Chan   p 13
Patrick Eagar   pp 1; 2; 3; 4; 5; 6; 7; 8 centre; 9 right; 10; 11 insert; 12; 13
insert; 14; 15 insert; 16 insert
The Gleaner Company Limited, Jamaica   p 11
Keystone Press Agency Ltd   p 9 left and centre
Cosmos Phillips   p 15
Fitzroy Rogers   p 16
The publishers have made every effort to trace the copyright holders, but if
they have inadvertently overlooked any, they will be pleased to make the
necessary arrangements at the first opportunity.

West Indians at the Wicket

Clayton Goodwin

Foreword by Clive Lloyd

MACMILLAN CARIBBEAN

Contents

Foreword

by Clive Lloyd

For just over ten years I had the privilege of playing in, and leading, one of the most successful teams ever to play Test Match cricket. In that time we defeated each of our principal opponents, and did so often by such decisive margins that people everywhere have come to think immediately of the West Indies when they talk about cricket. Apart from the natural joy of batting, fielding, bowling and taking decisions I have had the pleasure of being involved when history has been made.

It hasn't always been easy — however much it may seem to be so from the outside. So many people over the years have contributed to that success. There have always been great cricketers in the West Indies, but for many years conditions were against them. Take just one example. The battery of fast bowlers has been a key factor in our success. Yet who knows what could have been achieved if the great fast bowlers of the 1930s had been able to play together more often.

The heroes of the past have given us something to aim at. Just as I hope that we have encouraged the youth of today. People need heroes, and in the Caribbean we have had plenty. Everybody has heard of Learie Constantine, Gary Sobers, George Headley and Frank Worrell. Even so there have been many others whose memory lies more in their good name and reputation than in the record books. It has been so everywhere in the region.

The present side has been something special, and every member deserves consideration with the best in history. Whether it has been the greatest side ever is another matter. The experts will always argue that one, and I am not going to involve myself in that debate.

It would be wrong of me to pick out one match or one player for special attention. That wouldn't be fair, and it isn't possible. Everyone has their own memories. Taken together they make an impressive picture. One thing is certain — it is no longer possible for writers to patronise us as the brilliant but erratic calypso cricketers.

West Indians at the Wicket covers most of the important events, probably all of them. It describes the game through the careers of the players, and gives some indication of why the West Indies have become so popular. Each member of the side is a personality in his own right. Each has a particular skill to contribute to the overall team performance.

More than that, the book shows the background, a glimpse of the social conditions and domestic competition which has forged that character. It pays tribute to the tradition handed down from one generation to the next, and the next, and manages to say something about the issues that have swayed its development and to take each part of the region into consideration, and that isn't always easy.

A lot has happened since I played my first innings in a Test Match, scoring 82 and 78 not out at Bombay in December 1966, and led the West Indies for the first time at Bangalore almost exactly eight years later. They were favourite moments for me, two of several. What has been your favourite moments? As likely as not you will find it recorded in *West Indians at the Wicket*.

Thank you for sharing these few thoughts with me. I hope that this book gives you as much pleasure to read, as it has obviously given Clayton to write, and as the events have given to my colleagues and myself in participating on the field of play.

Preface

The West Indies have dominated world cricket in the past decade. They have beaten each of their opponents in both conventional matches and in the various forms of limited-over competition, and have been undefeated at home. The manner of that success cannot be measured solely in terms of results and statistics. Great and exciting batting, memorable and enthralling fast bowling, and superlative fielding has been impressed indelibly on the minds of all privileged to have been there or to have followed events through the medium of television, radio or newspaper reports. The names, like those of the captains at Agincourt, according to Shakespeare in King Henry V, have become familiar in our mouths as household words.

Yet the present generation could not have attained such consistent success without the traditions, inspiration, artistry and example of those that went before. It has not been a continuous progress. There have been so many ups and downs. Each member has brought to the team an unconscious echo of his past. The cricket of any country is difficult to understand without an appreciation of history, and for the West Indies it is impossible. We seek to look at some of the trends, the events and personalities along the way, which have led up to the victorious West Indies side of such recent recall.

West Indian cricketers, above all, cannot be confined to statistics or mere chronology. This is no history. It is more a catalogue of impressions around selected themes. There is injustice in that more attention has not been given to the contributions of George Headley, Learie Constantine, S.G. Smith, even the three Ws and Gary Sobers, or Deryck Murray, but their performances and personality have been documented well and are steadfast in the recollection of those that saw them. Everybody has their favourite cricketer, or an incident which lingers in the memory. Our purpose will have been served to a substantial extent even if this book only stimulates the reader to reflect fondly on what has been omitted.

In paying tribute to the several accomplished authors, and their

vi

work in books and articles, we admit that it is impossible for us to provide anything like an adequate coverage in depth of the individual territories. Nevertheless the day-to-day Jamaican enthusiast may know little of the club traditions, the legends and the personalities of Barbados or Trinidad, and vice versa, and those living outside the region, including the children of emigrants to the United Kingdom and to North America, are hardly aware of the present shape of the game in the Caribbean. It is anticipated that most readers will know more about the topic than is contained in some of the chapters but it is hoped that they will find the others useful in adding to their knowledge and experience.

West Indians at the Wicket originated from a conversation with Bill Lennox, the Caribbean Manager of Macmillan, during a lull in the play early in the Test Match at Lord's in June 1984. Just a couple of days later Gordon Greenidge hit his sparkling double-century, one of the most spectacular innings of international cricket, and it became even more obvious that such performances needed to be recorded for those who could not be present. That knock stimulated much discussion and the inevitable comparison with outstanding batting of the past. Where conversation after, before and during the match provide much of the enjoyment of the game, the action on the pitch is really only the tip of the ice-berg.

Our impressions of the game, and the locations in which it is played, are obtained, apart from our own personal experiences, from conversations with friends and from books. In many cases the books, themselves, have become as friends. Wherever possible we have tried to include those observations of other writers which have played a particular part in shaping my own appreciation, whether it has been in childhood, in the travel between matches, or in quiet nights at the hotel, and are grateful for their permission to quote from the works. The observations may be sometimes different to my own, but they are always complementary.

Because it is useful to have a common point of reference particular attention has been paid to one book, *Cricket in Many Climes* by Pelham Warner, for a consistent picture of the situation at the turn of the century, to *Through the Caribbean* by Alan Ross for that of the era 1959/60, and to the recollections of my contemporaries and myself for more modern times. Other books may give as good a description of an individual time or territory without relevance to the entire region. Johnny Moyes' description of the visit of Frank Worrell's side to Australia remains, in my opinion, one of the best books on a single tour. Wisden, as usual, has been invaluable in checking details and in sifting fact from fond illusion.

My unconscious judgement must have been influenced by the comments and opinions of those with whom the time has been passed at Test Matches and at all games of cricket in the Caribbean and England. If no specific acknowledgement has been given to Tony Becca, John Figueroa, Tony Cozier, Louis Braithwaite, Reg Scarlett, Geoff Cameron, Robert Best, Colin Cumberbatch, Reds Perreira, Bernard Pantin or Lionel St. Aubyn, they are invited to take consolation in knowing that they have contributed much to the overall understanding and that there is always a drink waiting for them, on the understanding that, hopefully, the hospitality will be reciprocated. The observations of the players, themselves, at all levels of the game, are usually perceptive and as always appreciated, as are those of taxi-drivers, bar-tenders and enthusiasts Winston Dalrymple, John Hanson, Philip Howell, Frank David, Cedric Best, Ricky Clarke and so many more, who make a point of passing on regularly their views and assessment.

One

Cricket Through the Region

In view of the vast distances between territories in the region, and the variations of culture, history and geography, the similarities in the development of the game of cricket in Barbados, Trinidad, Jamaica and Guyana are more remarkable than the differences. The same factors, however, have given cricket in the Caribbean a character completely unlike the pattern of domestic competition almost everywhere else in the world. In England, Australia, India, New Zealand and, initially, Pakistan the county, state or province has provided a tier of competition between that of club and country.

The West Indies Test Match team is regional, not national. Geography, the several hundred miles between territories and the small size of the islands, precluded for many years extensive inter-territorial competition, so that club cricket has thrived here as it has not done so anywhere else. Until the institution of the Shell Shield competition two decades ago, and often since then, a West Indian cricketer would cite his first-class debut as being his first game in his island's premier internal tournament rather than an initial appearance for his country.

Cricket was carried to the Caribbean, as it was to many other parts of the world, during the increased military and commercial activity immediately before and after the Napoleonic Wars. It was a time of much change and the development of new national identities. Some territories had already long-established ties with the United Kingdom, and others had been acquired as colonies only recently from the French and their Spanish allies. Barbados had been associated with Britain since it was colonised in 1627 — the island has the third oldest surviving House of Assembly in the western hemisphere, and the game had taken root there several years before the dawn of the nineteenth century.

There is a recorded reference to a meeting of St Anne's Cricket Club in Barbados in 1806, and similar clubs were established in Guyana, Trinidad and Jamaica before the mid-century. Throughout the

1

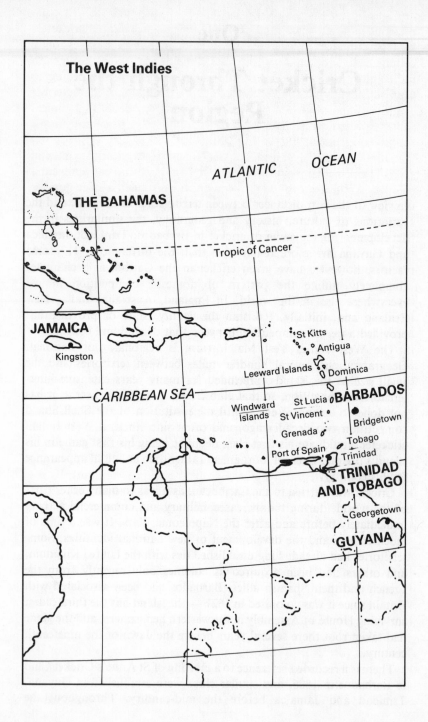

The West Indies

ATLANTIC OCEAN

THE BAHAMAS

Tropic of Cancer

JAMAICA

Kingston

St Kitts
Antigua
Leeward Islands
Dominica

CARIBBEAN SEA

Windward Islands
St Lucia
St Vincent
Grenada
BARBADOS
Bridgetown
Tobago

Port of Spain
Trinidad
TRINIDAD AND TOBAGO

Georgetown

GUYANA

previous hundred years, and probably longer, experienced cricketers from England had called at the islands in pursuit of their professional, commercial and military interests, and must have brought a rudimentary understanding of the game with them. According to Charles Dickens in 'The Pickwick Papers', the fictional character Mr Jingle had appeared in a single-wicket match, probably in Jamaica, some years earlier. Such an incident would not have been hard for his readers to accept.

Barbados and Guyana met in the first inter-territorial games in 1865. The principal players were the white commercial entrepreneurs, colonial administrators and army and navy personnel, a large number of whom had club, county or college experience in England. Lord Harris and Sir Pelham Warner, both born in Trinidad, looked to the 'old country' for their education and identification. By the time that the first touring sides arrived in the late 1890s, however, black professional bowlers were of sufficient importance to make the difference between success and failure.

Cricket was developed by the military classes — the first inter-territorial games in Georgetown were played at The Parade Ground and others in Barbados at the Garrison Savannah — the church, and the educational establishments. The real backbone of early competition was provided by the cricket clubs, as, indeed, it is still today. Wanderers C.C. of Barbados, the island's oldest surviving club, was founded in 1877, five years ahead of Pickwick, the great rivals against and by whom so many records have been established

In their first fully recorded game the Wanderers, victors over the Royal Artillery the previous Saturday, had the better of H.M.S. Rover whom they dismissed for 19 (C. Bascom and Rev. T. Clarke sharing the wickets) and replied with 94 (Pile contributing 33 not out). By the end of the 1880s Wanderers and Pickwick were joined in competition by clubs such as Garrison, Combermere, Alleyne School and Codrington School, all rich in memories and associations.

Harold Austin and George Challenor were among the several top West Indian cricketers who played for Wanderers in the earlier years. More recent Test Match representatives have included Roy and Norman Marshall, Denis and Eric Atkinson, Robin Bynoe, David Allan, Richard Edwards and Keith Boyce. Milton Small, who came into the regional side so swiftly against the Australians in 1984, and Mike Worrell, the brilliant young wicketkeeper raised in England, have been foremost in the younger generation. Clubs in each of the other territories have similar records of excellence and tradition dating from about the same time.

The early English visitors were often surprised by the standard of

3

play in the islands. Although Pelham Warner etched no description of the game in Jamaica because Lord Hawke's side did not include that country in its itinerary, their predecessors under R. Slade Lucas lost to an all Jamaican side in 1895. Nevertheless, the westerners did not always give a good account of themselves in those early exchanges. Lord Brackley's side played and drew the first three-day match there in 1905 and won the second by a massive innings margin. Four years later a Philadelphian team from the U.S.A. won two out of three fixtures against the island.

Jamaica held the first M.C.C. team to a tie, the first in the region, in 1910/11, a season in which the elder J.K. Holt, the Fosters and Charles Morrison made a good impression on the visitors. Sidney Smith, the Trinidadian allrounder who had performed so well on the West Indian tour to England in 1906 that he stayed on to play for Northamptonshire, was the M.C.C.'s most successful bowler. Just after the First World War the Kingston C.C., which had already scored over three hundred runs to just seven by Spanish Town in 1872, ran up 500-7 in one day against St. Catherine C.C. in 1921, in which Ernest Rae, Karl Nunes and George Da Costa were the chief scorers.

Because there was so little inter-territorial competition early touring teams had to be chosen on trust and balance. The strong side which went to England in 1923 comprised five Trinidadians, four Barbadians, four Guianese, and three Jamaicans. Local enthusiasts could not understand some of the selections and considered, for example, that Wilton St Hill of Trinidad and Herman Griffith of Barbados should have been taken. Nevertheless the team performed well and whatever selection had been made would have disappointed somebody.

C.L.R. James has captured in *Beyond a Boundary* the flavour of club cricket in Trinidad at this time. Membership depended to a considerable degree on social status, and, therefore, inevitably on colour. Queen's Park, the controlling influence in the island's cricket, was for the white and wealthy. Shamrock was the club of the old Catholic families. 'I would have been more easily elected to the M.C.C. than to either' the author exclaims. Constabulary was drawn from the exclusively white inspectorate.

Stingo was the club of the black working-class, tradesmen and unemployed. Maple drew members from the brown middle-class, and Shannon from the black middle-class, clerks and teachers. With such clear lines of identification it is easy to understand how matches were supported with such partisan fervour. The younger generation, less inclined to accept the established social strata, was influenced also by the standard of cricket, and this attraction was generally socially

4

'downwards'. It is difficult to accept that this hide-bound establishment was the first in the region to give black cricketers a chance to perform against touring sides.

James explains that he deliberated long over which club he should join and, in spite of inner misgivings, was persuaded eventually to join Maple on the advice of the father of Clifford Roach, the celebrated opening batsman, on the grounds that he should not let his feelings override the fact that Maple's members included the people he was going to meet in life.

'My decision cost me a great deal .... Faced with the fundamental divisions in the island, I had gone to the right and, by cutting myself off from the popular side, delayed my political development for years'

The writer observed the preference for white batsmen and black bowlers.

'The next generation of black men bowling fast was more sure of itself. In actual fact it produced the greatest of them all, George John. World War 1 interrupted his international career as it interrupted George Challenor's. These two, the gentleman and the player, the white batsman and the black bowler, were the two finest cricketers the West Indies had produced up to this time, and the most characteristic. John was a man of the people, and an emigrant from one of the most backward of the smaller islands .... John incarnated the plebs of his time, their complete independence from the values and aspirations that competed in the spheres above'.

Learie Constantine, the best-known cricketer to come out of Trinidad's club cricket in the early 1920s, was the son of Lebrun Constantine, a tower of strength for Shannon and the first West Indian batsman to score a century at Lord's. Old Cons was the most famous cricketer in the country and Major Bertie Harragin, the patrician of the period with and against whom the father had played, noted a spark of the same inspiration in the son. The youngster went to England in 1923 and, more than anybody else, represented Caribbean cricket in the eyes of the world.

In club competitions reputations could be made and lost in an afternoon. Constantine has described in Wisden how the young Wilton St. Hill, then unknown and casual, took on the bowling of the mighty Stingo, including George John, and with suppleness of wrist rather than muscular power despatched the ball to every part of the boundary. This young man, one of the first successful black batsmen, became a national hero and his memory still evokes a reverence which is difficult to understand from any assessment based solely on his below-par international record.

In Barbados the rivalry between Wanderers and Pickwick generated a crescendo of runs which reached a peak in two remarkable matches at the turn of 1920 and 1921. In the first encounter Wanderers reached 465-4 dec through a double-century from George Challenor and a single hundred by Ince; in reply Tarilton was undefeated on 139 in taking Pickwick to 320-3. In the second match George Challenor, making 206 and 133, and Ince with a century in each innings overwhelmed Pickwick for whom Tarilton and C.A. Wood reached three figures.

From its inception in 1892/93 to 1927 the island's 1st Division Cup was won by Pickwick seventeen times, Wanderers, eleven times, and Spartan four times. Then Harrison College broke the stranglehold of these three teams, and Empire won the honour twice in consecutive seasons in the mid-1930s. Competition was becoming more open as social conditions changed and new paths to recognition became available. In view of the country's renowned, almost notorious, excellent batting conditions the performances of the bowlers were especially commendable.

The Empire pitch at Bank Hall was an exception and provided fair encouragement to the club's fast bowling attack. Herman Griffith, who formed an effective partnership for island and region with George Francis, whose bowling in the nets had inspired Austin's confidence and won him preference in 1923, was one of the best bowlers for the West Indies in the early Test Matches. His club career overlapped with that of Manny Martindale, the spearhead of the regional attack in the 1930s. Their pace was supplemented by that of Foffie Williams, who played in Test Matches before and after the Second World War, and of Pampie Spooner.

Continued club and inter-territorial competition in the war years, when the game was suspended almost everywhere else, encouraged the growth of the splendid stroke-players of the late 1940s who gave England such a shock when international cricket was resumed. After Combermere's victory in 1940/41 no club won the 1st Division Cup in Barbados outright for two years in succession, though Carlton and Spartan had a share of the trophy in consecutive years, until Wanderers completed a hat-trick of wins from 1959 to 1961.

The career and cosmopolitan background of George Headley demonstrates just how similar, and different, was the game in Jamaica. He was born in Panama to a Barbadian mother and Jamaican father and spent his childhood years in Cuba. His early expectation of emigration was based on the U.S.A. rather than on the United Kingdom, as it would have been if he had lived in the eastern islands. In his youth he participated in baseball and Passailaique, with whom he shared so many fruitful partnerships, was also a regular baseball player.

Jamaican batting was particularly strong. Frank Martin hit 204 not out against L.H. Tennyson's team in 1927, but even that innings was dwarfed by the undefeated stand of 487, a world record for the sixth wicket between Headley, 344 not out, and Passailaique, 261 not out, when his lordship returned with another side five years later. England's huge 849 runs total at Sabina Park in the Fourth Test Match of 1930 was unusual but hardly out of keeping with the prevalent high scoring.

Although Headley, at least, deserved and received selection wherever the West Indies played, Jamaica's remoteness from the rest of the region was underlined by that season's team composition. 'Mass George' was the island's only representative in the three earlier matches, but no fewer than six others — Nunes, Martin, Ivan Barrow, Passailaique, Tommy Scott, Oscar Da Costa and George Gladstone (Marais) — joined him in the side at Kingston. In 1935 two Jamaicans, Headley and Leslie Hylton, travelled to the Test Matches in the eastern territories.

It is not surprising, therefore, that Jamaicans considered the tussles between Lucas C.C., whose players included Headley and Hylton as well as Kenny 'Bam Bam' Weekes who scored an explosive hundred at The Oval in London in one of his only two Test Matches before the Second World War curtailed his international career, Kensington C.C., Kingston C.C. and Melbourne C.C., which had real relevance to their allegiances, to be the ones which really mattered. Those of their compatriots chosen for the West Indies tours did not always spring immediately from the local population. John Cameron, whose father had gone to England with Austin in 1906, was picked as vice-captain and spin bowler in 1939 on the strength of his university and county performance in that country, and his brother, Jimmy, was at study in North America when the call came for him to go to India in 1948/49.

At that time Trinidad was still then the place in which to catch the regional selectors' eye. Family connections and traditions were important not so much in ensuring that an untalented player was included but more in giving a gifted youngster the platform on which to demonstrate his skill at the earliest opportunity. The Warner and Constantine dynasties were replaced by the families of the Grants, two of whom captained the West Indies consecutively, and the Stollmeyers. Six of the eleven who played in the Test Match at The Oval in London in 1939 were Trinidadian, four of them batsmen.

Tyrell Johnson, the only specialist fast bowler — Constantine being an allrounder, took a wicket with his first ball in his only Test Match. Jeff Stollmeyer looked back in his book *Everything under the Sun* on the controversy surrounding the selection of himself, an inexperienced teenager, for that tour:

'There no doubt was a certain amount of hit and miss but, as things turned out, it was not those who were criticised most who were the biggest failures. Of the Trinidadians who missed out, the most unfortunate were Cyril A. Merry and R.P. Tang Choon. The former, blooded in 1933 when he probably did not deserve selection, was now without doubt the best batsman in Trinidad. Experienced, mature and with a resounding cover drive, I can conclude that if he had been selected I would have been omitted'.

The youngster came back from England with his reputation enhanced by the two substantial partnerships he shared with Headley in the two Test Matches in London. He continued to prosper during the war years so that only he and Gerry Gomez of that team played regularly through the first international series after the war in 1947/48. Victor Stollmeyer, his brother, who captained the island in the early 1940s, was stumped for 96 in his only Test Match innings.

The wartime inter-territorial matches provided many batting records. The outstanding exception occurred at Kensington in 1942. Aided by the effect of the sun drying a rain-soaked pitch Derek Sealy, who had played for the West Indies as a wicketkeeper and batsman, routed Trinidad for just 16 runs, in which there were eight ducks, by taking 8 wickets for 8 runs. Tom Pierce, the home captain and later regional manager, held five catches at short leg.

Jeff Stollmeyer and Gerry Gomez made several double-centuries between them, and in 1947 they put on 434 for the third wicket against British Guiana at Queen's Park, of which the former made 324. By this time, however, chief batting attention had moved to Barbados, for whom Frank Worrell, 308 not out, and John Goddard, 218 not out, set a new record fourth-wicket stand of 502 runs against Trinidad at Kensington, and two years later Clyde Walcott, 314 not out, and Worrell, 255 not out, added 574 for the same wicket against the same opponents in Port of Spain.

The structure of Barbadian competition gave young cricketers an early chance to prove themselves. In his book *Cricket Punch* Frank Worrell recalled:

'I enrolled at Combermere School ... which meant first-class cricket, for the schools take part in first-class cricket in Barbados. The school teams are made up of both pupils and

8

masters, and we had on our staff Derek Sealy ... but even with a former Test star on your side, it was a bit tough for a thirteen year-old boy to be playing in top-grade cricket. Nevertheless, it was great experience, I found myself up against some of the best players in the West Indies, and there is no better way of learning anything than by coming up against the finest exponents'.

Walcott was in the Combermere side at the same time before moving to Harrison College. Everton Weekes, however, came to the fore during his service with the Barbados battalion of the Caribbean Regiment. His potential was recognised by Teddy Hoad, captain of the West Indies in the first home Test Match at Kensington in 1930, and moved into the Barbadian batting to replace Worrell, who had emigrated to Jamaica.

Sonny Ramadhin and Alfred Valentine, the young spinners who made such an impact on their first tour to England in 1950, demonstrated that there were still short-cuts to the top outside established club competition. The former was included in the pre-tour trials after bowling consistently well for the Trinidad Leaseholds Oil Company and impressed sufficiently to be preferred to Ferguson who seemed to have made the position his own. The selectors were even more perspicacious in spotting Valentine's potential because he had no success in the trials.

The M.C.C. tour of the West Indies in 1947/48, the first to the islands for 13 years, was a disappointment in spite of the success. Clyde Walcott explained in *Island Cricketers*:

'M.C.C. sent out a weak side, which was further weakened by a crop of injuries, and for the first time in cricket history M.C.C. went through a tour without winning a match. There is no doubt in my mind that M.C.C. seriously under-estimated the strength of West Indian cricket. Many key players ... couldn't be bothered to play cricket against lowly West Indies'.

The insult, whether or not it was intended, rankled with players and public and goes a long way towards explaining the jubilation of subsequent victories over the country which had treated them so disdainfully. The disappointment was particularly sharp then because the domestic first-class programme was suspended during this tour by an overseas team. The game against the visitors and the following Test Match provided the only opportunity for islanders to see top-level cricket.

The writing was soon on the wall as Taylor, Walcott and Weekes made hundreds as Barbados amassed 514-4 dec in the opening engagement in Bridgetown. Trinidad treated the bowlers with similar ease, Andy Ganteaume, Gomez and Rupert Tang Choon reached three figures in making 481-4 dec. Jamaica, for whom Colin Bonitto and Ken Rickard scored centuries, also declared, so that the tourists must have welcomed the rain in British Guiana ... which did not fall until after Peter Bayley had posted another hundred.

Guyana has a similar framework of youth and senior club competition. Clive Lloyd made his debut in the Case Cup at Bourda for Demarara C.C. against the Georgetown C.C., whose bowling included territorial representative Norman Wight. Although fast-medium bowler Berkeley Gaskin, who achieved even greater fame as a selector, manager and administrator, had played for the West Indies in 1947/48, no batsman from Demarara C.C. had been selected for the region. It was an incentive to succeed.

Even though he had been invited to the territorial trials after hitting a record run aggregate in the Case Cup competition, Lloyd was kept out of the side for some time by the selectors and by the weather. The standard of domestic competition was so high because the best cricketers had no other outlets for their talents. As a result a run of good scores over an extended period against such good quality bowling was the most sure way of making a correct impression. Batsman Andrew Lyght, as well as former international opener Roy Fredericks, fast bowler Colin Croft and the Harper brothers have come from the same Demarara C.C.

Walcott came to British Guiana in late 1954 as cricket organiser and coach on the estates of the British Guiana Sugar Producers' Association. Six of the players he coached were in the territory's side which won the quadrangular knockout tournament two years later. Many of the newcomers came from the Port Moraunt estate, where Robert Christiani, the former Test Match cricketer, was employed. Berbice, whose side included Joe Solomon. Rohan Kanhai and Basil Butcher and contained a high proportion of East Indian descent, was sufficiently strong to have its own match against the Englishmen in 1960.

Barbados were not successful in their challenge to the Rest of the World in the game at Kensington in March 1967 to mark the country's attainment of political independence. As the West Indies had just completed decisive victories over Australia, England and India, and as Barbados had won the newly-instituted Shell regional tournament for the second successive time, it was assumed widely that the island could hold its own as an international entity.

After the visitors had scored a commendable 308 against Wesley Hall, Charlie Griffith and Gary Sobers, the home batting fell apart for only 84 runs before the pace of Graeme McKenzie, the Australian new-ball bowler, and spinners Lance Gibbs and Mustaq Mohammad.

Wicketkeeper John Murray, following his hundred for England against the West Indies at The Oval in London the previous summer, hit 121 in putting the Rest of the World 500 runs ahead. Although the island fared better at the second attempt not one of this powerful batting side reached fifty in the match in which they went down by 262 runs.

The Shell Shield tournament, founded in the mid-1960s, was the first successful attempt to bring together the four conventional territories, and the smaller islands, into a proper competition. Hitherto first-class matches had been limited to some of the less regular tournaments involving Barbados, Trinidad and British Guiana (occasionally Jamaica), occasional bi-lateral fixtures, and contests against touring teams. Contemporary Shell Shield standards have been impaired by the absence of so many top cricketers on the region's increasingly frequent overseas tours.

Commercial sponsorship has led to a spectacular expansion in top-level competition. The Geddes Grant/Harrison Line Trophy is the premier limited-overs promotion, and the Neal & Massy Youth Tournament provides extended scope from which to pick up the stars of the future. The Texaco Beaumont Cup is contested in Trinidad, the Jones Cup in Guyana, and there are specific Windward Islands and Leeward Islands Tournaments. Because of the nature of such sponsorship the names of the competitions may be changed, or presentation may not always be regular, but good quality cricket now reaches every corner of the region.

The capital cities continue to be the cricket centre in each country. In Jamaica, the largest island and, therefore, the one in which the outlying districts are more remote from the centre, the difference between town and country is felt most strongly. In 1957 the Duke of Norfolk took a team of first-class cricketers which played at Prospect, Monymusk, Montego Bay, Frome and St Antonio as well as at the established national grounds at Sabina Park and Melbourne Park in Kingston.

Even now few of the island's regional representatives have come from outside the major clubs of the corporate area. Whereas it is argued effectively that the urban district acts as a natural magnet for those country cricketers with the right ambition and temperament, the point is not appreciated always by the few on the outside. The chief complaint is that the provincials are not accorded parity of treatment rather than of opportunity. A rural rude boy remains just that, while for the same offence a youth from an established Kingston club may be considered merely limmature and likely to improve.

The Neal & Massy Youth Tournament in 1983 provided an

11

opportunity to involve several venues in Kingston — Kensington Park, Melbourne Park, the Police Grounds and the Army Grounds — and the final, in which the home side suffered defeat by an innings and 230 runs to the fast bowling of the Barbadians Ricardo Ellcock and Milton Small, was presented at the Alparts Ground, St Elizabeth. The 1984 Australians went to Montego Bay, and so did the rain, and limited-overs games have been staged outside Sabina Park. The balance, though, is difficult to maintain.

The pent-up arthusiansm of the Leeward and Windward Islands had burst forth in a blaze of activity from Grenada in the south to St Kitts-Nevis in the north. Shell Shield matches are played at Mindoo Philip Park-Castries, Warner Park — Basseterre, Arnos Vale — St Vincent, Queen's Park — St George's, Windsor Park — Dominica, Grove Park — Nevis, and Sturge Park — Montserrat. Matches against touring teams, including limited-overs representative contests, are varied from location to location. Trinidad and Guyana now organise first-class games at Guaracara Park, Pointe-a-Pierre and Albion, Berbice respectively.

It is now almost impossible, at least in theory, for any youngster with real ability to fall through the net. The series of tours and representative matches between the West Indies Young Cricketers and the England Young Cricketers has given the first taste of international competition to several who have progressed to play in Test Matches. The first team went to England with financial backing from the Sir Frank Worrell Memorial Fund in 1970 and the visit was reciprocated two years later.

The first international matches took place in 1974. In that initial series Jeffrey Dujon and Wayne Daniel helped the West Indians to win by two victories to nil, but England won both of the fixtures in the Caribbean in 1976. Mike Gatting enjoyed great allround success and was supported by Chris Cowdrey in the batting, and Paul Downton who kept wicket. Winston Davis bowled well for the home side in the match in Trinidad.

There are too many private, semi-official and even official tours between the two regions to list even the most significant. Barbadian sides, as may be expected, are in the forefront. From the seemingly innumerable brochures, that of Ricks Cavaliers C.C. tour to England and Geneva in 1980, picked up at London, shows that the best-known member was Gregory Armstrong of the Empire club who made his debut for Barbados in 1974 but, in spite of some years with Glamorgan in the English county championship, did not make the international progress that had been expected of him.

The Desmond Haynes Cavaliers which went to England in 1984

contained an even better balance of promise and proven ability. The side was drawn extensively from St James parish on the western coast and gave untested youngsters the opportunity to play alongside and to learn from the celebrities of yesteryear, including fast bowler Charlie Griffith and off-spinner Albert Padmore. Hartley Alleyne and Collis King, also, represented the team in the three weeks tour which did much to stimulate interest in the West Indian community of the United Kingdom.

With so many competitions between and within the territories, and the giving and receiving of tours at almost every level of the game, it is somewhat sobering to remember that the first touring team to the region from the U.S.A. in 1887, returning a West Indian visit to North America in the previous year, dismissed the West Indies for a mere 19 runs. In cricket development a mere hundred years has been a very long time, and it is impossible to surmise where and how the game will be played a century hence.

Two

The West Indian Cricketer

The international concept of the supposedly typical Caribbean cricketer has changed considerably over the years, and yet it has remained very much the same. This contradiction derives more from the success attained on the pitch, and the accompanying respect, rather than from any variation in character. The present efficient professional is not that far removed from the so-called calypso cricketer, symbolised by brilliant though brittle batting, which lay more in the mind of the beholder than in reality. The distinctive vein of application has been always there. George Headley was no less disciplined than his successors. The grace of Stollmeyer, and Rae's watchfulness have complemented their colleagues' more full-blooded stroke-play. The conditions, the experience and the times have moved on.

From its inception West Indian cricket has contained ingredients of its own: traits which have contributed to the supremacy of recent years. Cricket is a game for the entire community, man, woman and child, rich and poor, across the whole age spectrum. Children are involved integrally in a way that is no longer so elsewhere. Coaching is more by experience and example than by textbook teaching. Celebrities of the past remain on hand to inspire with advice, intuition and encouragement. The essence of Caribbean cricket is seen most clearly in the careers and character of those cricketers who have come to embody that ideal most closely.

Collie Smith is the forgotten hero of the 'middle ages', namely the late 1950s. His premature death in a motor accident in England in September 1959 and the mass attendance at his funeral in Jamaica has obscured the memory of the contribution made while he lived. He was the contemporary of Gary Sobers and Rohan Kanhai, and lost nothing in comparison. The eulogies of his obituary give some indication of the affection in which he was held and the spirit which he brought to the game.

Sir Kenneth Blackburne, the then Governor of Jamaica, said:

'The name of Collie Smith will long live as an example not only of a fine cricketer, but also of a great sportsman. He will provide inspiration for our youth in the future'.

J.F. Dare, the President of the West Indies Board of Control, commented:

'He was one of a diminishing band who play a game for the game's sake and he had a great future before him'.

Gerry Alexander, captain of the West Indies at the time of his death, stated:

'His passing is a tremendous loss to those of us who came to realise what a wonderful spirit of cricket he was'.

His rise from Boys' Town to the West Indies was remarkable. He was selected for Jamaica only in 1955 and that same year scored 169 for the island against the Australians, which won him selection for the First Test Match at Sabina Park. There Smith made 104 on his debut, but was dropped swiftly after failing to score in either innings of the next match. To his credit he bounced back from that disappointment and often did particularly well when his colleagues failed. In England in 1957, Collie hit 161 in the run-feast at Birmingham and made a stubborn 168 to prevent defeat almost single-handed at Nottingham.

E.W. Swanton summed up his career:

'One does not, however, think of him in terms of figures and records. He was a happy cricketer with the broadest of grins, whose pleasure in the game infected everyone .... He was extremely popular with his opponents, and I can scarcely think of a young contemporary cricketer who was better company or who had a more admirable approach to the game'.

Children are born into cricket in the Caribbean. It is a continuing process. In such close communities the great players of yesterday are still a vital part of the social fabric, on hand to advise, consent and criticise. Current celebrities mingle with the public in an informal manner which would be impossible almost anywhere else. West Indians living abroad may well still identify their place of birth as being within so many yards of where such-and-such famous cricketer learned his art, or a mile or so from the home of a well-known batsman or bowler.

It is easy enough for boys to pitch make-shift wickets in an urban side-street, by a countryside clearing or on the seashore without the threat of prolonged interruption or physical danger from excessive motorised traffic moving at speed. There is no need to seek a specific, officially-recognised pitch. Cricket is brought to the community. Adults are on hand to provide encouragement and to participate. In this casual manner sub-teenagers may have their first experience of sharing a bat-ball knockabout with experienced players, whereas elsewhere they have to work up to that stage through the various tiers of formal competition.

Softball, played by even first-class cricketers when they join in, stimulates confidence in batting against even the fastest bowling, taking catches from the face of the bat, without the fear of injury. Youngsters have time to master fluency in stroke-play and anticipation in the field before they are introduced to the hard ball. The vagaries of street or cracked-earth pitches teach quick reflexes, the ability to change stroke and to improvise.

There are local variations of the game 'firms'. The batsman continues his innings until he is dismissed, at which point his place is taken by the person, whether bowler or fieldsman, who has effected his dismissal. As a result bowlers have to attack the stumps rather than to maintain a defensive length. The 'tip and run' code, in which the batsman must run if he makes contact with the ball, encourages the striker to hit the ball far and to place it accurately between the fieldsmen. There is no room for the defensive prod to mid-off or mid-on, or to block the ball in the crease.

Learie Constantine wrote in Wisden:

'In my boyhood there was an enthusiasm for Cricket in Trinidad such as I have seldom seen equalled anywhere else in the world. My father set the family to work to make a private pitch from rolled clay covered with matting; it was the fashion everywhere and tremendous cricket battles were fought out between neighbouring families. My mother could keep wicket almost as well as a Test 'keeper; my sister had as much aptitude for batting as I had; one of my uncles was an international player and another was just as skilled. When we small boys were not playing in bigger games, we incessantly opposed each other, using oranges for balls and coconut branches for bats'.

Constantine, himself, represents the complete Caribbean cricketer to most people living outside the West Indies, and so many of those in the region. It was more than his being an exciting and vigorous stroke-player, one of the best fast bowlers at a time of outstanding fast bowling throughout the world, and a breathtaking fieldsman. The Trinidadian played with an extremely rare, if not unique, zest and enthusiasm, and could win a match by what seemed to be his own exertions alone. Although his father was the outstanding cricketer of his day, the young Learie learned the game from the most rudimentary principles and went on to become the best-known West Indian of his generation, to many Englishmen and Australians the only known West Indian. His robust batting, bowling which could become extremely fast, and speed of fielding which deceived the eye summed up the the most dynamic qualities of Caribbean cricket.

Contemporary critics of current tactics may be surprised to learn that as long ago as 1926 Constantine was restrained only by the intervention of his colleagues from continuing a spate of short-pitched deliveries at visiting captain Calthorpe, after his own skipper, the then elderly Austin, had been subjected to similar treatment, and that he and Manny Martindale met fire with fire to great effect in the Test Match at Manchester in 1933.

Coaching is by example and intuition. This approach caused the downfall of the region's pioneer batsmen when they encountered unaccustomed conditions in England and Australia. Performance overseas has improved with familiarity. Learning comes with experience. Clyde Walcott has explained how he failed in his first game in Trinidad, in a heavy atmosphere which helped fast bowlers Prior Jones and Lance Pierre to swing the ball, because he applied too literally the Barbadian maxim of playing forward.

George Headley was the master of technique, and its application. For almost a decade after he hit a hundred as a 21 year-old on his international debut at Kensington in 1930 the Jamaican carried the regional batting and he lost nothing in comparison with his great contemporaries, Donald Bradman and Walter Hammond. All strokes were at his command and he had the exceptional timing and eye-sight to play the ball unusually late. Spectators came to the match to see his running between the wickets. His popularity, indeed the hero-worship, in his homeland was so strong that in his forties he was brought back from England by public subscription so that he could play in the First Test Match of the 1954 series.

George adapted by experience. He was essentially an off-side player when he went to Australia in 1930/31. Initial failure against spinner Clarrie Grimmett caused him to re-think his approach, and to change his stance and grip. He scored centuries in Test Matches at Brisbane and Sydney on the way to becoming also an outstanding leg-side batsman. The Jamaican had adapted himself to the surroundings and requirements of the game, though, undoubtedly, more speedily than most of his colleagues. It was the example which inspired the next generation.

Rohan Kanhai, inexperienced and impetuous, started the second innings of the Fifth Test Match at The Oval in London in the disastrous 1957 series by hitting Freddie Trueman, fast and hostile, twice to the on-side boundary. When he tried to repeat the stroke the wily bowler had him caught at the wicket. The critics contended that the youngster should curb his enterprising approach. Kanhai learned to temper his aggression with control but he never lost the cavalier spirit. The application, not the attitude, was adjusted.

Over-coaching is the cause of many present-day problems outside the region. West Indians are more natural cricketers who worry less about having the legs and arms in the correct positon than in feeling comfortable with their action. Coaches concentrate more on tactics than technique. Batting in the confined space of the verandah, or backyard, with the fieldsmen clustered around within touching distance, has taught the aspiring batsman already to drop the ball at his feet without giving a chance, and has imparted to the bowler the need for compensatory skills.

Walcott recalled that his schoolmasters, Derek Sealy, the former Test Match player, and Stan Gittins, and opening batsman for Barbados, took much interest in the pupils' cricket but proffered little coaching advice other than to play forward with the left elbow well up. He considered, too, that English batsmen psyched themselves into difficulties against Ramadhin by formulating all manner of theories about how to read him. In contrast, he picked the Trinidadian's leg-break by watching him bowl in the nets for an afternoon.

Recent rubbers between the West Indies and England, for example, have shown up an important difference of approach in preparation on the morning of a match. The Englishmen prefer to practise in the artificial atmosphere of the nets where the edge of competition is absent. The West Indians have engaged in physical training, exercises and jogging to hone the muscles and reflexes to respond speedily when demanded to do so by the contingencies of the real contest at the crease.

The strength of continuity, tradition and example is demonstrated effectively by the contrast to West Indian youth transported to another social environment. There is little physical difference between a boy brought up in Barbados and his cousin raised in inner-city England but the variation in the cultural current and behaviour is considerable. The latter, if he is attracted to sport at all, will share usually the interest of his neighbours in football, athletics or the martial arts. In England cricket is very much a rural pastime, and very few West Indians there live in the country.

Those first-class cricketers of West Indian descent raised from that community have developed from the smaller provincial towns rather than from the major urban areas — Stevenage (Roland Butcher), High Wycombe (Wilfred Slack), Reading (Gordon Greenidge) and Slough (Cardigan Connor). The vast crowds of their compatriots which support the West Indies against the host country do so primarily out of loyalty to their homelands and to the memory of the

18

game they played there. The West Indian competitions in England, though still popular with the middle-aged who came there as immigrants, attract hardly any of the younger generation born there.

Cricket, then, is seemingly endemic to the social conditions and climate of the Caribbean rather than being natural to West Indians as such. Successful cricketers have excelled throughout the world, and many have made their professional homes overseas, but the love of the game was kindled at home. Cricket, like religion, is essentially caught rather than taught.

Pelham Warner noted in *Cricket in many Climes* that from the earliest days the game was supported by the entire community, even in those territories which excluded black players from their team. Lord Hawke's side arrived initially in Barbados where:

'The whole population was mad on cricket; and when we appeared on deck, we were surrounded by an excited little crowd ... After breakfast we went on shore, where a huge swarm of black men awaited us on the wharf ...

As soon as we were landed from the Gulf steamer, we were swept down by a large gathering of black men, whose enthusiasm was simply — tropical!'

It was the same almost everywhere throughout the region: in Grenada 'A large crowd came to see us off' and the crowd in St Vincent 'mostly black, were very enthusiastic'.

Warner was very much opposed to racial discrimination particularly in an area where enthusiasm ran through the whole community:

'(In Trinidad and) in the smaller islands such as Grenada, St Kitts, St Vincent, Antigua, St Lucia, black men are always played ... but Barbados and Demarara have strenuously set themselves against this policy. With this uncompromising attitude I cannot agree. These black men add considerably to the strength of a side, while their inclusion makes the game more popular locally, and tends to instil a mutual and universal enthusiasm among all classes of the population'.

Barbadian bar-tenders, waiters and taxi-drivers are renowned for their knowledge of the game. They are more aware of the finer points then their own counter-parts in some other communities and some of the professional commentators from most countries. During the tense days following the cancellation of the scheduled Bourda Test Match in 1981 the cab-drivers waiting for custom outside the Holiday Inn in Bridgetown showed greater perception than many of the reporters lodged in the hotel.

Even when a bee flies into their bonnet, and it is usually a Barbadian bee, it is based on sound judgement. The restaurant waiter who declared consistently that 'he cannot compare to Conrad Hunte' whenever a guest praised an opening batsman could back his contention with statistics as well as sentiment. As many here will not mention Viv Richards or Lawrence Rowe in the same breath as Everton Weekes as there are Jamaicans who take to task anyone putting Gordon Greenidge and Roy Fredericks on a par with Rowe.

A couple of years ago I arranged to interview Wilfred Slack, the Vincentian left-handed batsman with Middlesex, during a match against Derbyshire at Lord's. A thunderous downpour, which emptied the ground in mid-afternoon, seemed to present the ideal opportunity. There would be no further play that day. Yet entrance was not permitted to the pavilion because my pass was valid only for the press-box and the steward did not consider it to be part of his responsibility to inform the cricketer of my presence. Such insensitive formality could not happen in the West Indies.

Images of first-class cricket, and cricketers, in the Caribbean are nearly always images of informality ... watching Andy Roberts and Michael Holding play the fruit-machines amid the thronging guests at the Caribbee Hotel in Barbados; seeing the whole team waiting outside the same hotel for their transport to the Oval in the morning; Conrad Hunte serving drinks at a get-together for Roland and Cheryl Butcher at Pegwell, and Joel Garner dropping in unannounced; the young Malcolm Marshall steering his moped between crowded pedestrians in downtown Bridgetown; Peter Short smoothing over the inconvenience of accreditation that had gone astray.

Trinidadians are always willing to talk, about cricket as much as anything else. It is impossible to pass through the shops and stores around Independence Square without running into two or three of the big names from the past. Andy Ganteaume stopped to talk not about his Test Match century but to recall being dropped down the batting order for a county game against Kent in 1957 because he had arrived late at the ground after taking the opportunity to visit Canterbury Cathedral. Gerry Gomez is available at his desk at Sports and Games for the occasional word between commitments.

Cricketers are always among us. It is not so in London. There they pass by incognito in cars or trains. Even at Lord's celebrities take motorised transport to the main gate and walk only the short distance to the pavilion and stand accommodation. Any former cricketers standing around chatting in the main concourse are likely to be West Indian, and as often as not with former Test Match offspinner Reg Scarlett. Children are not encouraged to seek autographs, contact or the advice of their heroes. There are many social occasions but they are held behind doors with invited guests and away from the prying eyes of the casual public. This erosion of the vital link of communication between cricketers and the community should not be exported to the Caribbean.

Cricket is the premier participatory sport activity of the West Indies. Those with an aptitude for games are directed towards the bat and ball. Michael Holding could have been a top-class athlete. Viv Richards, Clyde Walcott and Richie Richardson, among many others, have been skilled at soccer. Yet there was no serious risk that they would be lost to cricket. Most other top players could have made a comfortable career in some activity away from the pitch, but few of those who have had the chance to walk away from cricket have done so.

Attitudes are not the same everywhere. Sport provides a precarious living. Young men in most countries are encouraged to seek security in a profession or other alternative employment. Even those with the necessary sports potential are pointed towards soccer, golf, athletics or lawn tennis. Not many cricketers stay in the sport long. George Gunn and Wilfred Rhodes of England were each over fifty years old in the first Test Match series in the Caribbean in 1930, but their successors continue only rarely beyond their mid-thirties.

Although several games are played to a high standard of proficiency in the region, cricket remains paramount. Jamaica, closest to the North American colleges, has also a tradition of success in athletics, especially in the short-distance track events. The 4 × 400 metres relay team of Arthur Wint, Leslie Laing, Herb McKenley and George Rhoden which took the gold medal in the Olympic Games at Helsinki in 1952 is remembered with similar affection to the cricketers of that time.

There is much popular dissatisfaction, however, that so many top athletes have gone overseas for training and competition. They may win medals for their country, but from so far away their achievements do not seem to be really representative. Rural and urban youth can identify neither with them nor with those Jamaicans, and the children of Jamaicans, who have attained fame in English football. Whatever they may do, wherever they may be, the best cricketers are still at home when it matters most.

Enthusiasm for cricket, and participation in the game, seems to be in inverse proportion to the size of the territory. Since the turn of the decade Antigua with a population of 76 000 and 108 square miles has contributed as much to the regional team as Jamaica with a population of over two million and almost 4244 square miles. The compactness of the community enhances the sense of cohesion. It is unlikely that anyone in Antigua does not know, or, at least, has not seen Viv Richards. His people have a personal interest in his success. There are some in Jamaica, not many but some, who have not heard of Jeff Dujon or Michael Holding.

Young cricketers the world over learn a love of the game from their fathers. In the West Indies it is learned also from their mothers. Cricket in England and Australia is essentially a male preserve, but interest in the Caribbean is not so limited by gender. That is in keeping with the game's heritage. Dr. W.G. Grace, the genius who revolutionised cricket in England, was coached by the whole family, including, and especially, his mother. Cricket is far too important an enterprise to entrust to one sex, one generation, one race or one social class.

West Indian selectors are prone to back their own judgement, often when it has not been justified on previous performance. The choice of Ramadhin, Valentine and, to some extent, of Holding and of Sobers was a gamble on potential. Other similar inituitive stabs-in-the-dark have been less successful. To their credit the selectors have a reputation for standing by a player whom they consider to have ability. In some countries batsmen, particularly, are too afraid of being dropped after one failure that they do not play their natural game.

Richie Richardson and Gus Logie have been allowed to develop with much patience. Admittedly, though, it is easier to keep faith with one batsman in his disappointing spell if the other members of the team are going well. Desmond Haynes had no success in the first four Test Matches in England in 1984, but retained against the run of evidence he demonstrated his class by hitting a century at The Oval, the pitch on which run-scoring was most difficult that season.

Gary Sobers played in over four series before reaching his first hundred. Then he broke the world record and attained three figures in each innings of the following match. Rohan Kanhai did not pass fifty in any of his first eleven Test Match innings. Gordon Greenidge was badly out of touch against Australia in 1975/76. Yet in spite of the defeats suffered at the time the selectors did not desert those in whom they saw the spark of genius. West Indian administrators and selectors are prone to several faults, but disloyalty to their elect is not one.

The region has a very good record in recognising young talent. Derek Sealy was selected at 17 years 122 days, Gary Sobers at 17 years 245 days, Robin Bynoe at 18 years 31 days and Jeffrey Stollmeyer at 18 years 105 days, most of whom, if not all, converted their promise into performance. In spite of the country's much longer experience of Test Matches, Brian Close at 18 years 149 days is England's youngest player. Only Pakistan has shown greater confidence in youth, though quite a few of their selections have not lived up to expectation.

The series of representative matches between the West Indies Young Cricketers and England Young Cricketers in 1982 provides a yardstick in measuring the difference of attitude. Within two years Roger Harper and Courtney Walsh moved into the senior side, and, other factors being equal, George Ferris and Robert Haynes must have been close to serious consideration. Within that time, however, not one Young Englishman was a regular choice for his county let alone being in contention for his country's honours.

After an impressive season in the Neal & Massy Youth Tournament, in which he bowled Barbados to victory, Milton Small made his first-class debut against Trinidad & Tobago at Kensington in January 1984. Taking advantage of the absence of regular fast bowlers Wayne Daniel, Malcolm Marshall and Joel Garner with the regional side in Australia, and the departure of Hartley Alleyne to join Sylvester Clarke, Ezra Moseley and Franklyn Stephenson in South Africa, he took a wicket with his first ball and finished with 5 wickets for 57 runs.

The young Barbadian was moved straight away into the first one-day international match against Australia at Albion, Berbice, in which he failed to take a wicket, dismissed one batsman in the second at Queen's Park, and made his Test Match debut on the same ground. At the end of the series Small was taken to England and bowled with success and promise at Lord's before injury curtailed his further participation in the tour.

The fear of the late 1970s that the entire team would grow old together, as happened so dramatically after 1968, was not realised then because the selectors grafted new talent into the established line-up. The transformation has been handled effectively in respect of the bowling and, after some initial worry, the middle-order batting, but, perhaps, another opener could have been given a more extended chance to understudy Haynes and Greenidge.

Frank Worrell's career illustrates the difficulty of categorising the specialist skills of the successful Caribbean cricketer. Like Gary Sobers, Learie Constantine and S.G. Smith, he specialised in no one skill and yet he was a specialist of all. Wisden described his 261 and the 283 runs fourth-wicket partnership with Everton Weekes at Nottingham in 1950 as being 'in scintillating style', and his century at Melbourne on the following tour showed courage in the face of the short-pitched, fast bowling of Ray Lindwall and Keith Miller which cut through the other batting.

When the regular opening batsmen failed in England in 1957, Worrell went in first with the young Sobers at Nottingham and carried his bat throughout the innings for 191 not out. He had to turn round and go straight out again in the follow-on. That season Worrell opened the bowling as well as the batting, taking 7 wickets for 70 runs in the next match at Leeds. Bruce Harris was justified in declaring in *West Indies Cricket Challenge 1957* that:

'What the West Indian side would have done without Frank Worrell as a batsman and bowler it is hard to conjecture'.

After missing three rubbers through study he returned to the side by digging in for a patient 197 not out in the First Test Match against England at Kensington in 1960, sharing a record stand of 399 runs for the fourth wicket with Sobers. Frank came in on the evening of the third day and ground on until the declaration on the sixth. It was a sombre, not scintillating, tone. Even so before the end of the year he won acclaim for the enterprising manner in which he led the West Indians in Australia. Johnny Moyes in *With the West Indies in Australia 1960-61* has our last word in what a West Indian cricketer represented in the terms of Worrell and his team:

'Those who had the pleasure of watching the West Indian cricketers in action and of knowing them personally will never forget them. The impact they made on cricket in Australia was amazing: they turned the world upside down: they arrived almost unhonoured and unsung: they took away with them the esteem, affection, and admiration of all sections of the community. They gave the genuine cricket lover a thrill he had not felt for a quarter of a century. They brought back to the grounds many who had left them in disgust at the mediocre fare served up to them. They proved what so many of us had declared — that people would go to see cricket played as a game and entertainment . . .

The thrills were provided by the West Indians. No Australian during the series played with half the brilliance of Sobers at Brisbane or Kanhai at Adelaide. On those occasions these two grand players undoubtedly touched the skirts of Genius. Their stroke-play was superb; their timing precise; their placing of the ball amazing in the extreme. Except for brief out-pourings by O'Neill and that dazzling opening of the second Australian innings at Melbourne by Simpson there was nothing in the Australian batting to compare with the glorious artistry so often shown by some the West Indians, who exploded into their strokes as did the champions of other days. The West Indians were 'different'. The Australians often scored as quickly. It was the manner in which the West Indians made their strokes that was so attractive . . .

I believe that they put entertainment before victory, or perhaps they knew that they were natural entertainers and that by being natural they had a better chance of winning. Whatever it was, they left behind them from Perth to Brisbane and back again to Melbourne a trail of admirers who took them to their hearts and who will never forget them. After the Fifth Test at Melbourne the large crowd which waited to see the presentation of the Frank Worrell Trophy left no doubts about their loyalty to these 'Caribbean Crusaders', as Conrad Hunte once called them. The cheers and applause were so spontaneous that no one could possibly doubt that they came from the heart . . .

Gradually Worrell harnessed all this enthusiasm and put it to good use. He alone became the leader and his word was accepted. He had the affection and confidence of his team and gradually they began to improve. They began to play as a team, for Worrell was both realist and idealist and he inculcated these thoughts into his colleagues. They learned to fight as a team. There were no divisions in the side. But to the end they did not leave their laughter at the gate as they took the field. They took it with them. The spare parts came together to form a machine which could function efficiently under the guidance of a master mechanic'.

It was the beginning of a new era.

Three

Michael Holding

Michael Holding provides an unprecedented blend of skill, artistry, devastation and technical perfection. If they had the time to appreciate their own predicament opposing batsmen would be overwhelmed by the beauty of the action which had brought about their own destruction. The Jamaican is so much more than being merely a latter-day Lindwall to be praised for his poise, balance in delivery, mastery or technique, and outright bowling ability. He has such gentle grace that one commentator has written that even at full pace his approach to the wicket is so light that Michael could run on soft snow without leaving the imprint of his foot.

There is venom in his skill. Holding shows little of the visible belligerence of Malcolm Marshall or Roy Gilchrist, or the seasoned sublety demonstrated by Andy Roberts. He strikes with the sudden lethal majesty of a king-cobra. At Perth in late 1984, at a time when observers had relegated his contribution to that of senior seamer, Michael whittled down the Australian first innings with awesome authority. His 6 wickets, taken in 35 deliveries, cost him only 21 runs as the batsmen toppled out for just 76, the lowest total their country had ever registered against the West Indies.

Michael Anthony Holding, born on 16 February 1954, was wise in his choice of antecedents. His father, Ralph, no mean cricketer himself, was formerly President of Melbourne Cricket Club, which, no Jamaican needs reminding, is one of the strongest in the island. Compared to, say, Roy Gilchrist, who had to build his fame in country parts away from the centre of attention, Holding was in the right place for his nascent talents to be noticed. Yet it was not certain that cricket would benefit from his sports ability.

As a youth at Kingston College he was also a gifted athlete. Jamaican sporting tradition, unlike that of the territories of the Eastern Caribbean, extends deeply beyond the cricket field. Herb McKenley, Arthur Wint and Don Quarrie are as honoured as George Headley, Alfred Valentine and Collie Smith. Norman Manley, one of the two great pioneers of political independence, held records in both track and field events. If he had taken an athletics scholarship to the U.S.A., like several of his contemporaries, Michael would have been lost to cricket.

Fortune, though, continued to bless him, and us. It is reported that his sports master, Trevor Parchment, persuaded him to make cricket his primary aim, but the beauty of the athlete has remained in everything that he has undertaken. With his natural ability Holding progressed quickly through each level of competition. These years were exciting for West Indian cricket as the regional team emerged victorious from the frustrations of the late 1960s and early 1970s. That renaissance would be confirmed by brilliant batting and fast bowling of unprecedented quality, but for the moment that lay in the future.

Holding moved quickly from his debut in the West Indies youth tournament in 1972 to his first-class debut the following year. The visiting Australian batsmen were the first to experience the sting in his bowling. Within three years he was awarded the Karl Nunes Trophy as the young player who had done most for the game in character and ability. With one arguable lapse he has been ever since a model example in a generation which has not been that remarkable for its character and conventional good conduct throughout all sport.

Nevertheless, Holding's selection for the tour to Australia in 1975/76 was considered to be a gamble. A new partner was needed for Andy Roberts, whose speed had been a prominent feature of the previous tour to India and Pakistan. Keith Boyce had not maintained the promise of his first series in England, and neither the under-rated Vanburn Holder nor Bernard Julien had the extra pace needed for Australian conditions. Michael seized his opportunity — though as a batsman — by scoring halfcenturies in his first two games against South Australia and New South Wales.

Yet it was his bowling in the narrow victory over the State side at Sydney that propelled him into the Test Match team. New South Wales, ahead on first innings, needed to score only 199 runs to win. The target became academic when Holding whipped out McCosker and Beard, and followed later by dismissing Turner, Gilmour, O'Keeffe and Colley in his 6 wickets for 60 runs. All of his victims were current or future international players.

The First Test Match at Brisbane was an anti-climax in which he failed to take a wicket. When Keith Boyce bowled well against Western Australia the Jamaican seemed to be lucky to retain his place for the Second Test Match at Perth. Fortunately the selectors decided on that fast pitch to include four pace bowlers at the expense of spinner Inshan Ali. The practice would be repeated many times in the years ahead.

Although the match is remembered best for Roberts' match-winning performance in the second innings, Holding set up the victory with 4 wickets for 88 runs over the first four sessions. Three batsmen, including Ian Chappell, who had scored 156, were dismissed in his second over of the second morning. All three were bowled. Michael broke down in the second innings, missed the following Test Match at Melbourne and did not regain his impetus for the rest of the series. There seemed to be little to distinguish him from his predecessors.

Since the dawn of the international era Jamaica had contributed a sequence of good fast bowlers to the regional side. Yet after only a single outstanding performance — or, occasionally, a successful season — they had faded from further contention. No doubt the long intervals between Test Match series had an unsettling effect, but the same considerations had not impaired the consistency of the Barbadians (Francis, Griffith, Martindale). It seemed that there had been some flaw in the Jamaican character which had prevented them from rising to the occasion more than once.

Leslie Hylton shared the honours with Martindale and Constantine in the victories of 1934/35. He was not overshadowed in any way by his better-known colleagues and took 4 wickets for 27 runs in the first innings of the drawn Third Test Match at Georgetown. In low-scoring conditions England had hoped to move 2-1 ahead in the rubber. Although his then younger colleagues attest to his ability to read a tactical situation and to the personal assistance he had given them, Hylton was not successful on the tour to England in 1939. The outbreak of the Second World War terminated his international career, and Leslie hit the headlines thereafter only when he was hanged for the murder of his wife.

Hines Johnson, extremely tall and another whose best years had been lost to the war, gave England's batsmen more problems than they could handle at Sabina Park in 1948. He followed his 5 wickets for 41 runs in the first innings with 5 wickets for 55 runs in the second. The West Indies won that match by 10 wickets, and with it the series. On the strength of that performance Johnson was expected to spearhead the attack in England in 1950, but that season belonged to the spin of Ramadhin and Valentine. Spectators remember him well for seeking shelter under the wicket-covers instead of taking cover in the pavilion during a shower at Nottingham.

Esmond Kentish, with whom Johnson had shared the new ball for the island in the late 1940s, caused such a breakdown in England's batting in the First Test Match at Sabina Park in 1953/54 that an apparent draw was turned into a West Indian victory by 140 runs. His 5 wickets for 49 runs justified captain Stollmeyer's much-criticised decision against enforcing the follow-on. When he played for Oxford University against Cambridge University at Lord's in 1956 the then 39 year-old Kentish became the oldest cricketer to participate in that tradition of matches.

Tom Dewdney remained within and on the edge of international selection throughout the 1950s without having the extra degree of fire or penetration to realise his promise. He took 4 wickets for 125 runs against Australia at Kensington Oval in 1955, but the tourists did score 668. That was his problem. Dewdney's best opportunities came in contests against the extremely strong England and Australian batting sides of that decade. At another time or in another place he might have lasted longer.

That chance went to compatriot Roy Gilchrist. He had the speed and the hostility to continue well into the 1960s, but it was not to be. The Jamaican — like Ray Lindwall and Malcolm Marshall — was short in stature for a fast bowler. Against England in 1957 he generated great pace, especially at Lord's where he took 4 wickets for 115 runs, without the necessary control and direction. Gillie achieved something of the latter in the following home series against Pakistan where he chipped off the top of the opposing batting. He stamped his mark with 4 wickets for 32 runs in the first innings of 'the series at Kensington Oval and scarcely looked back. After a while even the great Hanif Mohammed dropped down the batting-order to avoid the initial assault.

The reputation of the partnership of Roy Gilchrist and Wesley Hall rests on their feats against India in 1958/59. The terror inspired in their victims has become a by-word for the severest ordeal by leather. Once more Gilchrist made an early impression with 4 wickets for 39 runs in the opening encounter at Bombay. Two matches later he overwhelmed the Indians at Calcutta by taking 6 wickets for 55 runs. Along the way he picked up more wickets and hit a few other bodies. Then he was sent home for disciplinary reasons and did not play again for the West Indies.

Chester Watson, another Jamaican, took his place when England came to the Caribbean the next year. He took 4 wickets for 62 runs in an exhibition of inspired fast bowling with Hall at Sabina Park. Nevertheless temperament proved to be his undoing on the next tour to Australia. Watson was the fourth fast bowler from the island in a decade to attain the grade but to be found wanting in consistency. The fifth failed similarly to win regular selection: in his case, however, the fault was not his own.

Charlie Griffith, a Barbadian, had become Hall's steady partner by the time that injury gave Lester King his only real chance at the highest level in the Fifth Test Match against India at Sabina Park in 1962. He responded magnificently by taking 5 wickets for 46 runs — effectively winning the match in his opening spell. Thereafter he was condemned to be the perpetual first reserve to the two Barbadians. When it seemed that they were teetering past their best, injury forced King to withdraw from the tour to England in 1966, for which he had been selected, and, thus, terminated his career.

Like Dewdney before him, Uton Dowe came to the fore in the interval between two eras of outstanding fast bowling. He took 4 wickets for 69 runs against India at Kensington Oval in 1971, but his bowling was rarely controlled and two years later the Australians hit him out of further international consideration. Pugnacious opening batsman Keith Stackpole was particularly severe on him. After his own decline following the success at Perth, there seemed to be no good reason to believe that Holding would be anything other than one more bright but transcient meteor. He soon set the record right.

After establishing his position as first strike bowler with Andy Roberts in the first two matches against India in 1976, the Jamaican ripped through the batting in the Third Test Match at Queen's Park. The fixture had been moved to Trinidad from its original venue at Bourda because of floods. Holding bowled splendidly on a pitch lacking either pace or bounce. Ironically his 6 wickets for 65 runs led to his captain declaring the second innings prematurely closed and, so, giving India the chance to record an historic victory.

There was no such reprieve for the tourists in the final Test Match at Sabina Park. Here Michael made the whole world sit up and take notice. In conditions conducive to uneven bounce Holding heightened the unpredictability by bowling short and around the wicket. The batsmen prospered initially to the extent that Sunil Gavaskar and Anshuman Gaekwad put on 136 runs before the first wicket fell. On the second morning Holding broke the back of the batting with 4 wickets for 82 runs in a declared 306-6 total.

Showing that there was nothing necessarily wrong with the pitch he scored 55. Admittedly, though, India had no quick bowler. The tourists' second innings became a debacle in that five batsmen failed to come to the crease. Holding had Gavaskar caught at short-leg before the score had reached double figures. The innings ended at 97 even though only five dismissals had been effected. The acrimonious aftermath and condemnation of 'intimidatory' bowling served only to make the players and public aware that the England side faced a new dimension of pace when the West Indians arrived there a month later.

Early in the tour Holding struck terror in his future opponents by scything through the country's best young batting talent in the game against the M.C.C. at Lord's, but the repercussions of ill-health kept him out of serious international contention until the Third Test Match at Manchester. That pitch on which even the gentle-paced Mike Selvey dismissed Viv Richards cheaply and broke through the early batting was obviously a nightmare for the batsmen. Roberts, Holding and Wayne Daniel gave them a torrid time. The first innings realised a meagre 71 runs, and the second was not much better.

The score crept painfully to 46-2 before Michael unleashed the assault which brought him 5 wickets for 9 runs in just 7.5 overs. Wisden describes some deliveries as lifting at 'frightening pace' and those dismissing Woolmer and Hayes as being 'all but unplayable and even the greatest of batting sides would have been severely taxed'. Batsmen who had fared better than anticipated against Lillee and Thomson the previous summer were reduced to impotence. It could well have been remembered as Holding's finest hour if another of even greater glory had not occurred in the Fifth Test Match at the Oval.

The magnificence of the achievement is confirmed by the context of the conditions. Viv Richards and Dennis Amiss each made a double-century on the placid pitch, and no other bowler on either side took more than three wickets in an innings. The previous Test Matches on the same ground against Pakistan and Australia had resulted in high-scoring draws. Yet in all Holding took 14 wickets for 149 runs. The history of international competition has no finer example of fast bowling. The Jamaican countered the lifeless nature of the pitch by achieving greater speed through the air. While Amiss defended admirably at one end Holding cut down his partners at the other. Chris Balderstone, who fell twice to the same bowler without scoring, and Bob Woolmer failed to reach double figures. Eventually Holding bowled Amiss as he moved too far over to the off-side to glance to leg, and he finished with 8 wickets for just 92 runs. Lloyd recognised the value of his fast bowlers by not enforcing the follow-on. While they rested the West Indian openers took another undefeated century partnership.

On the final morning England's first five second innings wickets toppled for 78 runs. Michael applied the decisive thrust by taking four, including those of Amiss and opposing captain Tony Greig. That purpose achieved he was taken out of the attack so that others could force the point home. Appropriately Holding was recalled to dismiss the last two batsmen and finished with another 6 wickets for 57 runs.

After that, injury and his participation in World Series Cricket kept him out of conventional Test Match competition for the greater part of three years. It was probably just as well. Otherwise this story would have become a sequence of statistics and Colin Croft, Sylvester Clarke and Joel Garner may not have had the chance to make their mark. On his return, after an outstanding series in Australia, Holding blotted his copy-book uncharacteristically by kicking over the stumps at Dunedin in the bad-tempered rubber in New Zealand.

His bowling spoke for him more eloquently when the West Indies returned to England in the extremely wet summer of 1980. The duel between Graham Gooch and Michael Holding on the first day of the Second Test Match at Lord's was one of cricket's great confrontations. The batsman hit a century and the bowler took 6 wickets, including that of Gooch, for 67 runs. In a blistering early evening spell in the second innings of the Fourth Test Match at The Oval the Jamaican dismissed Gooch and Larkins before either had scored and England slumped to 10-2. At such pace and in such form he was irresistible.

Nevertheless, his ability to switch from the apparently innocuous to the invincible, often with the old ball, was shown best against Leicestershire in the first week of that tour. The county was outplayed so much that the game seemed to be heading towards a close early on the second day. Michael did not appear to be moved to any great exertion. Gradually, however, David Gower and Brian Davison took advantage of the comparative laxity to score halfcenturies. Pressmen who had cancelled their hotel bookings for that night now cancelled the cancellation.

The same thought must have crossed the Jamaican's mind. He came back for another spell determined to end the charade. Wickets crashed with shattering regularity and he dismissed 5 batsmen for 57 runs in the innings. The commentator of the Pelham Cricket Year, David Lemmon, recorded 'the rest of the batting succumbed to Holding as if they wanted to get home early'. The recently reversed cancellations were now confirmed.

That season the West Indies fast bowlers worked out that Geoff Boycott, their potentially most formidable opponent, could be unsettled by extreme pace bowled from around the wicket. This tactic was effective from as early as the opening morning of the First Test Match at Nottingham but wicketkeeper Deryck Murray had a terrible time and chances were not accepted. Even so the message had been received and would be remembered well. Within a year Holding produced a spell of bowling against the same batsman on a fast Caribbean pitch that will be recalled for as long as cricket is played.

The Third Test Match at Kensington Oval in March 1981 came in the wake of the 'Jackman Affair' and was marred by the death of Ken Barrington, England's assistant manager. It would have been only too easy for the events off the pitch to have overshadowed those at the crease. The match, itself, was hardly a contest. The West Indies won at a canter as Richards and Lloyd plundered hundreds. It was a time for individual excellence.

The England innings began on the second morning. Roberts commenced with an over to Gooch. Then Holding was summoned from his place in front of the Challenor Stand. He tested Boycott with an over of electrifying pace. Each delivery was celebrated with near delirium by the spectators massed near to where he had been fielding. One excited onlooker whirled his machete to the hazard of his neighbours. When the Yorkshireman's wicket was shattered, the crowd erupted in delight. The Jamaican was given a hero's welcome as he walked back to his place in the field at the end of the over.

The opening moments of the second innings were even more dramatic. Boycott failed to get out of the way of a sharp lifter which lobbed up for the long Garner at gully to pitch forward and catch. With the next delivery Holding flattened Gatting's stumps. The batsman walked off the pitch looking ruefully for the hole in his bat.

Yet again Michael was rested once the initial break-through had been made. Ironically the opening batsmen contributed most to England's improved performance in the remaining two Test Matches, but by then it was too late to erase the memory of Bridgetown.

Wisden — through reporter Henry Blofeld — considered prematurely that 'there was evidence during their tour of Australia that the powers of Clive Lloyd's West Indian side had begun to decline' in 1981/82. None of that criticism could apply to Holding. In the three-match series he took 14 wickets at an average of 14.33. The aggregate was exactly double that of the next most successful bowler. Michael took five wickets or more in four innings out of six. Because of injury that season was the last in which he could bowl consistently at top pace off of his longer run.

In spite of his success in four continents Holding is still very much one of the most approachable members of a generally approachable team. His attitude and his accent remain unmistakably Jamaican. Not only is Holding unsullied by the taint of temptation from South Africa, but the public and the private Holding are essentially indistinguishable. There is no hint of a 'star' complex. In recent years Michael has cut down his run and speed with devastating effect. He has come into the attack after the initial shock has been dealt by Marshall and the rejuvenated Garner. Andy Roberts, Freddie Trueman and Dennis Lillee made the same transition, and the Jamaican's successful adoption of the new role has enabled the West Indies to dispense with Roberts' experience and still strengthen the thrust of the bowling. It would be wrong, however, to consider Holding to be regularly a stock rather than a shock bowler.

The manner in which he and Marshall combined to master the Indians in 1983/84 evoked memories of their hosts' earlier ordeal at the hands of Gilchrist and Hall a quarter-of-a-century previously. Mohinder Amarnath, whose form in the Caribbean and in the Prudential World Cup earlier in the year had won him the reputation of being the world's best player of fast bowling, was demolished. He made only one run in six innings. The Indians paid a heavy price for taking the World Cup from the champions.

In a team less well-endowed with batsmen Holding could have qualified as an all-rounder. His batting has few frills but he observes the basic principles. In the First Test Match at Birmingham in 1984 he and Eldine Baptiste plundered a record ninth-wicket stand of 150. The former made 69 before he was caught while hooking. The docile pitch was favourable to big hitting ... at least by the West Indians. His innings in the Third Test Match at Leeds was played in entirely different circumstances.

On the evening of the second day and the morning of the third Holding hit Bob Willis, the England captain and fast bowler, out of international cricket. He came in to bat with the West Indies still 64 runs in arrears and the last three batsmen out in seven balls from Paul Allott. Most cricketers would have opted for defence. The Jamaican showed that attack could be the best form of defence. He cracked five sixes off Willis alone and raced to 59 in an 82-runs stand with the patient Gomes. By the time that he was out the West Indies were already ahead.

Holding had always bowled well at The Oval, but now he seemed to play in the shade of the Barbadians. There was little in the early exchanges of his third Test Match in South London to suggest that his performance would live up to that of the previous two. Unlike its behaviour eight years before, the pitch aided those bowlers who could cut or move the ball. Few batsmen prospered, but the determined second innings batting of Broad and Tavare gave England hope that some of their reputation could be salvaged. Then the Jamaican was recalled to the attack.

A thrill of anticipation ran through the crowd as he marked out his run ... his long run. Since his injury it had been considered to be a medical impossibility. The effect was incredible. The pace eclipsed that of anything generated by Marshall. In one spell he determined the match and tied up the 'whitewash'. Broad fended a lifter to gully with memories of Boycott at Bridgetown, beaten by pace Gower was l.b.w. and three-times century-maker Allan Lamb fell to a superlative catch by Desmond Haynes at short-leg.

Holding excels primarily at the highest level of competition and is one of the few leading West Indians without a sustained and successful career to date in English county cricket. Although he has played for Lancashire and Derbyshire he has not yet become a regular county player in the manner of Garner at Somerset, or Roberts and Marshall at Hampshire. On tour he has been regularly more penetrative in the Test Matches than in games against county, state or provincial teams. A West Indies' cap — figuratively because he is inevitably bareheaded — brings out best the competitive instinct.

Michael's catching has been consistent rather than spectacular among his more brilliant close-field colleagues. Yet he has a safe pair of hands in the deep and matches have been settled by an injudicious lofted shot in his direction. By firm standing and accurate positioning he has secured the ball close to the boundary rope without the danger that the force of impact would carry him over. On the occasions he has been brought closer to the wicket he has not disappointed.

English observers, particularly, are surprised that this seemingly introverted and certainly modest character is the only serious long-term contender to Viv Richards as the team's principal pin-up. His appearance at the crease turns the heads of the young ladies automatically from what they have been doing. A celebrated beauty queen has stated that the highlight of her term of office had been the opportunity to meet the fast bowler at a social reception. His slim good looks, though more robust, are not unlike those of Michael Jackson.

Holding has been at the top of his profession for a decade, ten years of intense competition. Fast bowlers of Martindale's generation played in a dozen Test Matches in almost as many years. Their successors participate in perhaps even more within a single year. Conventional Test Matches, too, are supplemented by international limited-overs contests of equal importance. The stress is almost more than anything for which the human body and mind have been designed. It is a wonder that all fast bowlers do not burn themselves out by the time that they are thirty.

This consideration is particularly pertinent to Holding whose lean frame has broken down at critical points in his career. Yet like Dennis Lillee, the other fast bowling genius of the age, he has bounced back to even greater glory. In time, opposing batsmen might have come to terms with the sheer energy of his early years. They have not been able to cope with the later variation, subtlety and the retained ability to unleash one or more deliveries of exceptional, and controlled, pace.

Four

Wolmer's and
Wicketkeepers

Tony Becca, the respected cricket correspondent of the *Daily Gleaner* in Jamaica, has described the new three Ws of the game in the Caribbean as being .... Wolmer's, wicketkeepers and West Indies. He should know because he, too, is a former student of the same school. Yet by any standard Wolmer's achievement is exceptional. Whereas Barbadians have specialised in batting and fast bowling, Guyanese in stroke-play, and contemporary Trinidadians in spin, the Jamaican tradition has been in wicketkeeping.

Karl Nunes, Ivan Barrow, Alfie Binns, Gerry Alexander, Jackie Hendriks, Desmond Lewis and Jeffrey Dujon have served the region behind the stumps, a record unmatched by any other territory. Of these only Binns and Lewis· did not attend Wolmer's School, and neither of these kept for more than one whole series. Each of the school's quintet was also an accomplished batsman, three of whom have hit Test Match hundreds and the other two reached half-centuries. Generally they have stayed in the sport as administrator, manager, selector or commentator after their playing days were over.

Wolmer's School was founded over 300 years ago with proceeds from the estate of John Wolmer, a wealthy Kingston goldsmith. It is situated in Marescaux Road immediately to the north of National Heroes Circle, next to Mico College, one of the oldest teacher-training institutions in the world. Cross Roads, and the road leading to the modern commercial centre of New Kingston, stands to the north and Allman Town to the east. Wolmer's was initially solely a boys' school, but a girls' school was founded later.

Karl Nunes enjoyed the distinction of being both captain and wicketkeeper when the West Indies took the field for the first time in a Test Match on 23 June 1928 at Lord's. Veteran H.B.G. Austin, in many ways the 'father' of West Indian cricket internationally, had been nominated initially for the leadership, but well beyond his half-century in years he handed down the responsibility to his vice-captain from the previous tour in 1923. Nunes, who had been educated also at

Dulwich College, was well-suited to the social requirements for breaking the ice in the host country.

The Jamaican was not a specialist behind the stumps and missed a number of chances. The Cricketer magazine considered him to be little more than a 'target for fast bowling'. In spite of those that got away he made history by taking the first wicket ever to fall to a wicketkeeper for the West Indies by catching Herbert Sutcliffe from the bowling of Herman Griffith at Manchester. It was his only victim in the three-match series.

Nunes was much better as a left-handed batsman. His value in that capacity was demonstrated most forcefully in the Fourth Test Match, the first ever to be played at Sabina Park, in April 1930. That was the celebrated 'timeless Test' which England commenced by scoring a massive 849. Nunes hit top-score of 66 in the home team's insignificant reply. After Calthorpe, the visiting captain, had declined to enforce the follow-on, he scored another 92 in the massive second-wicket partnership with double-centurymaker George Headley which kept the game very much alive until torrential rain washed out any possibility of a result.

His contribution as an administrator, particularly in the important years immediately after the Second World War, went a long way to establishing the identity of West Indian cricket at Test Match level. Nunes was a member of the Jamaican Board of Control from its inception in 1926 until his death over three decades later, and he was President of the West Indies Board of Control from 1945 to 1952.

Teenager Ivan Barrow, another student of Wolmer's, kept wicket in that high-scoring match at Kingston in 1930, coming in for Errol Hunte of Trinidad who had held the position for the first three matches in the series. Immediately he achieved the first stumping for the West Indies in dismissing old-stager George Gunn from the bowling of Jamaican compatriot Frank Martin. The youngster had the reputation for high scoring, and the previous year had shared with Headley a stand of 248 runs against Lord Tennyson's team, but on his international debut Ivan was bowled without scoring.

By the visit to England in 1933 he had been promoted to open the innings with Roach, and that is where he showed his ability. At Manchester, a match marked by much intimidatory short-pitched bowling, he became the first West Indian to score a Test Match hundred in England. Headley, who joined him in a second-wicket partnership of 200, was on 99 as Barrow swept past him to the landmark. He was good enough to be retained as a batsman even after Cyril Christiani had taken over behind the stumps in 1935.

Christiani, one of two Guianese brothers to don the gloves for the region, was the first West Indian to be selected on specialist skill alone. He would have gone to England again in 1939 but died prematurely from malaria. By co-incidence Barrow, Christiani and Sealy, the three wicketkeepers in the decade after 1930, filled three of the first four batting positions in the 1935 Jamaican Test Match.

The selectors turned again to Barrow on Christiani's death, but the Jamaican had been out of the game too long. He yielded his place to Derek Sealy after just one match. All but two of his eleven international appearances were made outside the Caribbean. Sealy, who at 17 years 122 days was — and is still — the youngest player for the West Indies on his debut at Kensington in 1930, held his own as a batsman and returned some excellent bowling performances for Barbados. He was still a force in territorial competition in the late 1940s.

It is often forgotten just how good a wicketkeeper Clyde Walcott was between 1947 and the tour to Australasia four years later. A back injury sustained then caused him to give up keeping and concentrate on his batting . . . to such telling effect. Walcott's effective reading of Sonny Ramadhin's otherwise baffling spin was a decisive factor in the triumph over England in 1950. Robert Christiani, his deputy on tour, owed his own selection for the West Indies more to his batting ability. Simpson Guillen of Trinidad, who took over initially on Walcott's injury, went back to New Zealand to represent that country in future matches.

No one wicketkeeper kept the confidence of the selectors in the mid-1950s. Alfie Binns, Ralph Legall, Clifford McWatt and Clairemonte Depeiza were tried and discarded. McWatt, whose luck in batting won him the nickname Mc-Catt (nine lives), seemed to be favoured at first, but Depeiza's record 347 runs seventh-wicket partnership with Denis Atkinson against Australia at Bridgetown in 1955 seemed to clinch the choice in his favour. Both Binns and Depeiza were taken to New Zealand, and that, surprisingly, was the end of their international careers.

Gerry Alexander, a student of Wolmer's and Cambridge University, was the shock inclusion in the touring team to England in 1957. Even in Jamaica he was regarded below Binns and probably the young Hendriks, and could not compete with the regional reputation of the Barbadian, Depeiza. Reid of Dominica was another strong contender. When the side arrived in England it was not certain whether Alexander or the young Rohan Kanhai was the first choice wicketkeeper. The issue was still not settled by the mid-point of the Test Match series.

That team seemed to be exceptionally strong on paper. Frank

Worrell, Clyde Walcott, Everton Weekes, Gary Sobers and Kanhai provided the core of the batting, Roy Gilchrist and Wesley Hall should have contributed pace and penetration, and Ramadhin and Alfred Valentine seemed to be still at the height of their powers. Yet it was hammered out of sight. Allowing for every other relevant factor, and there were many, the balance of the side was compromised fatally by the selection of opening batsmen and wicketkeeper which seemed to be inexplicable at the time and even more so afterwards.

The attempt to make Kanhai the successor of Walcott in all his capacities could have ruined his career. If he was not the target for fast bowlers that Nunes had been, it was more because the type of bowling was no longer so important. He had neither the expertise nor the experience to cope with Ramadhin. Thankfully for both cricketers after the Third Test Match at Nottingham the decision was taken to play Alexander as wicketkeeper and Kanhai as a batsman. Although the Jamaican was an improvement on his immediate predecessor, it seemed to be inevitable that the position would be overhauled on the return to the region.

There, however, Alexander was appointed to the captaincy. Worrell, the obvious candidate, was deemed to be pre-occupied with his studies, but Walcott was still there and he had been vice-captain in England. Following John Goddard, Denis Atkinson and Jeff Stollmeyer in the leadership in rapid succession, Gerry seemed to maintain the social tradition which stretched back to the beginning of cricket in the hemisphere. Whatever its other merits, or otherwise, the decision made certain that Alexander was not lost as wicketkeeper.

His selection ensured, he was one of the several successes of the home series against Pakistan and the following tour to India. His keeping co-incided with the renaissance in fast bowling. The Jamaican's most spectacular work seemed to be achieved always when he was standing back, and the errors that are remembered, including the fatal fumble at Melbourne in 1961, came usually when he was up for the spinners. As batsman, captain and wicketkeeper Alexander's form was a revelation.

The West Indies seemed to be the stronger side when England came to the Caribbean in early 1960, but the series was lost on the batting breakdown in the Second Test Match at Queen's Park. As skipper Alexander, whose slowness in tactical approach contributed to the lost initiative, paid the penalty for the overall lacklustre performance. With Worrell back in the team and challenging strongly for the position which many people considered should have been his already, the failure to win from a position of apparent strength brought its own retribution. Although he lost the captaincy, the Jamaican, who had just set a record for catches at the wicket, was the only realistic choice as wicketkeeper.

Gerry was an outstanding vice-captain to Worrell on the memorable tour to Australia in 1960/61. As such he deserves much of the credit for blending a real sense of regional identity in a team which could have split so easily into its territorial components. His keeping reached a consistently high standard, particularly in the several nail-biting finishes in that rubber, including the heart-stopping conclusion to the tied Test Match at Brisbane. Yet he excelled also as a batsman and finished ahead of even Gary Sobers, Frank Worrell, Rohan Kanhai and Conrad Hunte in the Test Match averages.

Alexander started the series modestly enough with 60 at Brisbane, where even Wesley Hall made a half-century, and scored 108, his only first-class hundred, at Sydney. From there he finished the season in a blaze of runs by hitting 63 not out and 87 not out at Adelaide and 73 at Melbourne. His value to the side impressed Johnny Moyes who in his book *With the West Indies in Australia, 1960-61* noted that the tour was a triumph for him in every way, that his wicketkeeping improved day by day, and that he took so many difficult catches.

'As a batsman his value is not completely portrayed by the averages, for figures never tell the whole story. They cannot, for example, demonstrate just how his stroke repertoire developed; how his reliability affected his team-mates; how inspiring was the knowledge that there was still Alexander to come; from time and again he made runs so splendidly when they were needed . . . . He could be relied on when things were going badly . . . . No finer wicketkeeper-batsman has been seen in Australia within living memory'.

Jackie Hendriks, also of Wolmer's, the under-study for that tour, took over when Alexander retired immediately afterwards. He could have anticipated a long tenure of office, because even then opinion of him was high, but a finger injury sustained in his First Test Match against India at Queen's Park in 1962 put him out for the rest of the season, and even longer. Players of that era are convinced that day-in and day-out Hendriks was consistently the best wicketkeeper ever to have represented the West Indies, at least within their experience.

The Jamaican was also extraordinarily unlucky in respect of injury and in being in the wrong place. Apart from the curtailment of his first series, he missed selection for the tour to England in 1963 through working out of the region. After regaining the position for the visit of the Australians two years later he was side-lined again by back injury for the next home rubber against England. Back in the saddle for the tour to Australia and New Zealand in 1968/69 he was replaced by

Mike Findlay later in the year.

Ivor Mendonca of Guyana and David Allan, a Barbadian, appeared to benefit initially from Hendriks' first injury. Even when he had seemed to make the position his own the latter was cheated by fortune. Illness forced him out of the First Test Match at Manchester in 1963 and Deryck Murray, the teenaged Trinidadian, took over and set a new record. Throughout the next decade he and Hendriks jostled for preference which was determined as much by the former's studies and the latter's injuries as by individual skill.

In spite of his build Jackie hardly put a foot, or a glove, wrong. Unlike others of his calling who are required to specialise in keeping to either speed or spin, the Jamaican served the best balanced attack of the era. He faced the pace of Wesley Hall and Charlie Griffith, the orthodox off-spin of Lance Gibbs, and the variety of deliveries sent down by Gary Sobers. Although he was not a wicketkeeper-batsman in the manner of Walcott, Alexander or Dujon, he has one or two international half-centuries to his credit.

Hendriks' catches have turned matches. His leg-side dismissal of Colin Cowdrey off Griffith ending his 169 runs partnership with Tom Graveney prevented England from gaining an impenetrable grip on the Third Test Match at Nottingham in 1966. The first innings deficit was reduced to less than a hundred runs, and the West Indies rallied on the strength of Basil Butcher's unbeaten double-century to win the match and take an unassailable lead in the rubber.

After his playing career had ended Hendriks followed the example of previous wicketkeepers in moving into management and serving on the selection panel. He won additional honours by managing the triumphant team which overwhelmed England in all five Test Matches in 1984. Even before that result had been achieved he had earned respect for the firm and knowledgeable manner with which he handled public relations without the brusqueness associated with some of his predecessors. The players admired the example of a mentor who had been there before them and, at the same time, recognised that all of the good players didn't come from the past.

Deryck Murray, the long-serving vice-captain to Clive Lloyd, was the outstanding wicketkeeper of the 1970s. Nobody challenged seriously for the job as long as he wanted it. Name-sake David Murray of Barbados took over during the World Series Cricket 'schism' and stayed on as his deputy. He succeeded to the post when the Trinidadian was considered to be past his peak, not without public protest, in 1981. Randall Lyon of Trinidad and Milton Pydanna of Guyana had filled the reserve positions to the Murrays.

Peter Jeffrey Dujon, yet another from Wolmer's, has had to keep to an almost ceaseless pounding of pace. Much of the fast bowlers' success has depended on the sharp catching of himself and the ring of close fieldsmen. His spectacular one-handed dives in the goal-keeping manner come easily to someone with a tradition in football. It is debatable whether his specialist skills have prevented him from achieving even greater success as a batsman, for it was in that capacity that he came first to regional attention.

Dujon made his first-class debut for Jamaica against the Combined Islands in 1975 when he was not yet twenty years old. The previous year he had gone to England with the West Indies Young Cricketers. There he made his mark by scoring 74 in the second representative match at Arundel Park and top-score of 62 in the one-day match at Lord's. It was in this series that Wayne Daniel made such an impressive impact. Jeffrey maintained his promise throughout the 1970s. He was well situated in Kingston to catch the administrative eye.

There is certainly a suspicion in the island that cricketers from the countryside do not compete on an equal footing with those of the capital city and corporate area. The discrepancy, it is said, is illustrated most clearly in the treatment of 'bad boys'. Indiscipline and petulance by players from the outlying areas usually brings firm retribution, whereas displays of dissent and temperamental tantrums from Kingston's club cricketers are put down all too often to youthful indiscretion. Roy Gilchrist, for example, considers that he would have been recognised earlier and disciplined differently if he had been socially more than a country boy.

Dujon was a strong contender for selection in the home series against England in 1981. In the event the selectors preferred Everton Mattis, another Jamaican who without really failing did not justify their faith, and recalled Larry Gomes. The Trinidadian's renewed success secured the only available place, and with the abundance of established middle-order batsmen shut out any immediate prospect of the newcomer forcing his way to regional recognition. Honours were won less easily now than at any previous time.

The Jamaican returned to contention as the reserve wicketkeeper to David Murray on the tour to Australia in 1981/82. He was preferred to his several rivals because of his batting ability. Ironically after scoring an undefeated century against New South Wales he was chosen as a batsman for all three Test Matches. Dujon made forties in each of his first four innings and reached his fifty at Adelaide. On that occasion he took over from the Barbadian behind the stumps. His three catches in each innings contrasted with the several chances dropped by the Australians and probably tipped the balance.

The performance could not have come at a more opportune time. Before the next series commenced Murray placed himself beyond consideration by joining the 'rand rebels' in South Africa, and Jeffrey was in the right place. He put any doubt out of the question by scoring a hundred for Jamaica against the Indians in the opening match of their tour. In the Fifth Test Match at the Recreation Ground he became the first wicketkeeper to reach three figures for the West Indies in over two decades. He and Clive Lloyd put on more than two hundred runs for the fifth-wicket.

Dujon has an attractive style at the crease. He flows into his strokes with a flourishing backlift and wristy action. In his first series Henry Blofeld observed that he still had much to learn about the need to concentrate. He described one innings as 'Dujon played as if he was batting in the Jamaican nets'. The former observation was made in the light of the batsman's failure to progress from his several forties to a more substantial score, but, in spite of the subsequent centuries, the criticism would be valid for the apparent inattention which has cost him his wicket early on.

There was no lack of attention in the 130 he hit in the Second Test Match against Australia at Queen's Park in early 1984. To that point the tourists, though not on top, had given a good account of themselves. The *Benson & Hedges West Indies Cricket Annual 1984* confirmed

'he was never less than completely in command, dazzling the eye with his elegance and sense of timing which brought him two successive hooked sixes off Hogg and 15 fours'.

It was his highest innings to date but even in a more brief encounter he has the power to enchant.

Jeffrey's wicketkeeping was fallible in England in 1984. He missed chances, and more culpably permitted extras that could have been prevented, off the fast bowlers — though it is difficult to envisage any wicketkeeper, contemporary or otherwise, taking the thunderbolts of Malcolm Marshall and Michael Holding, or coping with Joel Garner's unusual bounce, with consistent accuracy. These were isolated incidents and he did not suffer quite such a nightmare match as that endured by even Deryck Murray at Nottingham on the previous tour. Any short-comings were compensated by his eye-catching dives and one-handed catches.

Dujon's temperament as a batsman was tested at Manchester. On the first morning the West Indies stuttered to 70-4 with Viv Richards and Clive Lloyd dismissed for a single each. The wicketkeeper came to the crease just before lunch and stayed almost to the end of the day. He scored 101 in a 197 runs partnership with Gordon Greenidge in which the Barbadian did not overshadow him. Indeed, if anything, the Jamaican took the play away from his partner, who, in contrast to his usual flamboyance, set about providing the innings with a solid foundation.

He exhibited his full repertoire, driving the faster bowlers and cutting the spinners. He moved delightfully into the ball. Christopher Martin Jenkins reported in *The Cricketer International* magazine:

'Dujon, simply, is a batsman of high class, a classical player with all the strokes, not least the late cut which he was able to play with delicate precision all too often by Cook and Pocock .... They were faced by batting of the highest class from Greenidge and Dujon, who punished any indiscretion of length and whose concentration never wavered'.

There is a definite advantage in playing a wicketkeeper-batsman, in that a place is opened for an extra batsman or bowler. Yet traditional wisdom dictates that the wicketkeeper above all other should be a specialist, that his name should be written down first and the rest of the team built around him. The practice is often different. Dujon is a competent 'keeper, and by the standard of some of his specialist predecessors could be expected to hold the position by that skill alone. Even so the argument lacks total conviction.

Mike Worrell, who made his name in club competition in England before returning to Barbados, is regarded as the best wicketkeeper to develop in the early 1980s. Nevertheless, he has been overlooked as reserve to Dujon for two consecutive tours in favour of Thelston Payne, another Barbadian whose infrequent appearances behind the stumps take second place to his left-handed batting. Although he went to Zimbabwe with the West Indies 'B' side in 1983, Worrell would lack real representative experience if he were required to step up to Test Match class now.

Everything points to Dujon continuing as wicketkeeper-batsman. There are those, however, an increasing number, who consider that he would serve the side best as a specialist batsman, particularly now that Clive Lloyd has retired and Viv Richards cannot be too long in following him. Whether he could take on an extra responsibility as a batsman while tending to his present duties is debatable. Much may depend on how Richie Richardson, Gus Logie and the emerging generation mature in the middle-order.

Even greater responsibility is not impossible. Dujon is captain of his country and is mentioned freely as an alternative to the assumed devolution of the regional leadership on Roger Harper. Nunes and Alexander, also from Wolmer's, led the West Indies from behind the stumps, but it is agreed generally that their best achievements came after they had given up one or other of these responsibilities. If the captaincy beckons, Dujon could yet move away from the wickets.

The Jamaican continued to prosper in Australia at the end of 1984. He scored 139 runs of sparkling stroke-play in putting on 147 for the sixth wicket with Larry Gomes in the First Test Match at Perth after the early batsmen had been dismissed cheaply, and shared a partnership of 160 runs for the same wicket with Clive Lloyd at Adelaide.

Pelham Warner considered that the absence of a regular wicketkeeper was one of the two main weaknesses of the first touring team to England in 1900 — the other was poor judgement of a run. Although Lebrun Constantine, father of the celebrated Learie, and George Learmond shared the task, both were required also for other skills. There have been several times since then when it has seemed that the stumper has served little purpose other than as stopper. That is no longer the case, and has not been so for a long time.

Nunes and Barrows were products of their age. Hendriks and Alexander yielded preference to no-one in their generation. Jeffrey Dujon, too, is in the modern mould shown throughout the world in wicketkeeper-batsmen Syed Kirmani, Paul Downton and, until his recent retirement, Rodney Marsh. Whatever the circumstances, the former students of Wolmer's School have served the West Indies well.

Five

Sabina Park, Kingston

Jamaicans are the individuals of the Caribbean, or, indeed, of anywhere. Outside influences and fashionable attitudes do not easily shake them out of their sense of independence or self-reliance, much to the frustration and grudging admiration of their friends. Test Matches at Sabina Park have a character of their own in which anything can happen, and from which explosive action on the pitch and controversy away from it result naturally if not inevitably. Kingston has been the scene of many outstanding individual performances and several swift changes of fortune.

Let Barbados have its waves of fast bowlers and free-scoring batsmen, Trinidad its tradition of spinners, and Guyana its stroke-players, Jamaica produces one genius in each generation, each one different to the other. Since the island made its first impact on world cricket George Headley, Alfred Valentine, Frank Worrell (by adoption), Collie Smith, Lawrence Rowe, Michael Holding and now Jeffrey Dujon have been among the first in talent. Others have flared with meteoric brilliance and have faded just as spontaneously.

Sabina Park has seen more dramatic incidents, exciting contests and individual excellence than any other Test Match ground in the region. The West Indies have no reason to be dissatisfied with their overall record here. Twelve matches have been won, ten drawn, and only three lost. The traditionally lively pitch has helped the fast bowlers to the advantage of the home side. All the defeats were sustained in consecutive engagements in the mid-1950s when the pace attack was unusually weak.

Kingston, the capital city, is on the southern side of Jamaica, an island which is mountainous in the interior and has low coastal plains and scattered hills and plateaux. It is 146 miles long but only 51 miles wide. Jamaica is the sole centre of cricket in the Western Caribbean, several hundred miles from the concentrated activity in the eastern territories from whose development it was divorced for many decades before air travel made communication easier. The nearest geographical neighbours are Cuba, Haiti, the U.S.A. and the Central American mainland.

The Norman Manley International Airport, situated on the Palisadoes isthmus 8 miles from the city centre, and the Douglas Sangster International Airport at Montego Bay on the northern coast provide air links with the rest of the region and beyond. Kingston, itself, is still a principal port. The city is overlooked by the Blue Mountains in the eastern part of the island, in which the highest peak rises to over seven thousand feet. The tropical, humid climate at sea-level is punctuated by frequent, though often brief, showers.

The cricket ground, still somewhat cramped in capacity, is located in the main urban area quite close to St. George's College and the Roman Catholic cathedral. Unlike the other main sporting venues, such as Caymanas Race Track and the National Stadium, which are sited either in the northern suburbs of the Corporate Area or outside the city limits altogether, Sabina Park is within easy access of the Franklyn Town, Passmore Town, Allman Town and Vineyard Town, pockets of high-density population.

A decade ago Brunell Jones, the Trinidadian writer, commented: 'The Sabina Park ground, which was surrounded by evidence of plans for improvement of the venue, was packed with spectators, and the view from the Press Box presented a riot of colour. Northwards were the beautiful Blue Mountains, one of the many wonders of the Caribbean, forming a backdrop for the sight of mango and ackee trees laden, not with juicy fruit, but scores of worshippers of the best game on earth!'

Cricket is known to have been played at St George's College since the middle of the nineteenth century, and the Vere C.C. was formed in 1857. Kingston C.C., the oldest surviving club, which in one extraordinary early game scored 356 against Spanish Town and dismissed their opponents for only 7, was founded six years later and occupied Sabina Park in 1880. Because of the difficulty in extended sea-journeys the island missed out on much of the developing inter-territorial competition until 1896.

In that same year G.W. Chandler took 126 wickets in club cricket, the first time the aggregate had been achieved in the West Indies. L.D. Samuel made 207 not out, the region's first recorded double-century, for Kingston C.C. against Melbourne C.C. in 1903. The early English touring teams brought the island within the scope of international cricket. Jamaica's games against the M.C.C. side in 1925/26 and those led by L.H. Tennyson in the years immediately afterwards were marked by exceptionally heavy scoring.

The first Test Match at Sabina Park in April 1930 was remarkable in many ways. It was intended that the contest should be played to a finish. George Gunn, then past 50 years-old, opened the innings with Andy Sandham, who scored 325, which set a new record highest individual Test Match score. The first six men in the order reached at least fifty as England amassed the record total of 849. Spinner Tommy Scott, the most successful bowler, yielded 206 runs for his 5 wickets. The West Indians, perhaps tired by their stint in the field, offered scant resistance in being dismissed for 286. Surprisingly Freddie Calthorpe, the visiting captain, did not enforce the follow-on in spite of such a massive advantage. He was aware doubtless than his own bowlers, who included Wilfred Rhodes, also in his fifties, would be fatigued and, in theory, he had as much time as he wanted at his disposal. England pressed on and declared their second innings a massive 835 runs in front.

George Headley, who had shown his ability by scoring three centuries earlier in the series, took up the challenge in partnership with home captain Karl Nunes. The latter was out eight runs short of his hundred. Headley kept going until he was stumped for 223. Clarence Passailique, with whom he put on an unbeaten 487 for Jamaica against L.H. Tennyson's team two years later, was still there when rain interrupted play at 408-5. It rained incessantly for two days, the eighth and ninth of the match, so that the teams agreed to call it a draw.

Headley was the central figure in the historic victory by an innings and 161 runs in 1935. The outcome of the series depended on this game. 'Mass George' hit an attacking 270 not out in which he dominated partnerships of 202 with Derek Sealy for the third wicket and of 147 with future captain Rolph Grant for the seventh. It was the only century for the West Indies in the entire rubber. The 535-7 dec total gave the fast bowlers an opportunity which they exploited to the full.

Manny Martindale's opening attack was devastating. A rising delivery broke opposing captain Bob Wyatt's jaw. Townsend, Paine and Errol Holmes followed closely, so that half the team were in the pavilion with the total at 26. As on so many previous occasions wicketkeeper Leslie Ames led the counter-attack, but England followed on 274 runs behind. Nobody saved them in the second innings as Martindale and Constantine hastened the tourists to defeat and the West Indies to their first Test Match series victory.

Fast bowling was the main factor in another one-sided win by 10 wickets over the same tourists in 1948. Hines Johnson, the exceptionally tall paceman, dismissed five batsmen in each innings — 'looked a truly great bowler' commented Wisden 'no time did he attempt to intimidate the England batsmen by pitching short'. Everton Weekes recalled, because of Headley's withdrawal, to the team from which he had been omitted initially, hit a sparkling 141 in sustaining support batting throughout the order. The Barbadian went on to reach three figures in his next four innings against India to establish a record of five hundreds in successive Test Match innings.

There was further high scoring in the Fifth Test Match against India in 1953. The tourists, for whom Polly Umrigar made a century, moved comfortably to 277-4, from which point left-arm spinner Alfred Valentine limited the final total to 312. The West Indian batsmen were rampant. Frank Worrell made 237 and Weekes and Walcott contributed single centuries. India, 264 runs behind, were rescued by a 237 runs second-wicket partnership between Pankaj Roy, the patient yet erratic opening batsman, and Vijay Manjrekar.

The West Indies were in command throughout the First Test Match against England in 1954. J.K. Holt, a Jamaican whose l.b.w. dismissal for 94 sparked popular displeasure, was one of five home batsmen to reach fifty. The tourists, in contrast, batted unevenly and trailed by 247 runs. Stollmeyer's decision not to invite them to follow on caused surprise at the time. Quick-scoring by Weekes in reaching 90 not out permitted his captain to declare 456 runs ahead. In this innings Headley's long international career came to an end with his dismissal by Tony Lock from a delivery of dubious legality.

England set off strongly in pursuit of the target. Left-handed opener Willie Watson was so much at ease that the second wicket did not fall until the total had reached 277. Then fast bowler Esmond Kentish brought about a complete transformation of fortune. Seven wickets toppled for just six runs, and the Jamaican fast bowler took his analysis to 5 wickets for 49 runs. In spite of some belated defiance for the last wicket England went down by 140 runs.

The tourists' confidence increased throughout the season and they needed only to win the Fifth Test Match at Sabina Park to share the rubber. The issue was settled effectively in the opening overs. Fast-medium bowler Trevor Bailey took 7 wickets for 34 runs in dismissing the home side for 139. Len Hutton scored 205 in taking England to victory by 9 wickets. The highlights for the West Indies were Clyde Walcott's secure batting, which contrasted greatly with that of his colleagues, and the international debut of Gary Sobers, played here as a left-arm spinner.

In the First Test Match of 1955 the Australians showed what to expect for the rest of the season as Neil Harvey and Keith Miller followed a three-figure stand from the opening batsmen by putting on 224 runs for the third wicket. In spite of yet another hundred from

Walcott, the West Indies batted disappointingly against fast bowlers Ray Lindwall, Miller and Ron Archer and had to follow on 256 runs behind. Collie Smith's hundred in his first Test Match was the consolation of the brittle second innings, from which the West Indies lost by 9 wickets.

The Fifth Test Match on the same ground bristled with batting records. Miller gave Australia a great start by taking 6 wickets for 107 runs. This time the West Indies, for whom Walcott made one more century, flattered to deceive. At one point 205-3 they were bowled out for 357. The dismissal of the first two Australian batsmen before the total reached double figures raised hopes that the scoring could be kept within bounds.

Alas, doublecentury-maker Harvey, the dapper left-hander, and opener Colin McDonald put on 295 runs for the third wicket, and Miller and Archer powered the tourists ahead with 220 runs for the fifth. Richie Benaud raced to his own hundred in 78 minutes to establish a record five centuries for a Test Match innings. The 758-8 dec total was the highest to date by any country outside England. Five bowlers were hit for over a hundred runs each, and a sixth, Sobers, failed by just a single to join them.

Walcott and Sobers scored 179 runs for the third wicket, after which the tourists swept on to the seemingly inevitable success by an innings and 82 runs. The match was a personal triumph for Walcott. He added 110 to his 155 in the first innings, and having achieved something similar at Queen's Park he became the first batsman anywhere to record the feat twice in the same series. In five consecutive matches at Sabina Park he had scored five hundreds and two half-centuries, and he was not finished yet. Beaten in Jamaica thrice in succession the West Indies have not lost there again in over three decades.

There were even more records against Pakistan in 1958. Imtiaz Ahmed, the opening batsman and wicketkeeper, saw the visitors to a sound enough start in reaching 328, and, in spite of the absence of two batsmen through injury, Wazir Mohammad fought a sturdy rearguard second innings. The aggregate would have been sufficient to evade defeat in a normal match, but this match was not normal and the West Indies won easily by an innings and 174 runs shortly after the start of play on the last day.

Conrad Hunte set the pace in seeming to chase the record individual score in a Test Match, which was then the 364 scored by Len Hutton for England against Australia at The Oval in London in 1938. The Barbadian was run out for 260 after sharing a stand of 446 runs for the second wicket. His partner, Sobers, carried on where he left off and set the new record of 365 not out in only his first international century. Walcott, who had scored so heavily on previous visits to Kingston, was on 88 not out when the left-hander reached that landmark. Delighted fans running onto the pitch caused play to be abandoned for the rest of the day. At this point the West Indies declared at 790-3, which is still the highest Test Match score by any team other than England.

The dominance of bat over ball was broken in 1960. Wesley Hall bowled magnificently to take 7 wickets for 69 runs, in which only Colin Cowdrey offered recognisable resistance. Sobers was again irresistible as the West Indies reached 299-2 on their way to what seemed to be a substantial match-winning total. The rest of the batting fell away so suddenly that the eventual lead was only 76 runs. Even so victory was still likely on a pitch generating pace.

Geoff Pullar and Cowdrey, the opening batsmen, countered a determined assault by the fast bowlers and were not parted until 177 runs were on the board. The latter was caught at the wicket just three runs short of registering his second hundred of the match. The rapid loss of wickets prevented the tourists from prospering by this success. Eventually the West Indies needed to score 230 runs to win in just over four hours and, in spite of a valiant attempt in which at one time they seemed to be ahead of the clock, and not without controversy, they finished 55 runs short with four wickets in hand.

Alan Ross in *Through the Caribbean* was not very impressed by the old press-box in this 'steeply enclosed cockpit of a ground':

'The Press Box at Sabina Park must rank high among the most uncomfortable on Test Match grounds .... It was also a box so hot and airless that a pressure-cooker could scarcely have been less inviting. Lunch had to be fetched from the pavilion a long way off .... There was danger in the box too. Glasses crashed to the ground, beer bottles got crunched underfoot .... There were few incident-free days within the box .... There were compensations, however. We were directly behind and above the bowler's arm, and so near that Trueman could wink or scowl at us on his walk back. Wesley Hall almost disappeared from sight under us as he turned at the end of his run'.

Two years later the Indians came to Kingston twice, and twice they were defeated. The West Indians enjoyed a batting feast in the high-scoring Second Test Match in which Sobers, Kanhai and Easton McMorris made hundreds. Although the tourists achieved 395 at their first attempt they lost by an innings and 18 runs. Hall whittled through their second innings with 6 wickets for 49 runs.

Jamaican fast bowler Lester King excelled in his one real

international chance to take 5 wickets for 46 runs in the Fifth Test Match. His initial spell demoralised the Indians after they had dismissed the West Indians comparatively cheaply. Sobers enjoyed allround success in scoring 104 and 50 and in taking 5 wickets for 63 runs in the victory by 123 runs. Frank Worrell, the triumphant captain, made 98 not out in his last Test Match innings on the home ground of his adopted country.

Fast bowler Wesley Hall was the match-winner again in 1965. The early sessions were hard fought. The West Indians disappointed in making only 239. Yet because of Hall's 5 wickets for 60 runs the Australians could not capitalise on that advantage. Ahead by 22 runs the home team regained its confidence and went on to win by 179 runs. This comparatively low-scoring match in a season dominated by high scoring was vital to the outcome of the series.

The Second Test Match against England in 1968 was rich in incident and controversy. The pitch was fast and fiery from the outset, but Cowdrey and John Edrich survived further good bowling by Hall to take the visitors to the apparent safety of 376. That total seemed to be even more commanding as fast bowler John Snow shot out the West Indies for a modest 143 by taking 7 wickets for 49 runs. After his previous success here Sobers was l.b.w. without scoring. His team followed on 233 runs behind.

Although second innings resistance was more determined five wickets went down before the arrears were cleared. Then Basil Butcher's dismissal to a diving catch by wicketkeeper Jim Parks sparked a bottle-throwing riot. When play was resumed Sobers batted magnificently in adverse circumstances to score 113 not out It was similar to and as important as his innings at Lord's two years earlier. The initiative changed hands so completely that he declared, leaving England to survive almost two hours. The West Indians almost snatched a spectacular victory. Two batsmen were out without a run on the board, four were out for 19, and England hung on at 68-8. That collapse may have inspired the less successful declaration at Port of Spain two matches later.

E.M. Wellings, the Wisden correspondent, submitted a report that was not sympathetic to the West Indian point of view:

'Until the bottle throwing riot in mid-afternoon on the third day England looked like winning comfortably. After the trouble ... they never regained their zest. In the end they struggled to avoid defeat in a final innings marked by strange umpiring. They made the mistake of agreeing to resume after the trouble had been put down. It would have been wiser and fairer to the visiting players to abandon play for the day'.

Sardesai scored 212 which enabled his captain to ask the home team to follow on. Rohan Kanhai, who had made top-score in the first innings, banished fears of a further breakdown by hitting 158 not out, in which he was supported well by Sobers and by Clive Lloyd.

Lawrence Rowe was the hero of the drawn match against New Zealand the next year. On his international debut he scored 214 and shared a 269 runs second-wicket stand with Roy Fredericks. Glenn Turner, the tourists' opening batsman, carried his bat for 223 and clipped the West Indian lead to 122 runs. Rowe excelled again in scoring a second innings 100 not out. Chasing a target of 341 runs the visitors were soon in trouble and were indebted to Mark Burgess for saving the game over a hundred runs adrift with four wickets in hand.

There was another high-scoring draw when the Australians came to Kingston in 1973. Both sides scored exactly the same first innings total. Maurice Foster hit a hundred on his home ground, and the West Indies batted consistently against the pace of Max Walker and Jeff Hammond. Opening batsman Keith Stackpole struck a punishing century which killed further competitive interest.

Batsmen had the better of the exchanges in the next match against England. Rowe and Fredericks repeated their feat of two years earlier in putting on 206 runs for the first wicket. Five West Indian batsmen attained fifty in establishing a first innings lead of 230 runs. Opener Dennis Amiss fought a magnificent rearguard action for England. He scored 262 not out, being still at the crease with the last batsman at the close. In one respect it is a pity that his partner was not dismissed in the closing stages so that Amiss could have been recorded as carrying his bat.

India have sad recollections of their meeting with Michael Holding in the concluding Test Match in 1976. Although Sunil Gavaskar and Anshuman Gaekwad started with 136 for the first wicket, the fast bowlers were later unplayable on a fiery pitch and two batsmen retired injured. The Jamaican paceman performed to near perfection in the first example of the blitz of speed with which the West Indies would dominate international competition for at least the next decade.

Rowe and Fredericks began with yet another century stand, but the home team led by only 85 runs. To every appearance the match was still open. Mohinder Amarnath steered the score to 97-2, and there the match ended. Three wickets fell at that total and, because of injury, the remaining five batsmen failed to come to the crease. It was a remarkable anti-climax, and the home team won easily by 10 wickets. The sudden decline of the Indians established the reputation of the West Indian speed attack as a formidable force.

Brunell Jones recaptured in *Cricket? XI* the impact of Holding's bowling on one unfortunate batsman:

'Gaekwad's confidence had by now been completely shattered. He was absolutely nothing like the fellow who had batted so well for his century in Trinidad. The blows he received from the fast bowlers the day before had him cowed. On this day, with Holding bowling as fast as the wind; with the pitch provoking fire-cracking hostility, Gaekwad began backing away; turning his face away and ducking, from the moment Holding began his run-up from the Press Box end and he paid dearly for it. In one unforgettable over, the last before lunch, Holding hit Gaekwad on his gloved, injured fingers; next ball kicked and hit the batsman on the left side of his body and the painful climax came when Gaekwad, taking his spectacles away from the flight of the ball, was struck under the ear'.

The West Indies beat Pakistan by 140 runs in a more straightforward match in 1977. Gordon Greenidge took the honours by scoring 100 in the first innings, in which fast bowler Imran Khan otherwise carried all before him in taking 6 wickets for 90 runs, and in the second shared a century opening stand with Fredericks in their last partnership together before the latter retired from international cricket. Asif Iqbal made a spirited fight back in the final stages, but by then the match had been decided.

Controversy returned with the Australians in 1978. The tourists wanted to win the Fifth Test Match in Kingston to salvage some honour from a disappointing tour. They began purposefully. Peter Toohey's hundred was followed by some incisive overs from the quicker bowlers which reduced the West Indies to 63-5. Centurymaker Larry Gomes was well supported by the lower-order in taking his side to within 63 runs of the Australian total. The visitors did not surrender the advantage. Graeme Wood and Toohey added 180 runs for the second wicket and made a declaration possible.

West Indies, set to score 369 runs to win, lost half of their wickets before reaching three figures. Alvin Kallicharran battled single-handed against the spinners. He made a painstaking 126 and shortly after his dismissal Vanburn Holder was given out l.b.w. The home team was then 258-9 and as 6.2 overs still remained to be bowled defeat was virtually inescapable. The crowd began to hurl missiles onto the pitch and play was suspended for the day. Although the administrators consented to continue into a sixth day the umpires, who had been neither consulted nor informed, refused to proceed, so that the match was abandoned as a draw.

Graham Gooch, hitting 153, and Michael Holding, taking 5 wickets for 56 runs, resumed the most enthralling of modern duels in the drawn match in 1981. The West Indies, for whom Haynes and Greenidge commenced with the now customary century stand, batted well throughout the order to lead by 157 runs. The tourists sagged to 32-3 but the prospects of victory receded as soon as David Gower got into his stride in scoring 154 not out.

Rain seemed to destine the First Test Match against India in 1983 to a similar conclusion. The visiting batsmen experienced such difficulty against the fast bowlers, especially Andy Roberts, that they were 127-7 before Yashpal Sharma and Sandhu took them to 251. The West Indies, for whom Greenidge made the only half-century, found run-scoring to be just as difficult and edged ahead by only three runs. The loss through rain of the entire fourth day dampened the competitive interest.

India reached 168-6 by tea on the final day. Immediately on the resumption Roberts dismissed three batsmen in his first over and took the outstanding wicket shortly afterwards. The home team had to score 172 runs to win in a very tight race against the clock. They went for the target from the start. Viv Richards hit a sparkling sixty with four sixes. Although wickets tumbled in the final overs the West Indies won convincingly by 4 wickets.

The Australians were outplayed even more decisively the following year. Malcolm Marshall and Joel Garner humbled their batsmen for 199, a stark contrast to their astronomical scores on the same ground just under thirty years earlier. Gordon Greenidge, hitting the only hundred of the match, maintained his tradition of a century first-wicket partnership here, and his partner, Haynes, was not out until the tourists' total was in sight at 162. The other batsmen did not maintain the momentum, but the lead of 106 runs was decisive.

The visitors were hampered by the absence of injured opener Steve Smith. Allan Border, coming in at first wicket down, defied the bowlers tenaciously in scoring 60 not out while his colleagues at the other end faltered. Marshall curtailed any hopes of survival by cutting through the middle- and lower-order in taking 5 wickets for 51 runs. The West Indies cantered home by 10 wickets.

The New Zealanders broke down so completely against the fast bowlers, spearheaded by Winston Davis, in early 1985 that they had to follow on 225 runs behind. Only opening batsman John Wright's half-century kept them in the contest after the West Indies had batted soundly, rather than spectacularly, throughout the order to reach 363. Yet the tourists seemed to ensure a draw when Jeff Crowe and Wright, who scored 112 and 84 respectively, took them to a comfortable 223-1 in their second innings.

Marshall turned the match by catching Crowe and, himself, swiftly dismissing Rutherford, Ian Smith, Bracewell and Richard Hadlee in a blistering spell early on the fourth day. With Jeremy Coney unable to bat after sustaining a broken arm in the first innings the New Zealand innings terminated suddenly and the West Indies won again by 10 wickets. As with the Indians nine years earlier the visitors' resolve had crumpled against the fast bowlers after an initial display of defiance.

That match confirmed also the keen appreciation of the future by the regional selectors, and the continuity of the Jamaican tradition of pace, in taking Courtney Walsh, a then promising youngster, to Australia at the end of the previous year instead of one of the established fast bowlers. Although there were few opportunities in that series, Walsh showed that the faith was not mis-placed by sharing the honours in the defeat of New Zealand at Sabina Park.

Six

Clive Lloyd and the Captaincy

Clive Lloyd is almost certainly the best-known contemporary West Indian, even in those countries where cricket is not followed with such fervour as it is at home. Whereas statesmen appeal solely to the politically-minded section of society, and entertainment 'super-stars' essentially to the young, Lloyd's appeal has been to the entire community. He, his wife Waveney, and the children, are for many people the first family of the West Indies. It has been difficult to contemplate either the cricket team or the public communications media without him at the forefront.

Although Lloyd has been the best left-handed batsman since Sobers and an exceptional fieldsmen with cat-like reflexes, his most significant contribution to cricket has been as a captain. He was the captain who had most in common with the majority of West Indian cricket followers. As stated in my previous book *Caribbean Cricketers from the Pioneers to Packer* he

'has apparently stepped straight from the crowds on the terraces onto the field of play and shares the public's hopes, their fears and their sentiments. He has opened up the game when they would, closed it down when they would and has made mistakes when they would'.

Clive has steered West Indian cricket successfully through the World Series Cricket schism, the defections to representative competition in South Africa and the many pressures of the modern game by winning the respect of the men under his leadership. It is doubtful if any of his predecessors, save only Frank Worrell, would have had the breadth of understanding and sympathy, originating from a common background, to have represented their aspirations so effectively.

The early captains were drawn from the social elite. Aucher Warner of Trinidad, leader of the first overseas touring side in 1900, was the brother of Pelham Warner, the future England captain knighted for his services to cricket administration. Harold Austin, a

Barbadian, forged the identity of the regional team in the pioneer days, especially in putting together the pieces immediately after the First World War. He was succeeded by his vice-captain, Karl Nunes, a Jamaican, and by the Grant brothers, Jackie and Rolph, who had no real previous experience of representative cricket.

There were four different captains in the first home series against England in 1929/30, each of whom led in his own territory. Teddy Hoad was appointed for Kensington, Nelson Betancourt for Queen's Park, Maurice Fernandes for Bourda, and Nunes for Kingston. Something similar happened when the Grant dynasty came to an end. Although the practice was not conducive to continuity in leadership and inspiration, not all of the captains were lightweights who did not merit selection on playing ability or the quality of their captaincy. The West Indies were led far better than were India in the same period.

Wisden commented of Jackie Grant after the tour to England in 1933:

'In Grant, they were very fortunate to have not only a clever, but an enthusiastic captain. Astute in the management of his bowling and the placing of his field, he inspired the whole team by his own admirable example for very few men in England last summer fielded so brilliantly close to the wicket as he did ... Grant played the game, and insisted on those under him doing so, in the most sporting spirit'.

His adventurous declarations at Sydney in 1931 showed justified confidence in his bowlers.

The selectors had no clear-cut policy for the first home series after the Second World War. George Headley was the logical candidate, and he was black. The Jamaican led the West Indies in the opening engagement in Bridgetown without being appointed for the whole rubber. In the event, injury ruled him out for most of the season. Gerry Gomez took over from his compatriot Jeff Stollmeyer in Trinidad, but fortunate to inherit the mantle for the successes at Bourda and Sabina Park newcomer John Goddard, a Barbadian, secured the position.

There was little controversy when he was succeeded by Stollmeyer, his long-serving vice-captain. Nevertheless, the appointment of Denis Atkinson, who could not be sure of a regular team place, to replace the injured Trinidadian against Australia in 1955 underlined the change in social attitudes. Although he enhanced his reputation by scoring a double-century at Kensington, it was no longer acceptable to appoint a leader just because he was fair-skinned and had the right social connections. Even hitherto reactionary India had moved ahead of the West Indies in this respect since the ending of the Second World

War. There were now some first-class black candidates.

Gerry Alexander's captaincy at the end of the 1950s concluded this tradition. The Jamaican, not then successful as a wicketkeeper, would surely have been dropped if he had not been made captain ahead of more experienced and seemingly better qualified contemporaries. Ironically his later career revealed such batting, wicketkeeping and leadership skills that he might well have advanced to the position on his own merit. Henceforth, however, the captaincy would be won and lost on the field of play.

The selection of Frank Worrell to lead the team to Australia in 1960/61 was a landmark in the development of West Indian cricket. The man was matched with the hour. In the preceding decade there had been a series of frustrations made worse by the high expectations after the triumphs of the late 1940s. The region did not hold together. Worrell, however, had the right qualifications of being a Barbadian who now represented Jamaica, an independent spirit yet in tune with the aspirations of his colleagues, and an allrounder who knew the requirements of each department of the game.

Although that first series was lost (by the narrowest possible margin), only a stubborn last-wicket stand at Adelaide and a disputed umpiring decision at Sydney stood between the West Indians and a surprising victory. Freshly confident they exacted full vengeance on the visiting Indians in making a clean sweep of the five-match rubber and, then, defeated England in the memorable summer of 1963. Worrell, who retired then, had led the region in three series from the depths of despair to the top of the world.

On Worrell's premature death from leukaemia in 1967 former opposing captain Richie Benaud commented:

'He was a great leader of men and one of the finest cricketers on and off the field in the history of the game. It is difficult to realise that the indolent drawl, the feline grace known all over the world are no more. Few men have had a better influence on cricket'.

In the same Wisden obituary Billy Griffith, Secretary of the M.C.C., stated that he had

'been impressed by his ever growing stature as a leader of cricketers, by his tolerance and understanding and by the contribution he was making to the game'.

During his leadership all members of the team deserved their selection on merit. There was no obvious example of the previous embarrassing practice of one or more deserving player being left out of the side without good reason. Leeward and Windward Islanders might dispute that assertion, but Worrell was aware of their destiny.

As a result the team played up to its full potential and surprised many with their success.

There was no time for the contending territorial loyalties which had destroyed the team's cohesion. It has been said that on the disappointing visit to Australia in 1951/52 Barbadians and Trinidadians had formed different camps looking to different sources for inspiration. Because each member of Worrell's side was conscious of playing for the West Indies (it was also the age of the Federation) the selectors had less need to 'balance' the team by including perhaps an inferior cricketer at the expense of a better merely to soothe territorial pride. Adjustments may still be made, but nowhere to the same degree as hitherto.

Discipline was tight under Worrell. Outward signs of dissent with umpiring decisions were reprimanded. Even neutral observers considered that the West Indians had cause of complaint with some of the adjudication in Australia in 1960/61. Unnecessary short-pitched bowling also was kept in check. Wesley Hall did not need to resort to blind intimidation and the more mercurial Chester Watson played little part in the proceedings after sending down too many loose bumpers at Melbourne. Roy Gilchrist, who had been sent home from Alexander's tour of India as a disciplinary measure, might well have been more inclined to accept correction from Worrell.

Frank was at the helm in two of the most exciting finishes in the history of Test Match cricket, the tie at Brisbane in 1960 and the tense draw at Lord's three years later. His cool control prevented the panic measures which had snatched one-wicket defeat from the jaws of victory at Melbourne in 1951/52, and the practical advice to Hall, the bowler of the final over on each occasion, was that above all he should guard against delivering a no-ball.

Gary Sobers, instead of incumbent vice-captain Conrad Hunte, took over the reins for the victorious home series against Australia in 1965. He had a strong combination and under his mentor's guiding eye continued to dominate international competition. It was a happy honeymoon. Yet the dynamo had begun to run down at the time Worrell died. Sobers' personal allround brilliance in England in 1966, when he won the rubber off his own bat, hid for the time just how far the impetus had slowed. The full extent of the decline did not become clear until the next home series against England.

By the Fourth Test Match at Queen's Park in March 1968 the West Indies seemed to have survived the shocks in the early matches and come through without defeat. A first innings total of 526-7 declared put them in the driving seat, especially after England broke down against Basil Butcher, a very occasional leg-spinner. Instead of building up the moral advantage with a view to the final and deciding clash at Bourda, the captain gambled on a second innings declaration at 92-2. His depleted attack was reduced to two front-line bowlers and the tourists recovered to win by 7 wickets. That decision cost him the series.

Nothing quite went well for Sobers, as captain, after that. The Australians tore apart the remnants of the great team, and even the unheralded New Zealanders shared the honours. After further defeat in England the West Indies lost to India and drew with New Zealand in home rubbers in which man-for-man they were far away the superior side. The captain took the blame for the jaded performance and was relieved from the position for the visit of the Australians in early 1973.

Although that series, too, was lost, the West Indians bounced back under the leadership of Rohan Kanhai, the first Guyanese to be appointed permanently to the captaincy, to overwhelm England with quick bowling and an avalanche of runs, in which, appropriately, his predecessor participated to the full. That three-match series in 1973, in which they shared the billing with New Zealand, was the last mini-rubber the West Indies have played in England. Since then they have been the star attraction.

Nevertheless, in spite of ending the run of failure and in inspiring confidence Kanhai's captaincy was not accepted universally. The acrimony which affected the Birmingham Test Match, whatever the arguments on either side, was not considered to have been in the spirit associated with Worrell. The failure to press home the advantage in the return home series, in which England squared the honours in the last match, hastened his departure. Perhaps precipitately the selectors decided to bring in a new broom.

Clive Hubert Lloyd was born in Georgetown, Guyana on 31 August 1944. As the cousin of off-spinner Lance Gibbs he was raised in an atmosphere of cricket and destined to make his mark in the game. He followed Gibbs and other young cricketers of the neighbourhood into the celebrated Demarara Cricket Club and made his debut in the Case Cup while still only 15 years old. Yet in spite of some good club performances the youngster did not play for Guyana until 1964. Once more he had to experience initial disappointment before meeting with success.

Lloyd's first match against Jamaica at Bourda was not outstanding and he was dropped. The following season he failed similarly to impress against the visiting Australians. The domestic season of early 1966 provided the first crux of his career. His future looked bleaker still when he failed to score in the first innings against Barbados. In the second, however, Clive hit a century and has not looked back. That Barbadian attack was particularly strong, and a year later the island challenged the rest of the world.

Guyana came into Caribbean cricket in a big way in the 1960s. The batting success of Roy Fredericks, Steve Camacho and Lloyd, himself, showed that the earlier breakthrough of Kanhai, Butcher and Joe Solomon had been more than temporary. It demonstrated also that Georgetown was capable of matching the excellence of Berbice. Disappointed to be omitted from the tour to England in 1966, the young left-hander was the discovery of the ensuing visit to India at the end of that year.

Although he did little in the opening games Lloyd was included in the side as a replacement for the injured Seymour Nurse in the First Test Match at Bombay. In the first innings he made 82 in a three-figure stand with Conrad Hunte, and in the second was there at the finish with 78 not out as the West Indies won the match by 6 wickets. Described as 'looking scholarly behind thick-rimmed spectacles' the newcomer hit centuries against the Prime Minister's XI at New Delhi and against Ceylon (now Sri Lanka) at Colombo, and failed by only five runs to reach the same target in V.S. Hazare's benefit game at Nagpur.

Lloyd held firm while the rest of the batting disintegrated around him at the turn of the decade. Against England he hit hundreds in crises at both Queen's Park and Sabina Park, and reached a match-winning 129 on a spinning pitch at Brisbane. The retirement of Butcher, Nurse and, temporarily, Kanhai following that disappointing Australasian tour reduced further the stability of the batting. Clive was now a senior player on whom much depended, but his dominating touch seemed to desert him.

After that century at Brisbane he reached fifty six times in the next five rubbers without going on to three figures. Particularly he could not get going in the Caribbean. His inclusion in the side to oppose the Australians in 1973 was disputed and touched with political overtones. He replied to the criticism in the most convincing manner and in the most appropriate place. Clive plundered 178 from the opposing attack at Bourda, in which he and Kanhai scored all but 31 runs in the total of 366. From there he went on to make one century and two half-centuries against England.

At this point in his career Lloyd was more than just a world-class batsman. He was a more than competent bowler and an acrobatic cover-point to compare with the best in history. His fielding in the covers outshone even that of Colin Bland, the brilliant Springbok whose ground-work attracted spectators to see just that alone. Clive was one of the first West Indians to take advantage of the opportunity to make a professional career in the English county championship. His blitz batting made Lancashire the undisputed kings of limited-over cricket in the early 1970s.

Lloyd was not the automatic successor to Kanhai. Yet, with the decision in favour of youth, there were few of the younger players with his depth of experience. Gibbs was a bowler, and captains are not chosen often from these ranks, and wicketkeeper Deryck Murray, who had toured first under Worrell over a decade previously, had not played regularly enough to be a more serious contender. The Trinidadian became a stalwart vice-captain during the first half of Clive's captaincy and led the side in his absence. Several of the debutants on the tour to India in 1974/75 became long-serving members of the team.

After winning the first two matches by decisive margins, the West Indian express almost ran off the rails. The inexperienced batsmen were smothered by spinners Bishen Bedi, Erapalli Prasanna and B.S. Chandrasekhar at Calcutta and Madras. Each time the two sides finished almost level on first innings, but the tourists, batting second, failed in the final run-in. Lloyd, who already had scored 163 in the victorious First Test Match at Bangalore, needed to lead by example in the deciding encounter at Bombay.

The West Indians were rampant in reaching 604-6 declared. Clive did play a captain's innings. The 242 not out, his highest in a Test Match, contained a century third-wicket stand and a huge partnership of 250 with Murray for the sixth wicket. Although the Indians managed to keep in the fight by scoring 406 the initiative had passed to the visitors. They won decisively by 201 runs to take an exceptionally hard-fought rubber. The new West Indians were obviously a force to consider, but recent experience indicated that the traditional instability as well as brilliance had not been eradicated.

Clive's century crowned the first Prudential Cup Final at Lord's on 21 June 1975. The West Indies were firm favourites to thrash Australia whom they had beaten earlier in the tournament. Even so the start was not encouraging. Three batsmen were dismissed cheaply, including Fredericks who dislodged a bail with his foot while hitting the ball over the boundary. Then Lloyd set about the bowling hitting 102 and dominating a match-winning stand of 149 with a restrained but responsible Rohan Kanhai.

The euphoria did not last long. The team went to Australia that winter and suffered a hammering. Honours were even at a victory each after the first two matches. Then the fast bowling attack of Jeff Thomson, Dennis Lillee, Gary Gilmour and Max Walker rolled over the West Indians. The new leader had much to learn against an exceptionally strong home side guided by the Chappell brothers. Yet the greatest humiliation of Lloyd's captaincy sowed the seeds of future success.

He had a comparatively good season with the bat. Clive made centuries in consecutive matches at Perth, a convincing victory, and at Melbourne, where the West Indies could not come back after a first innings breakdown. He finished the series on 91 not out in the return fixture at Melbourne. Apart from some sound scoring by Viv Richards in the later stages the younger batsmen failed to make the progress expected of them. Somebody would have to pay for the debacle, and it was the Indians.

Once more Lloyd led from the front. He struck a century in the opening engagement at Kensington and half-hundreds in the following two matches. Now his own strategy was based on pace, which had been so decisively destructive for the other side in Australia, and it did not change appreciably in the next decade. He found the right penetrative striking-force in the smooth-action Holding. Clive could afford even to blunder with his declaration at Queen's Park — the Indians scored a record 406-4 to win in the fourth innings — and still win the rubber impressively.

The West Indies were mature and confident in both batting and bowling when they hit England in 1976. It was a spectacular summer. After two sparring draws the tourists scythed through the opposition. Apart from half-centuries in the two London matches, Lloyd was not required to score runs in a season in which Richards and Greenidge blasted their way to the forefront of world batting. The strength of the side is illustrated by the necessity for Alvin Kallicharran and Lawrence Rowe to contest one available position.

The success of the fast bowlers was just as encouraging. The combined assault of Holding, Roberts and Daniel succeeded where even the Australians had been thwarted after some initial success the previous year. Excessive short-pitched deliveries wasted the opportunity in an evening session at Manchester, but when the bowling was directed to better effect it was irresistible. Thereafter Lloyd's outstanding ambition was to defeat Australia in an even contest over five Test Matches. That confrontation was an unexpectedly long time in coming.

The Australian team which came to the Caribbean in 1978 was weakened already by the omission of the leading players contracted to World Series Cricket. The full-strength West Indies won by an innings at Queen's Park and by 9 wickets at Kensington, but there was little satisfaction in such one-sided traffic. Then the contest was thrown wide open by the withdrawal of the greater part of the West Indies team on the eve of the Third Test Match at Bourda.

The selectors left out Desmond Haynes, Richard Austin and Deryck Murray, all of whom had signed to World Series Cricket and whose participation in the forthcoming conventional tour to India could not be certain. Lloyd and most of the other players withdrew as a demonstration of their lack of confidence in the selectors. It says much for their loyalty to Clive that only one of the regular team members did not follow his example. Without his guiding hand the under-strength side went down to its first ever defeat in India.

Because the decision was almost unanimous the schism did West Indian cricket little long-term harm. The region was at full strength again in 1979 for the Prudential Cup competition, which was won even more convincingly than on the previous occasion. Clive made top score of 73 not out against New Zealand at Nottingham in the tournament's tightest contest. It was good preparation for the abbreviated tour to Australia. There Lloyd hit 121 in the rubber-clinching match at Adelaide. Anyone less ambitious would have considered that victory to be compensation for the earlier defeat, but Clive would not be happy until he was successful over the full distance.

Rain, the wettest summer for over seventy years, washed out the competitive edge of the English season in 1980. The West Indies scrambled home by 2 wickets in the First Test Match at Nottingham, the only one decided. The weather ruined the Third Test Match at Manchester. Yet Lloyd, coming to the crease with the total at a precarious 25-3, held the side together and reached a century which was welcomed by the local crowd as one of their own.

Clive passed fifty every time that he went in to bat against England at home in early 1981. He and Larry Gomes steadied the innings at Kensington after Richards had fallen without scoring. Their fifth-wicket partnership realised 154 runs in which the captain made exactly 100. He was caught at the wicket for 95 in giving his side a 157 runs lead at Sabina Park. The enjoyment of that series was impaired by the inadequacy of the opposition, the death of England's assistant manager Ken Barrington, and the repercussions of visiting bowler Robin Jackman's South African connections.

The question of South Africa would not go away. Frustrated in their attempts to gain re-admittance to conventional international competition the Springboks sought to lure the world's leading players to an alternative representative competition. Although they had some success in attracting current England cricketers, the venture failed at the time because too many top West Indians stayed away. No

65

tournament could have credibility without the participation of the world champions.

Lloyd must take credit for the example and persuasion which prevented all but a handful of former players and impatient aspirants from joining the 'rand rebels' under Rowe and Kallicharran. The loyalty which he and the administrators showed to those who resisted the considerable financial temptation was reciprocated. It remains to be seen, however, whether or not more will yield to the attraction once his influence has been withdrawn and the side re-constituted on the basis of new talent.

From there it was triumph after triumph. The Indians came to the region in early 1983 and were seen off decisively. In the Second Test Match at Queen's Park the captain joined Gomes with the first three batsmen out for just a single between them. They put on 237 runs together, of which Lloyd made 143 and followed with another century at the Recreation Ground. After losing the next Prudential Cup Final to the same opponents, the West Indies returned the visit at the end of the year and won in even more impressive style. Clive headed the batting averages in hitting 103 when the team was under pressure at Delhi and 161 not out at Calcutta.

The Australians, too, were humbled at the beginning of 1984. They could withstand their hosts in neither batting nor bowling. Once more the runs flowed and the wickets tumbled. Even so Lloyd was still not satisfied that it was the vengeance which he sought for 1975/76. Full compensation could not be exacted until Australia had been defeated on their own grounds. The chance for that would come in just under a year, but en route there was a record to be set in England.

That 5-0 'whitewash' was the culmination of his captaincy. No previous team had achieved the feat in over a hundred years of Test Matches in that country. The opposition was not so much beaten as crushed. The exchanges were not all one-way and England often held their own on the first innings. Nevertheless the West Indies always had the batsman for the moment and had the stamina to keep going until resistance crumpled. Lloyd, himself, saw the tourists through a testing time on the first day at The Oval, in which his 60 not out was top score. His example to the younger players was now taken for granted.

The relentless wave of fast bowlers kept up incessant pressure. Although critics commented adversely on the short-pitched bowling, the real damage was achieved by right-arm bowlers delivering at speed from around the wicket. The ball zipped across the batsman's body for induced snicks to the wicketkeeper and slips or to be popped up to short-leg. Since an earlier injury Clive had moved into the slips where he, Richards and Harper, Garner or Greenidge at gully, and wicketkeeper Dujon snapped up every possible catching chance and some that seemed to be impossible.

The revenge over Australia was achieved in Lloyd's last series as captain. The West Indies won the first three Test Matches of the rubber and came within a couple of wickets of winning the fourth as well. Even so Clive's captaincy ended in anti-climax both in a flare-up of passions between the players, the sporadic disappointment of his otherwise commendable leadership, and by surprise defeat on a pitch at Sydney whose capricious nature gave victory to the side which won the toss.

Lloyd enjoyed a good measure of success with the bat. In the first innings of the series at Perth he was caught by wicketkeeper Wayne Phillips from Alderman's bowling without scoring, but in the next outing at Brisbane he hammered 114, the century coming from just 114 balls, and shared a partnership of 152 runs with Richardson for the fifth-wicket. His 72 at Sydney, his last Test Match innings, has been described as a masterful display of batting on a bad pitch. The victorious team which he blended so well kept the momentum by beating New Zealand in the first rubber under his successor's captaincy.

Seven

Roger Harper

Roger Harper is the only specialist slow bowler to have penetrated successfully the present preference for pace. He is without doubt a very good off-spinner, but he is also fortunate in his time. In discussing the favourable press reports of Harper's performance for the President's Young West Indies XI against an England XI at Pointe-a-Pierre in 1981, early in his career, a former West Indies spinner told me, with only a touch of envy, that once they had written similarly about himself. The point is taken. Ability in itself is not enough — so much depends on the prevailing conditions and attitudes.

Because he has been able to rely on the fast bowlers to make the initial impact Harper has been employed essentially as an attacking bowler. Throughout his brief career to date the opposing batsmen have never really got on top of the bowling, and he has been spared the ordeal of spinning away for hours without realistic expectation of success. No batsman of the present generation, at least outside the West Indies, has been able, or permitted, to inflict on slow bowlers the suffering sustained by Sonny Ramadhin at Birmingham in 1957.

Slow bowlers have never been totally absent from top-level competition in the Caribbean, but they have been overlooked for too long in the international aspect. The West Indies Young Cricketers played four spinners on their tour to England in 1982 — the ill-fated Shervan Pragg, who was killed in a road accident before the year was out, David Cumberbatch, the mercurial Robert Haynes and Harper the captain. Although the ferocity of George Ferris, and to some extent that of Courtney Walsh, took the eye of the press, the renaissance of spin was not missed by those involved in cricket.

Comparisons between Harper and the young Lance Gibbs are inevitable. Both are conventional right-arm finger-spinners, a rarity in the West Indies, hail from the same territory, and have a lean and languid look. In the dozen years since his retirement Gibbs has not been effectively replaced. The tradition of slow bowling, though hidden too often under a bushel, has flickered since the dawn of the international era. Victor Pascall contributed much to the impact of the 1923 tourists to England which did so much to impress the game's administrators and win Test Match recognition.

Tommy Scott bowled well enough in the opening engagements against Australia in 1930/31, but he was opposed by batsmen who played day in and day out against quality spinners in the mould, if not of the calibre, of Clarrie Grimmett. He stuck to his task well when the batsmen of both teams mugged the bowlers mercilessly at Sabina Park in April 1930. The Cameron brothers, John and Jimmy respectively, filled the slow bowler's role on either side of the Second World War.

The West Indian batsmen of the 1930s were vulnerable against spin, especially in England where the ball turned, stopped and deviated. Batsmen who seemed to be comfortable enough against the thunderbolts of Harold Larwood were humbled by 'Tich' Freeman, Vallance Jupp, Walter Robins, Hedley Verity, James Langridge and 'Father' Marriott, several of whose names remain only in the record books. A similar failure against spin cost the West Indians dearly on their first tour to Australia.

Wilfred Ferguson was the region's first match-winner when Test Matches were resumed in 1947/48. He spun his way to 11 wickets in the drawn encounter at Queen's Park and, then, in partnership with John Goddard destroyed England on a rain-affected pitch at Bourda. Wisden commented:

'Ferguson, a short burly fellow who caused much merriment among the crowds when occasionally he removed his cap and revealed a bald head, gained more success than anyone else on either side by taking 23 wickets in the four Tests with his slow, well-pitched leg-breaks'.

The Trinidadian's aspirations of a prolonged career evaporated on the unresponsive pitches of India where the West Indians toured the following year. He did not bowl badly, but the home batsmen were experienced in playing his type of bowling. The fast bowlers made the only decisive break-through of that series. Even so Ferguson's omission from the tour of England in 1950 was unexpected and considered at the time to have been a tactical error.

There is no way of knowing how he would have fared if he had toured. His replacement, the inexperienced Sonny Ramadhin, reaped a rich haul of wickets. It is tempting to surmise that Ferguson would have prospered equally against spin-shy batsmen, but the Englishmen were destroyed as much by the youngster's mystique as his performance. They handled the spinners as badly as the earlier West Indians had handled England's own slow bowlers. For the next decade

69

Ramadhin was the region's most consistent shock, as well as stock, bowler.

In these years the new-ball attack was so negligible that Sonny was brought on after only a couple of overs. There were fears then the well of pace had run dry and the West Indians would have to depend for ever on spinners and on medium-pacers in the style of the two Atkinsons. The young team which went to New Zealand in 1956 could afford to leave behind experienced batsmen Clyde Walcott and Frank Worrell, but even to blood newcomers the bowling dared not be without Ramadhin and Valentine.

Alfred Valentine spun the ball with such force that his finger often bled. He did not always receive the credit which his effort and his genius demanded. The Jamaican was left out of the side in the mid-1950s when the West Indies could ill afford to miss him. Everything went wrong for him in England in 1957 from the sun glinting on his glasses and causing him to miss a catch at Lord's to his sustaining an injury on the eve of the Fifth Test Match at The Oval and, thus, forcing him to miss the one pitch that would have suited him.

Seven years earlier Valentine had made a remarkable international debut at Manchester. He owed his surprise selection for that match almost solely to a good performance against Lancashire on the same ground. Alfred took eight wickets on the opening day but lacked sufficient support for the blow to be decisive. Although he was overshadowed by Ramadhin for much of that summer the Jamaican delivered the thrust that knocked the final nail into England's coffin by taking 6 wickets for 39 runs at the Oval.

Valentine's bowling in Australia in 1951/52 is probably the highwater mark of West Indian spin bowling — Gibbs not excepted. He and Ramadhin bowled the visitors to the brink of victory at Brisbane, but, thereafter, he carried the burden of the attack almost alone. Alfred spun Australia to defeat with 6 wickets for 102 runs at Adelaide. In the following fixture at Melbourne he suffered the frustration of seeing the opposition sneak from under his own 5 wickets for 88 runs to win by a single wicket.

At the end of the decade the selectors introduced Ivan Madray and Lance Gibbs of Guyana, Charran Singh of Trinidad and Reg Scarlett of Jamaica in the search for a possible successor. The burly Scarlett, who was a more than competent batsman — and is an active cricketer today in England almost thirty years later, missed inclusion in the side touring Australia in 1960/61 and with it his chance of securing the position. The administrators fell back on the experience of Ramadhin and the recalled Valentine, supplemented by young Lance Gibbs.

The Third Test Match at Sydney marked the change in West Indian fortunes. For the previous couple of years they had promised much without realising the potential when it mattered: here they humbled the mighty Australians by 222 runs. The batsmen never got into the contest against Valentine and Gibbs. The latter recorded a hat-trick in the next match at Adelaide which the West Indies did everything but win. Thereafter the place in the team was his for almost as long as he wanted it.

Gibbs was positive in all that he undertook, in his brilliant fielding — who can forget among much excellence, his running out of Colin Milburn at Manchester in 1966 — as in his bowling. He played an integral part in the four-man attack which served the region so well in the 1960s, and would be unlikely be have been restrained by the current conception of slow bowling as an essentially defensive capability. He bobbed up to the wicket like a hare, but his striking power was more that of the mongoose. Throughout his career the West Indies hardly ever required the services of an additional specialist spinner.

The Third Test Match against India at Kensington Oval in 1962 was played in the shadow of the injury sustained by opening batsman Nariman Contractor against fast bowler Charlie Griffith. Spin seemed to pose fewer problems. By lunch on the last day Dilip Sardesai and Vijay Manjrekar were well on the way to achieving a draw with the score on 158-2. After the interval the batsmen made the mistake of assuming the defensive. Gibbs bowled with real 'bite'. The eager fieldsmen held a cluster of catches. In one session Lance took 8 wickets for just 6 runs, and had only 38 scored from him in the whole innings.

The victorious rubbers in England in 1963 and 1966 had several common features, not the least of which was the off-spinner's match-winning performances in the opening Test Matches at Manchester. He took eleven wickets on the first occasion and ten on the second. Thence England were fighting a rearguard action for the rest of the summer. The result was ironic because the home batsmen had reckoned on holding the tourists on pitches favouring spin to set against their own known disadvantage when the ball came through at any great pace. In 1966 Gibbs sent down almost a hundred overs more than fast bowler Hall.

Between these tours Lance bowled the West Indies to their first ever series victory over Australia. This otherwise high-scoring rubber was determined in the Third Test Match at Bourda. Gibbs pounced on the last day when the Australians seemed to be edging towards a draw. He was aided by some astute wicketkeeping by Jackie Hendriks and Gary

Sobers' acrobatic catching. The fast bowlers had hardly a look-in as the tourists tumbled to a historic defeat by 212 runs.

The off-spinner's greatest frustration must have occurred in the closing stages of the Fifth Test Match against England in Georgetown in 1967/68. The West Indies had to win to draw the rubber after they had lost the previous match from a premature declaration. Within an hour and a half on the final day the tourists collapsed to 41-5 against Gibbs. Colin Cowdrey and Alan Knott brought some relief but there was always a race against time. In spite of the bowler's efforts — Lance took 6 wickets for 60 runs — the last batsman played through the final over to ensure a draw.

Spin bowlers generally have served the West Indies well in Australia. The overwhelming victory in the opening engagement at Brisbane in 1968/69 gave little indication of the disappointment to follow. Century-makers Bill Lawry and Ian Chappell punished the fast bowlers, who seemed to age suddenly, but the batting was spectacularly at sea against Gibbs. Denied the vital first innings lead the Australians succumbed a second time to the spinners. The West Indians would not be in such command again in that country for a generation.

Gary Sobers, who shared that triumph with Gibbs, was a world-class left-arm spinner as well as being the leading batsman, superlative seam bowler, exceptional fieldsman and team captain. He had made his international debut back in 1954 as the prospective successor to Valentine . . . the batting came later. The success at Brisbane obscured temporarily the decline which had set into the side and was revealed immediately afterwards.

The fine balance of bowling talents made the West Indies attack of the 1960s economic and suited to most conditions. In his dual role Sobers linked the outright pace of Hall and Griffith to Gibbs' orthodox spin. The saving permitted the team to include an additional batsman. The disadvantage was the lack of cover which the breakdown in any one sector placed on the other. The decline of the fast bowlers and Sobers' pre-occupation with shoring up the batting exposed Gibbs to the vagaries of fortune.

Although he could not be expected to reproduce the consistency of his youth the Guyanese spinner provided the fulcrum of the attack throughout much of the lean years between 1968 and 1973. His bowling still won Test Matches at Queen's Park in 1973/74 and at New Delhi a year later, and he continued to bowl well into the Clive Lloyd era. Gibbs retired rich in honours and with a record harvest of 309 wickets in Test Matches. There has been no recognised successor until Harper came to the fore.

Albert Padmore of Barbados was given the first chance to claim the succession. He contested the one slow bowling position with Inshan Ali, but by then tactical opinion was moving in favour of an all-pace attack. The three-pronged assault of Roberts, Holding and Daniel in 1976 pushed spin out of serious consideration for a decade. Padmore remained a force in his island's cricket and led Barbados to success in the Shell Shield.

Trinidad & Tobago has remained a nursery for slow bowling. Imtiaz Ali, Inshan Ali, Raffick Jumadeen, Harold Joseph, Jack Noreiga and Ranjie Nanan have found their way into the regional team where few have held consideration for long. Noreiga was already a veteran when he took 9 wickets for 95 runs, the best inning analysis ever returned for the West Indies, against India at Queen's Park in 1971. Visitors to the twin-island state, including the powerful Barbadian batting battery, have had their limitations against spin bowling shown up embarrassingly.

For several years Derek Parry of Nevis seemed to be marked for preference. He was selected for the West Indies immediately prior to the withdrawal of the players contracted to World Series Cricket in 1978, and he took advantage of their absence to bowl Australia to defeat in Port-of-Spain. Parry was there or thereabouts for the next several years. He was probably the best slow bowler available at a time when there wasn't really a suitable place.

The increase in the number of limited-over matches induced the selectors to rely on either Larry Gomes of Viv Richards as the statutory fifth bowler. This practice was carried over into conventional cricket. In the instant code batsmen have been induced to take risks, and frequently get themselves out, against these part-timers rather than to take on the specialists. A slow bowler, especially an attacking slow bowler, has become even more redundant than the reserve wicket-keeper on tour.

By the dawn of the 1980s a new generation of spinners emerged in regional and internal-territorial competition. In addition to the inevitable Trinidadians, Marlon Tucker, Robert Haynes, Roger Harper, Noel Guischard, Derek Kallicharran and Clyde Butts pushed themselves into contention. There was probably greater depth in talent in this department here than in either England or Australia, but that impression was not carried into the international arena. Any way, it was difficult to change a winning combination.

The choice fell ultimately on Harper, whose elder brother, Mark, had made his Shell Shield debut for Guyana in 1976. Roger played his own first match in the competition four years later and, though he did not participate in a Test Match for another three years, he was regarded immediately to have world-class potential. His appointment as captain of the West Indies Young Cricketers in England in 1982 was an important step forward, after which it was only a matter of time.

The tall off-spinner was taken on the extended tour to India and Australia in 1983/84 and showed how much he had learned in the First Test Match in the return rubber against Australia at Bourda. His bounce and turn on a rain-affected pitch dismissed four batsmen for 56 runs. By scoring 86 for Guyana against the tourists he ensured his selection to the team to visit England later that summer. His arrival was awaited with interest, even though it was expected that he would play second fiddle to the fast bowlers.

The surfeit of speed has produced its own counter-effect. Two years earlier Abdul Qadir, the Pakistani leg-spinner, had run riot against England batsmen starved of the experience of playing against high quality slow bowling. Conceivably Clive Lloyd would have introduced Harper as his 'secret weapon' earlier in the series, but the apprehension generated by Malcolm Marshall's initial assault on the first morning at Birmingham indicated that the opposition were even more vulnerable to pace.

There is some suspicion that the pitch at Manchester for the Fourth Test Match had been prepared to off-set the West Indians' superiority on faster surfaces. The home side selected two spinners, Nick Cook and Pat Pocock, but the tourists needed only one to win. In the northern city's traditional rainy weather England were required to follow on 220 runs in arrears. Their batsmen were trapped on the pitch intended for the West Indians. Harper jostled them out with 6 wickets for 57 runs. Gibbs had done the same thing twenty years earlier.

Roger delivered his off-spinners from great height with unexpected maturity. He sent down 28.4 overs, more than the combined total of Garner, Davis and Holding. Batsmen whose earlier misfortunes had been blamed on short-pitched fast bowling were found to be equally wanting against the turning ball. Harper exacted a grim revenge for the humiliation which previous generations had suffered at the hands of Jim Laker and Tony Lock. Only Marshall and Garner took more wickets either in the series or on the tour.

Harper holds spectacular catches even in a side noted for spectacular catches. The practice of fast bowlers delivering from around the wicket depends on the ball crossing the batsman's body at great speed. There it is either snicked to the wicketkeeper and echelon of slips, or it is lofted into the square-leg/mid-wicket area. Safe catching is essential to its success. Harper, Richards and Lloyd form a formidable slip ring, and the former has thrown his long body length-wise to hold some breath-taking chances in the leg-side deep field.

Early in his professional career the impression developed that Harper was being groomed for the captaincy of the West Indies. He must have been ear-marked as a long-term prospect from the moment he handled the Young Cricketers with such success, but he has been brought along with studied attention. Unlike other slow bowlers left dangling on the edge of selection, Roger has been introduced steadily into international limited-over competition and into Test Matches.

No specialist spinner has captained the West Indies since John Goddard immediately after the Second World War, and, following his first season of success, he played an increasingly minor role in the attack. An even more pertinent consideration must be whether any slow bowler, however good, can be sure of selection on merit for every Test Match the captain is required to play. Mike Brearley of England was probably the last international captain to owe his position to leadership quality above batting or bowling expertise.

Current opinion is substantially removed from that of the 1960s when Lance Gibbs played in a balanced attack in which each skill had its place. The present emphasis on pace ensures that whenever a slow bowler is selected he performs as an alternative to the fast bowling, not as a complementary part of the overall entity. There will have to be a major revision of thought throughout the entire tactical approach. It is not impossible, but it would require a more drastic re-appraisal than is presently evident to the outside observer.

The potential of a spin-orientated policy should not be under-estimated. The Indian team which defeated the West Indies and England in 1971 permitted only a token couple of overs of medium-slow pace, if that, before Bishen Bedi, Chandrasekhar, Venkataragha-van or Prasanna was called upon to bowl. The last two named, both orthodox off-spinners, gave the West Indies most trouble and in 1974/75 brought their country back from a 2-0 deficit to square the rubber temporarily when Clive Lloyd took his first team to India.

The West Indies dominated the home series against England in 1973/74 until the final Test Match at Queen's Park. Then they suffered the lone defeat to cancel out their advantage achieved earlier on the same ground. Batsmen who had run up totals of 392, 583-9 declared and 596-8 declared in previous matches broke down against part-time off-spinner Tony Greig, whose 13 wickets in the match cost 156 runs. Like Harper, he brought down the ball from a greater height than usual.

The success of spinners Murray Bennett and Bob Holland in New South Wales' victory in late 1984 was regarded again as exploiting the West Indians' Achilles' heel. By introducing only one slow bowler into the side for the subsequent Test Match they employed a pace-first policy that was little different in conception to that engaged without the spinner. Then on a more responsive pitch at Sydney they were both included, where, ironically, Harper was omitted, and with Holland taking 10 for 144 and Bennett 5 for 124 the West Indies were beaten for the first time in three years.

Wrist-spinners will always have a part in international cricket, especially if they are gifted and 'mysterious'. Abdul Qadir and Laxman Sivaramakrishnan have made their impact on the Indo-Pakistan sub-continent. Their effect, for good or ill, is often immediate, which suits current preference for instant appeal. Within an over or two it is apparent whether the bowler or the batsman has the upper hand. It is unlikely that Ramadhin would have been given his chance so early if he had been a conventional finger-spinner.

The latter require time to develop an art based on experience. They need the lattitude to work out the weaknesses of opposing batsmen in a contest based on wits rather than on intuition. Off-spinners progress on the stepping-stones of their own mistakes. Laker took much hammer from the Australians in 1948, but the perseverance paid off eight years later. Gibbs worked for a couple of years at the highest level to become an 'overnight' sucess. Developing off-spinners depend more than most on the tolerance of their captain and selectors.

The restrictions of limited-over competition have caused left-arm spinners to adjust to a different role rather than to disappear. Those who have survived have done so by eliminating flight and lowering the trajectory. They have become bowling's defensive arm. As a similar discipline is required also of off-spinners in English domestic cricket it must be hoped that Harper's service with Northamptonshire daily from May to September will not hinder his attacking approach.

The natural inclination of young boys is to hit the ball as hard or bowl it as fast as possible. That is the essence of spectacle. Watchful defence or probing spin are acquired arts. It is easy to assume that today's mass radio and television audiences are less willing to follow the game's intricacies than spectators on the terraces. On the contrary, the slam-bang excitement of a limited-over thrash-around appeals almost solely to the crowd in the ground. The more sober followers are often one medium removed.

The now almost universal covering of pitches has done as much as anything to make the spinner obsolete. Conditions may be more even for each batting side, but there are hardly any sticky wickets on which the slower bowlers can taste a kill. The difference in the state of the pitch from the first day to the last is comparatively less. This change is reflected in the increase in the number of captains inviting the opposition to bat first. Yet the improved pitches have lowered the standard of batting — it is now less important to develop a sound defence to counter nearly impossible conditions.

With the ball less likely to deviate, greater attention has been paid to exploiting the moisture in the pitch in the opening overs. The new tactics require four faster bowlers, or three and a medium-paced substitute. Eldine Baptiste filled this role competently on the tours to India and England. He had the collage of talents to plug the breach wherever it might come, in batting or in bowling. New Zealand's considerably improved performance in the 1980s derived from its several 'jacks-of-all-trades' rather than on outstanding individual talent.

Few wicketkeepers now have adequate experience in taking top quality spinners. Used to standing back to pace they have fumbled stumping chances and missed deliveries which have deceived the batsman and slipped by the stumps. Jackie Hendriks, who kept to both speed and spin, is regarded justly as the best allround West Indian wicketkeeper. The spectacular dives and one-handed scooping catches of Dujon and his contemporaries illustrate no lesser talent, but the experience is less complete.

Overseas tours have been pruned back to comprise mainly Test Matches and other international contests. The programme of three-day first-class games has been cut to a minimum, and it was there that the off-spinner learned skill and patience. The captain is forced to go into a series with a pre-ordained plan and a pre-selected team, in which a newcomer can expect to be included only through injury to an established player or through changes forced by defeat, which, in itself, is hardly an auspicious beginning.

Rober Harper's international success, and that of the region's other slow bowlers, depends on much more than whether or not the captain tosses the ball to him enough times. If spin bowling is to come back into its own there must be a comprehensive re-thinking of tactics, itinerary and team composition, and in pitch preparation. It has happened before. The present age of pace dates only from 1974, though to those who admire the spinner's guile it has been a life-time.

Eight

Bourda, Georgetown

Georgetown is differrent to the other Test Match locations. It is situated on a mainland territory which has as much Dutch as British colonial heritage and, though the racial/religious mix of the population has similarity to that of Trinidad, the country seems to have developed at a different pace to the islands. Once considered to have been the bastion of conservatism, Guyana has now the most steadfastly radical administration. In respect to matters relating to South Africa it is prepared to give up its cricket for its political principles.

For decades the territory was virtually ignored in the composition of the regional cricket team and offered ineffective opposition to touring sides. Yet within a year of Willie Watson and Tom Graveney knocking-up double-centuries against British Guiana in 1954 the then colony commenced a policy of rebuilding which has made it now a foremost power in the Caribbean. Visitors do not come to the Bourda ground in Georgetown to mess around, either socially or at cricket.

From the moment the young Guianese surprised their neighbours in the quadrangular tournament at the end of 1956 the country has contributed a high proportion of representatives to the Test Match side, chiefly at the expence of Trinidad whose involvement has declined accordingly. There is much application in their attitude. Rohan Kanhai, Basil Butcher, Clive Lloyd, Alvin Kallicharran and Roy Fredericks, depending on the dictates of tactics, have mixed innings of attrition with a more general free-scoring approach.

The rainy climate must take much of the blame for there being more drawn matches than definite results at Bourda. Compared to eleven inconclusive finishes four matches have been lost and four won. The victories, however, include the landmarks of the first Test Match ever won by the West Indies and the triumph of completing the first victory in a series over Australia. Three times, against India both in 1962 and in 1976 and against England in 1981, either inclement weather or political considerations have caused Georgetown to lose a

Test Match from a rubber that was played out everywhere else in the region.

Guyana is the only South American mainland territory in which cricket is played at full international level. It is a comparatively huge country bounded by the Atlantic Ocean to the north, by Brazil to the south, by Suriname to the east and by Venezuela to the north-east. The bulk of the population live in the coastal plain. The land is low-lying in this coastal region but rises towards the interior. The people are mixed ethnically with those of African or Asian descent predominating, and from the point of view of religion.

Georgetown, the captial city, is situated at the coast on the east bank of the Demarara River. Before the country attained political independence in 1966 it was known initially as Demarara and then as British Guiana, which could cause some confusion to those outside researching its cricket history for the first time. The district around the Berbice River, round and about New Amsterdam, an important port on that river's eastern bank, has been a particularly fruitful nursery for cricket talent.

Clive Lloyd has described in his book *Living for Cricket* the city's enthusiasm for cricket:

'When a Test match is played at Bourda, in the capital of Georgetown, the queues start to form as early as 4 a.m. and the ground is filled to its capacity long before the first ball is bowled. When the Tests are overseas, radio sets are to be seen everywhere and it's easy to tell whether the West Indies are winning or losing. You have only to look at the expressions on people's faces!'

Apart from the one-off experience of Maurice Fernandes leading the West Indies successfully on his home ground in 1930 no regular regional captain was appointed from this territory until Rohan Kanhai succeeded Sobers in 1973. Then three Guyanese — Kanhai, Lloyd and Kallicharran — held the position consecutively and both Faoud Bacchus and Roger Harper were considered confidently as potential heirs apparent. That decade was the most successful which the West Indies has ever enjoyed in international competition.

Guyana has contributed much more to the Test Match team in batting than in bowling. There has been no tradition of pace to compare with that in either Jamaica or Barbados, and Colin Croft has been the only fast bowler to date to command regular selection. The success of Lance Gibbs and Roger Harper has given an impression of slow bowling talent that was not distinct until the former and Ivan Madray came to the fore in the late 1950s. Yet centuries by Guyanese batsmen have graced grounds around the world. The colony has a prominent part in pioneering the game. Georgetown C.C. was formed in, or about, 1857 and was the governing body for almost the next hundred years. The club occupied Bourda in 1884. Matches were played against Barbados and Trinidad by the end of the 1860s. E.F. Wright's score of 123 against Trinidad at the Parade Ground in Georgetown in 1882 was the first century recorded in a first-class match in the region, and five years later he made over a thousand runs in all matches. By the turn of the century Guyana began to lose ground regionally and internationally to Trinidad and Barbados. S.W. Sproston, who took over the captaincy on Aucher Warner's illness during the first tour to England in 1900, failed by only five runs to reach a hundred for British Guiana against Lord Hawke's team. Opening bowler King — 'the best of the British Guiana bowlers kept a very good length all through, with a little work from the offside. On a wicket to help him he would be a dangerous man' — gave the visiting batsmen a testing time, but the home side's prospects were ruined by inadequate batting in the first innings. The colony's performance did not come up to expectations, because, unlike Trinidad, they did not play their black professionals.

Pelham Warner noted in his book *Cricket in Many Climes* that the territory was different to the settlements seen elsewhere on the tour:

'Georgetown, the capital of British Guiana, which was originally a Dutch possession, cannot be called particularly beautiful when seen from the river. The lower portion of the town lies below the level of the sea at high-tide, and is consequently protected by an extensive sea-wall, which is a fashionable resort on Sunday afternoons. A stone house is scarcely to be seen, a circumstance due to the extreme difficulty of obtaining good foundations. Indeed, the houses are usually built upon heavy balks of greenheart timber, which are piled one on another till a certain security of base is reached.

Many of the streets in the town are intersected by canals, in which that wonderful lily, the Victoria Regis, grows to perfection. The size to which some of the leaves grow is almost incredible, and I was shown a photograph of a man standing on one of them, and he certainly did not look a light-weight. The Georgetown Club ... is extremely comfortable, and the town generally is about the best in the West Indies, being laid out in broad and well-kept streets'.

The West Indian batsmen punished the English bowlers heavily in the opening stages of the first Test Match played at Bourda in February 1930, and, although the tourists made something of a recovery, they were crushed by 289 runs. Clifford Roach, who had been dismissed without scoring in each innings of the preceding match, made 209, the first double-century for the West Indies, and shared partnerships of 144 with wicketkeeper Errol Hunte and 196 with George Headley for the first and second wickets respectively. From such a commanding start the 471 runs total was disappointing.

England collapsed completely to fast bowlers George Francis and Learie Constantine, each of whom took four wickets. The follow-on was not enforced. With patient batting Headley completed his second century of the match — the first time the feat had been achieved for the West Indies — and 'Snuffy' Browne cracked a very fast 70 not out. Chasing over six hundred runs to win Patsy Hendren, who had scored a fifty in the first innings, inspired belated resistance by making a hundred. The West Indians, however, would not be denied their triumph. Constantine took 5 wickets for 87 runs in bringing the match to an end with barely a quarter of an hour to go.

In contrast to that excitement, the next Test Match at Bourda in 1935 resulted in a very tame draw. The English batsmen were far from convincing against the home fast bowlers. As Ken Wishart and Headley reached their half-centuries it seemed that the West Indies must take a substantial lead, but the lower-order batsmen were spun out by Eric Hollies, taking 7 wickets for 50 runs. Although England were 42 runs ahead on first innings they lacked the confidence to seize the initiative and interest in the game faded.

Victory by 7 wickets in 1948, after failing to convert winning positions into victory in the preceding matches at Kensington and Queen's Park, was the first step in the West Indies' immediate post-war period of supremacy. Frank Worrell gave them an excellent start by hitting 131 not out, and John Goddard, captaining the region for the first time, brought about a batting collapse by taking 5 wickets for 31 runs. The tourists were invited to follow on 186 runs behind. Wilfred Ferguson, the Trinidadian slow bowler, took five wickets in the second innings to bring his haul to nineteen from two matches.

Rain ruined the Fourth Test Match in 1953. The Indians, disconcerted by Valentine's bowling and by the run out of two leading batsmen, recovered from 64-5 to 262 all out. Their own slow bowlers presented similar problems, but Clyde Walcott, who made a hundred, and Everton Weekes shared a century stand in putting the West Indies ahead by 102 runs. By the close the tourists, just 88 runs in front with five wickets in hand, were in the worse position, but, because of the weather, safe from the prospect of defeat.

England's visit to Georgetown the next year was explosive in more than one way. Beaten in Jamaica and Barbados the tourists had to win here to stand any chance of squaring the rubber. The first innings developed into a confrontation between Len Hutton, the austere captain and opening batsman, who scored 169, and Sonny Ramadhin, taking 6 wickets for 113 runs. The Trinidadian bowled without real support in the first indication of the scarcity of bowling resources which became only too obvious throughout the rest of this series and the next.

The West Indians began their reply badly as three wickets fell to fast bowler Brian Statham before the total passed 16. Something similar had happened at Kensington, where Walcott had come to the rescue with a double-century. The dismissal of Weekes for 94 by left-arm spinner Tony Lock ended aspirations of a similar recovery. John Holt, the regular opener coming in lower in the order due to injury, and wicketkeeper Clifford McWatt took the side towards the safety of avoiding the follow-on. Then it happened.

On his home ground and with the stand worth 99, McWatt was run out. The decision provoked the bottle-throwing riot which has become infamous. Holt, 48 not out, continued in his regular first-wicket position as the West Indies followed on 184 runs in arrears. He made top score of 64, but although several of his colleagues settled in they could not reach fifty. England won easily by 9 wickets and went on to win again in Sabina Park and share the series.

The Australians beat British Guiana by an innings and 134 runs in 1955. The margin of defeat obscured a historical turning-point. For too many years the territory had been a cricket backwater. Now, however, Walcott had moved here on an official assignment and had inspired the renaissance that has continued until the present time. The first six batsmen in the order were either current or future international batsmen — Pairaudeau, Glendon Gibbs, Kanhai, Walcott, Basil Butcher and McWatt.

Australia won the Test Match by 8 wickets. It was the only one in the series in which the scoring was modest. Weekes made a half-century as the West Indies were bowled out for a fragile 182. For once the touring batsmen did not take advantage of the situation. Colin McDonald and Richie Benaud pushed them ahead by only 75 runs. Walcott and Worrell took the home team to 150-3, from whence a fight-back seemed to be possible. Ian Johnson, captain and off-spinner, took 7 wickets for 44 runs, including three stumpings and one catch by Gil Langley, and his batsmen were under no pressure.

The West Indies beat Pakistan by 8 wickets in 1958 after a tight contest for a first innings lead which they won by only two runs. Saeed Ahmed, top-scorer with 150, and Hanif Mohammad gave the tourists a good chance of making it a real fight. Gary Sobers, going in first after his record score in the preceding match at Sabina Park, and

Clyde Walcott took the score so easily to 279-1 that another mammoth score appeared to be inevitable. Teenage spinner Nasimul Ghani, however, troubled the later batsmen.

Wazir Mohammad, undefeated just three runs away from a century, put the Pakistanis in a seemingly strong position in spite of a good spell by Lance Gibbs. The West Indies were expected to struggle in making the 317 runs to win on a pitch which was taking some spin. Centurymaker Conrad Hunte and Kanhai got them away to a sound start, putting on 125 runs for the first wicket, after which Sobers took over again. The Barbadian attained yet another record in hitting 109 not out, his second hundred in the match.

The drawn Fourth Test Match against England in 1960 was disappointing to the West Indies who came into it one match down in a series in which they were probably the stronger side. England's tailenders rescued them from an early breakdown to fast bowler Wesley Hall, taking 6 wickets for 90 runs. Sobers, hitting his third century in four matches that season, gave the home team a lead of 107 runs. Raman Subba Row and Ted Dexter, both of whom reached a hundred, prevented the breakthrough necessary for a decisive result.

The opinion of Alan Ross in *Through the Caribbean* echoed much of Warner's observations from sixty years earlier:

'The town itself has the air of Holland transported to the tropics, though in fact the French, during their short tenure between the Dutch occupation and its secession to Britain in 1812, laid it out. The main avenues, with canna lilies, samantrees and flamboyants in the central walks, are wide and shady. Intersecting streets are lined with white, weather-boarded houses, usually on stilts with a kind of bell-tower. Most of them are clouded in bougainvillaea, stephanotis, zinnias, gladioli and poinsettia, so that, driving by, one flashes past a blur of pink, purple, scarlet, orange, green and white .... Many of the roads were once canals, and though the dykes remain, only a handful of canals, with slow-moving clouds mirrored between punts and barges, still exist ...

The Georgetown streets at night bear a liberal sprinkling of ... 'sport girls'. The city as a whole has a dead, desolate air by early evening, but from the white pavilion of my mosquito-net I could hear far into the morning the blare of music from isolated pockets of resistance ... Whatever its defects as a country to visit, British Guiana is a real place. One is out of the false world of tourists and into the hard world of affairs, of strident nationalist politics, of economic struggle'.

The Third Test Match against Australia in 1965 was hard-fought, decisive and historic. The West Indies battled tenaciously against tight seam bowling by Neil Hawke, taking 6 wickets for 72 runs. Rohan Kanhai made 89, the only half-century of the match, but although three other batsmen reached forty they could not get to fifty. The Australians, in turn, batted without conviction against the varied home attack. There were 176 runs between the teams at the end of the first innings and batting became more difficult as the pitch took spin.

The West Indies were dismissed for 180, setting the tourists to score 357 runs to win. They started confidently enough in reaching 91-2, but Sobers had seen enough to take off the fast bowlers after they had bowled only eight overs and to rely on himself and Gibbs. The off-spinner was almost unplayable — how often that has been written about him — in taking 6 wickets for 29 runs. Australia made only 144, losing by 212 runs. The West Indies were now two-up in the series and, as the next match at Kensington was drawn, won a rubber against Australia for the first time.

The Fifth Test Match against England in 1968 was fraught with tension and controversy. The West Indies needed to win to make up ground from their opponents' shock victory after the gambled declaration at Port of Spain. Sobers led the way in hitting 152 in a fourth-wicket partnership of 250 runs with Kanhai, who scored 150. The lower-order batsmen failed to maintain the initial impetus. The final 414 runs was not decisive one way or the other. The match was building towards its climax.

England faded similarly after centurymaker Geoffrey Boycott and Colin Cowdrey put on 172 runs for the second wicket. Veteran left-arm spinner Tony Lock, recalled to the side midway through the tour from a professional assignment in Australia, surprised everyone with his batting ability. Coming in at number nine he scored 89 and dominated a three-figure ninth-wicket stand with Pat Pocock. The first innings lead of 43 runs gave the West Indies a narrow but important advantage on a pitch known to turn as it wore down.

The second innings revolved again around Sobers. The Barbadian batted masterfully to reach 95 not out at the time the innings ended. Fast bowler John Snow, who spearheaded the attack so incisively throughout the season, cut down the West Indian captain's partners in taking 6 wickets for 60 runs. Insufficient time remained for England to chase the 307 runs needed to win, but they had to survive the whole of the last day to draw and, thus, protect their lead in the series.

The tourists were soon in deep trouble. Gibbs struck immediately and the first five batsmen were out for 41. Cowdrey, playing a captain's innings, and wicketkeeper Alan Knott stopped the decline and frustrated the bowlers by putting on 127 runs and, more importantly, taking the match into the final session. Wickets fell steadily again after Cowdrey's dismissal. Knott encouraged the tail-enders through the closing moments as Gibbs completed his return of 6 wickets for 60 runs. Jeff Jones, the last man, the fieldsmen clustered almost in his pocket, scrambled through the final over to save the match.

The drawn Third Test Match of 1971 was balanced evenly. Century-maker Sunil Gavaskar put the tourists ahead by a mere 13 runs. Charlie Davis and Sobers hit hundreds in taking the West Indies to a 307-3 declaration in the second innings. The Indian opening batsmen, Gavaskar and Ashok Mankad, played out time to finish at 123-0.

The Fourth Test Match against New Zealand the next year was even more pointless. Alvin Kallicharran made 100 not out on his debut and the West Indies declared at 365-7. Glenn Turner, whose sequence of double-centuries around the Caribbean was reminiscent of Patsy Hendren's scoring in 1929/30, and Terry Jarvis put on a mammoth 387 runs for the first wicket. The former made 259, but the runs were acquired so slowly that, although the visitors did declare 178 runs ahead, no time remained for either side to effect a decision.

Australia came from behind to win by 10 wickets in 1973. The West Indies, starting their second innings 25 runs in front, were dismissed by pace bowlers Jeff Hammond and Max Walker for just 109, exactly the same score as Ian Chappell had made for the tourists. Opening batsmen Keith Stackpole, burly and attacking, and Ian Redpath, lean and patient, hit off the 135 runs needed to win. The outstanding feature of the match, however, was Clive Lloyd's batting in the first innings.

Because of a poor run of recent form his inclusion in the side had been disputed. He put the issue to rest with a convincing display of stroke-play in which he scored 178 in what should have been the formidable foundation to a match-winning total. Lloyd and Kanhai made all but 31 runs in the total of 366. The batting plunged sharply from 307-4 against the mild pace of Doug Walters. Clive's career was saved for the time being and was assured by his scoring one century and three fifties in the next four Test Matches.

The weather prevented a decision even on first innings for England's visit in 1974. Tony Greig, the tall blond allrounder, and opening batsman Dennis Amiss helped England to reach 448, an average total in a series in which high scoring was prevalent. Roy Fredericks, caught and bowled by Greig just two runs away from a hundred, was the principal West Indian scorer in the 198-4 permitted by the rain. The greatest talking-point of the fixture was the with-drawal from the team of Gary Sobers on the grounds of fatigue.

Pakistan came back from a 254 runs deficit to achieve a draw through excellent batting in 1977. Lloyd's gamble of giving the tourists first innings paid off. They were dismissed by the quick bowlers for 194. No batsman managed to reach fifty. The West Indian innings was marred by slow scoring, riot and bad temper, especially in reaction to umpiring decisions. Long-serving Irving Shillingford, whom Test Match opportunity seemed to have passed by, made 120. With three other players hitting half-centuries the West Indies were in a strong position.

Majid Khan showed a positive approach to the task of saving the match. He scored a dashing 167 and the 219 runs first-wicket partnership comprised 60 added with Sadiq Mohammad before his injury and another 159 in 2½ hours with stroke-master Zaheer Abbas. Most of the Pakistanis made some runs in the 540 runs total. With no prospect of a result Gordon Greenidge and Fredericks, the West Indian openers, put on 154 in the final stages.

There was drama before and during the Third Test Match against Australia in 1978. The walk-out of the greater part of the West Indies team in the dispute involving the World Series Cricketers promised that the match would be more evenly contested and exciting, because the weakened Australians were no match for the West Indies at full strength. Alvin Kallicharran was appointed captain of the newly-cobbled combination, several of whom were new to territorial, let alone representative, competition.

Encouraged by this unexpected opportunity Jeff Thomson and Wayne Clark, the fast bowlers, gave the early batsmen more trouble than they could handle. Kallicharran was bowled without scoring and five men were out while the total was still in double figures. Sieuw Shivnarine's half-century took the score to 205. The Australians, themselves, began badly against the pace of Norbert Phillip and Sylvester Clarke, and they were indebted to veteran captain Bobby Simpson and wicketkeeper Steve Rixon for achieving a 81 runs lead.

The West Indians rallied strongly in the second innings. Opening batsman Basil Williams scored exactly 100 on his debut and Larry Gomes marked his own recall to the regional team with a century. The batting was confident throughout the order. Shivnarine's second fifty and another by off spinner Derek Parry brought the final total to 439. The tourists made an appalling start. The first three batsmen failed to score and were out before their side passed 22. Graeme Wood and Craig Serjeant, both from Western Australia, joined then in a 251 runs partnership which changed the cause of the game. Although further wickets fell after their dismissal, Australia's win by 3 wickets kept the hitherto one-sided series open.

The proposed Second Test Match against England at the end of February 1981 was cancelled. The Guyanese Government declared that Robin Jackman, a recruit to the touring team to replace injured fast bowler Bob Willis, was unwelcome because of his cricket contacts with South Africa and his visa was revoked. To make matters worse the first-class game against Guyana was abandoned due to torrential rain. The frustrated cricketers had to sit around in an atmosphere of growing political tension without the opportunity to play or practice.

When Test Match cricket returned to Bourda with India in 1983, rain ruined a match that could have been interesting. Richards made a hundred which because of rain and the rest day extended over four days, and Greenidge and Lloyd helped him to a 470 runs total. Sunil Gavaskar made 147 not out as the tourists, with further help from the weather, played out the draw at 284-3. Bourda has not been kind to the Indians. On their five visits to the region Georgetown has been twice withdrawn from the schedule, two matches were ruined by rain, and the other was a stagnant stalemate.

The Australians provided a more interesting contest in the First Test Match in 1984. On a first day restricted by rain Joel Garner gave their batsmen a hard time and finished with 6 wickets for 75 runs. Greg Ritchie saw the tourists through the early difficulty, but the real backbone of the innings was the unlikely 97 runs partnership for the last wicket between Hogan and Rodney Hogg. The West Indies, for whom Desmond Haynes scored the only half-century, were left 49 runs adrift on the first innings.

The tourists' second innings followed a similar pattern to their first, in that the bulk of the runs came from one partnership. The pugnacious lefthander Allan Border and wicketkeeper Wayne Phillips put on 125 runs for the sixth wicket. Australia declared 322 runs ahead. Gordon Greenidge and Haynes set off in pursuit of the target with such purpose that victory seemed to be possible until well into the final session. By the close each had reached his century and had put on 250 runs without being parted.

In 1985 the New Zealanders participated for the second consecutive time in a high-scoring draw at this ground. Richie Richardson, who scored 185 after being dropped early in his innings, and Haynes put on 181 runs for the second wicket and paved the way for sound scoring throughout the order. The tourists saved the follow-on, thus ending the possibility of victory for either side, and finished only 71 runs behind due mainly to Martin Crowe's dominating 188. Much to local disappointment spinner Clyde Butts, on his debut, yielded over a hundred runs without taking a wicket.

Nine

Asian Community

Larry Gomes is at first sight so seemingly limited in his range of strokes and lacking in panache that it is difficult to appreciate accurately just how much has depended on him in recent Test Match series. In England and in Australia he has held the innings together when all others have failed. It has been said often that whereas some gifted cricketers have played below their full potential, Gomes has given 110% of his talent. Alvin Kallicharran, too, has contributed more over a longer period than is usually recognised.

Both batsmen, apparently batting against the tide, represent different traditions which have blended into the mainstream of West Indian cricket. Gomes stands in the line of watchful application which has always been a counter-balance to the more popular concept of the volatile Caribbean calypso cricketer. Kallicharran belongs to those batsmen of Asian descent who have added a new dimension to stroke-play over the past three decades. Asian players have been prevalent in both Guyana and Trinidad & Tobago.

Trinidad and British Guiana were developed principally in the mid- and late nineteenth century, and the labour shortage was met by recruiting extensively from the Indian sub-continent and, to some extent, in the Far East. Hindu, Muslim and Chinese traditions grew up alongside those of the descendants from Africa and from Europe. The Asians brought to cricket wrist-artistry in stroke-play and guile in slow bowling, but their impact was not felt substantially before the breakdown of the pioneer concept of white batsman / black bowler prevalent in the regional hey-day of Trinidad club competition.

There is still a residual loyalty to the Orient, emphasised by religion, culture and often language, which has withstood the century-old diaspora. Indian taxi drivers in Port of Spain, and not them alone, remember affectionately the innings of Sunil Gavaskar and Mohinder Amarnath as much as those of more local heroes. The Indian tourists are probably more at home in the southern territories of the Eastern Caribbean than anywhere outside their own homeland. Their perfor-

Michael Holding bowling during the 3rd Test West Indies v England at Barbados in 1981

Clive Lloyd with the Worrell Trophy, 1980

Gordon Greenidge hooks Cowans for 4 during his innings of 223 in the 4th Test
England v West Indies at Old Trafford in 1984

Viv Richards batting during the 3rd Test West Indies v England at Barbados in 1981

Gus Logie batting during the match Worcester v West Indies at Worcester in 1981

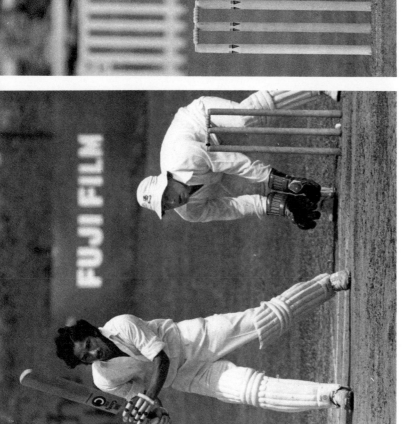

Larry Gomes batting during the England tour of the West Indies in 1981

Richie Richardson batting during the match
Worcester v West Indies at Worcester in 1981

Joel Garner bowling during the 5th Test England v
West Indies at the Oval in 1984

Malcolm Marshall bowling during the
1st Test England v West Indies at
Edgbaston in 1984

Alvin Kallicharran batting during the Prudential World Cup match,
Australia v West Indies, in 1975

Jeff Dujon catches Downton at Headingley in 1984

George Headley

Jackie Hendriks

Ivan Barrow

Gary Sobers batting during the 3rd Test
England v West Indies at Lord's in 1973

Frank Worrell

Learie Constantine

Rohan Kanhai batting during the final of the Prudential World Cup in 1975

Lawrence Rowe batting during the 1st Test Australia v West Indies at Brisbane in 1975

Courtney Walsh

The Sabina Park ground at Kingston, Jamaica

Queen's Park Oval at Port of Spain, Trinidad

Roger Harper

The Bourda Park ground at Georgetown, Guyana

Kensington Oval at Bridgetown, Barbados. *Inset*: Desmond Haynes

Eldine Baptiste

The Recreation ground, Antigua

The St Vincent ground. *Inset:* Winston Davis

mances in Trinidad confirm that impression.

Ellis 'Puss' Achong came into the West Indies side for the Second Test Match against England at Queen's Park in 1929/30, after bowling the island to the only victory by a territorial side over the tourists. He dismissed Patsy Hendren, the top-scorer and ultimately the match-winner, without posing the same problems when international honours were at stake. Achong played in all three Test Matches in England in 1933, did not fail, and took more wickets on the tour than any bowler save Manny Martindale, who was head-and-shoulders above his colleagues.

Rupert Tang Choon was a surprise omission from the team which toured England in 1939. He was an explosive batsman and held his own as a bowler and fieldsman. The Trinidadian did not do himself justice in the pre-tour trials and may have suffered from his island having too many contenders for the same berths. After the Second World War he scored a century for Trinidad against the England tourists in 1947/48 but missed selection for the ensuing Test Match. After that the success of Worrell, Weekes and Walcott left no vacant middle-order position.

Nyron Asgarali was one of the three specialist opening batsmen chosen to visit England in 1957 — the others were Andy Ganteaume and Bruce Pairaudeau. Though batting well against the counties he did not take his chances in the Test Matches. To some extent Asgarali was unfortunate on his two appearances to encounter an exceptionally fast pitch at Lord's and a spinning track at The Oval. Because of the brittleness at the top of the innings Frank Worrell, Gary Sobers and even international debutant Rohan Kanhai were drafted to go in first.

Few selections on speculation, if any, have succeeded like that of Sonny Ramadhin in 1950. He was preferred for the tour to Wilfred Ferguson and for the Test Matches to C.B. Williams. After five days at Lord's in June the slight, boyish figure had achieved total mastery over the home batsmen. Ramadhin enhanced the sense of mystery by bowling in his cap and by wearing his shirt-sleeves buttoned down to the wrist.

The introduction of Ramadhin and Valentine into the attack at Lord's had immediate effect. Openers Len Hutton and Cyril Washbrook had taken the score competently if not confidently to 62. Thereafter both were stumped off the spinners. The total toppled to 86-5, then to 122-9, from which point defeat was inevitable. Wisden commented:

> 'No blame could be attached to the pitch . . . . Ramadhin bowled
> with the guile of a veteran. He pitched a tantalising length,
> bowled straight at the wicket and spun enough to beat the bat.

No English batsman showed evidence of having mastered the problems of deciding which way Ramadhin would spin'.

Seven years later he repeated the performance in the First Test Match at Birmingham by taking 7-49 to dismiss England for 186 on a good batting pitch on the first day. It is a matter of record that in the second innings Peter May and Colin Cowdrey destroyed Ramadhin's magic with excellent batting and excessive pad play. Sonny sent down 98 overs, the most delivered by one bowler in any Test Match. Due to injuries suffered by other bowlers the Trinidadian's effective career was sacrificed to save his side.

Ramadhin was never quite so spectacularly successful in the West Indies. He won only one Test Match — that against India at Kensington in 1953. Undoubtedly he was overbowled. The regional attack was thin in talent, and he was forced into the front-line against the powerful English and Australian batting. Ramadhin's consistency when others wilted nailed for ever the suspicion laid in his early days that he could not cope with punishment. He was still good enough to merit selection when the emphasis was switched to pace at the end of the 1950s.

None of the Trinidadian slow bowlers who came after him have attained his stature. Several youngsters have acquired the 'new Ramadhin' tag without making the grade. Harold Joseph impressed the Englishmen with his bowling at Port of Spain in 1981, but, though taken to Australia at the end of the year, he did not settle. Shervan Pragg's performance for the West Indies Young Cricketers in England in 1982 earned a similar accolade. His untimely death deprived cricket of a potentially rare talent.

Not surprisingly Queen's Park has been kinder to spinners than have the other venues. Jack Noreiga's 9-95 in the Second Test Match against India in 1971 is still the best innings bowling analysis for the West Indies. The Indians won then and achieved another historic victory on the same ground five years later. They feel at home in Trinidad in more than one way.

Cricket is recorded in British Guiana since c. 1840, and twenty-five years later the territory took part in matches against Barbados. In 1887 E.F. Wright of the Georgetown C.C. became the first batsman to score a thousand runs in a West Indian season. Although the Guianese had played a prominent role in the pioneer development of the game in the region, the mainland colony yielded precedence to Trinidad and Barbados by the end of the first decade of the present century. Nevertheless the first West Indies Test Match victory was achieved at Bourda in February 1930.

Smarting from defeat by 167 runs in the preceding game at Queen's

Park, where they had led on the first innings, the West Indies took command from the outset. Clifford Roach hit the team's first double century, and young George Headley made a hundred in each innings. Although the tourists rallied again from a disappointing start they had lost too much ground to fast bowlers George Francis and Learie Constantine. The West Indies won by a decisive 289 runs. True to the practice of the time Maurice Fernandes, the successful captain, was not selected for another Test Match outside his home territory.

After spending decades in the doldrums Guianese cricket burst into prominence in the mid-1950s. Rohan Kanhai, Basil Butcher and Joe Solomon came to the fore together, co-inciding with the arrival of Clyde Walcott from Barbados as coach. British Guiana, an exceptionally strong batting side, won the quadrangular tournament in 1956, and Kanhai went with Walcott to England the following year. If the bowling had enjoyed similar strength the territory, whose success ended Trinidad's ascendancy, would have challenged Barbados more consistently as the power in Caribbean cricket.

The failure of others almost cost Kanhai his career at the outset. In his first international series he was required to open the batting and to keep wicket, for neither of which did he have sufficient experience or the temperament. Rohan's impetuosity was not suited to facing the new ball — though he fared better than most on the quickfire pitch at Lord's — and he was little more than a stopper behind the stumps. To the credit of his character he survived the experience to become a major influence in world cricket over the next two decades.

Few batsmen have dominated the opposing bowlers so decisively. On the twin-tour to India and Pakistan in 1958/59 he hammered double-centuries at Calcutta and Lahore. Two years later he scored a century in each innings at Adelaide. At that time he was still inclined to give the bowler a chance before his eye was in, and his running between the wickets was often hazardous to his partner and himself. Later he learned circumspection and, although there were fewer really high scores, his batting became more consistent.

Kanhai's unconventional approach was his greatest asset to the team. His rapid scoring could change the tactical course of a match in a session, and he took his runs where and how they were least expected. Rohan is remembered best for hitting to the leg-side with both feet off the ground and losing his balance from the force of the stroke as the ball sped to the boundary. It should not have been possible to score from that position. He took off in the air also for some spectacular catches at square-leg or mid-wicket. He prospered, too, at the times when his colleagues found batting to be most difficult.

Although he retired temporarily from international cricket after the tour to Australasia in 1968/69, Kanhai became a mature stalwart during the lean years that followed. In spite of his earlier reputation for being unorthodox he was appointed captain, the first Guyanese to hold the position for more than one match, in an attempt to revitalise the Test Match team after the stagnancy of Sobers' later years. More defensive in leadership than in his personal approach he has not always been given the full credit for what was achieved.

The sweeping victories in England in 1973 ended the drought of seven frustrating series in which the West Indies had had overwhelming individual talent but had had to settle for second best. Kanhai's captaincy was impaired by the tetchiness of the Test Match at Birmingham and the failure to repeat at home the success expected against an inferior England side. Even so he had presided over a resurgence in confidence and a renaissance of fast bowling, so that his dismissal for the leadership for the tour to India in 1974/75 was unexpected. The West Indies had shown that they could win, and since then, under Clive Lloyd, they have done so consistently.

Alvin Kallicharran, left-hander with deft wrist artistry and a fine sense of timing, made centuries against New Zealand at Bourda and Queen's Park in 1972 in his first two Test Match innings. He had learned his cricket at Paidama in rural Guyana. After progressing through the West Indian Schools tournament he became at 16½ years the youngest player ever to represent Guyana in the Shell Shield. Ever since then he has continued to pioneer new avenues of approach, but hardly such as he or his contemporaries could have foreseen at the time.

In the early-1970s Alvin appeared to be the most able in a formidable batting side. The West Indies team which toured England in 1973 had the unusual line-up of five left-handers in the first six positions — Ron Headley, Roy Fredericks, Clive Lloyd, Gary Sobers and Kallicharran. These were his most productive years internationally, but there is no knowing what he might have achieved if he had not taken part in South African domestic competition. It must be said, however, that most observers, including probably the player himself, had considered that his best days were behind him by the time that he took the rand.

Kallicharran graduated from the Port Mourant club in Berbice, whose former cricketers include Kanhai, Butcher, Solomon, the Christiani brothers and bowlers John Trim and Ivan Madray. His inspired hooking has annihilated short-pitched bowling from even the fastest bowlers, and he has placed the ball with equal ease through the offside field. Like most touch and timing batsmen Alvin has struggled

92

and looked ordinary when those talents have deserted him.

Controversy touched him first in the opening Test Match against England at Queen's Park in 1973/74. When the umpire signalled the end of the first day's play Kallicharran walked off the pitch without undergoing the formality of grounding his bat. Fieldsman Tony Greig threw down the wicket and appealed for a run-out. In the letter if not the spirit of the law Umpire Sang Hue had to uphold the appeal. In the interests of diplomacy the decision was reversed overnight and the next morning Alvin took his score from 142 to 158 before his dismissal was permanent.

Kallicharran's mugging of Dennis Lillee at The Oval in a preliminary round of the Prudential Cup in 1975 was one of the outstanding innings of representative cricket. The Australian whirlwind was then at his fearsome best. Described by Gordon Ross as batting 'like a firecracker, exploding all around' the lefthander slammed one six and seven fours in a ten-ball sequence. The faster and the shorter Lillee bowled the further he was hit. That mid-afternoon blitz shattered Australia's challenge.

Three years later Alvin renewed his acquaintance with controversy. He was the only established player who did not follow Clive Lloyd into World Series Cricket. When the other members withdrew from the side on the eve of the Third Test Match at Bourda he led the make-shift West Indies team on to the field against Australia. Two centuries and a ninety in the series indicated that he thrived on responsibility and stilled the contention that the captaincy should have been offered to Vanburn Holder. Disillusion was just around the corner.

At the end of the year Kallicharran became the first, and to date the only, West Indian captain to lose a Test Match series in India. His personal form remained above criticism in scoring 187 at Bombay and 98 at Madras. He could claim extenuating circumstances in that the World Series Cricketers were still missing. Nevertheless defects in his tactical approach were considered to be decisive to the outcome. Dicky Rutnagur stated bluntly in his report for Wisden: 'Kallicharran's captaincy was one of the major weaknesses of the touring team'.

Sieuw Shivnarine was one of the several players owing an international opportunity to the Packer schism. His allround performance was impressive in Guyana's game against the Australians preceding the contraversial Bourda Test Match. He hit three half-centuries in his first five innings for the West Indies. Probably the most unexpected choice he seemed to fit easily into the side. In spite of his match-saving batting at Calcutta, Shivnarine's reputation was not enhanced in India: his was not the only one.

Kallicharran's career blossomed for Warwickshire in the English county championship in the 1980s. He had played with Rohan Kanhai, Deryck Murray and Lance Gibbs in the county's side in the previous decade. With his international aspirations seemingly over Alvin scored more than 2000 runs, including three championship double-centuries and five single-centuries, in 1982, and repeated his success in the next two seasons. Such form demanded a Test Match recall even for a veteran, but by then Kallicharran had put himself beyond the pale.

At a time when passions were high concerning association with South Africa, especially after the 'Jackman affair' had threatened to curtail England's tour of the Caribbean in early 1981, he became the first West Indian to participate in that country's Currie Cup competition. By accepting a contract with Transvaal he had gone further than either John Shepherd or Gary Sobers, whose involvement with Rhodesia had aroused popular wrath. He was swimming more strongly against the tide than at any time in the World Series Cricket crisis.

The Guyanese left-hander was condemned further for his part in the 'rebel' West Indian tours to South Africa. In the event the defections did not impair the strength of the official team. Nevertheless those English commentators who blamed their country's poor performance on the absence of Graham Gooch and his associates should speculate on the margin of West Indian superiority if Kallicharran, Lawrence Rowe, Sylvester Clarke and others had been available to them.

Faoud Bacchus, also from Guyana, was one of the few West Indians to make a favourable impression in India in 1978/79. Bedi bowled him just four runs short of his century at Bangalore, but at Kanpur in the final match Bacchus stroked 250 in the face of a massive home total. At the time he showed much in common with Kanhai's march of progress twenty years earlier. Faoud had a double-century to his name, and at times had been dismissed through his own impetuosity. Yet the similarity ends there.

Whereas Kanhai scored his runs by powerful drives, hooks and pulls, Bacchus wafted an air of oriental artistry. His style was both attractive and adventurous. Moving from the middle-order to open the innings he came into competition for selection with Gordon Greenidge and Desmond Haynes once the Packer rift had been healed. He drifted back to contest a middle-order place with Kallicharran and Gomes. Faoud lacked sufficient authority to stamp his mark on the team.

Due to the instability of the middle-batting Bacchus hovered on the edge of selection for several years without achieving anything of lasting merit. His appointment to lead the Young West Indies in Zimbabwe in 1981/82 enhanced speculation that he was considered to be a long-term candidate for the captaincy of the senior side. Although the tourists won the only representative match to be decided, he lost ground to the more successful batting of potential rivals Everton Mattis, Timur Mohamed and Jeffrey Dujon.

During his brief international career Bacchus shone as a short-leg fieldsman. It was not easy fielding there to the fast bowlers, especially in England's unpredictable weather conditions in the wet summer of 1980. Desmond Haynes, his vice-captain in Zimbabwe, replaced him eventually as permanent opening batsman and at short-leg.

Although in early 1983 he represented the West Indies against India in the limited-over matches, Bacchus was dropped in favour of Gus Logie for the Test Matches. He was unfortunate that the tourists' scheduled game against Guyana, in which he could have pushed his claims, was abandoned. Overlooked for the tour to India at the end of the year, Bacchus threw in his lot with the 'rand rebels'. As a second-wave defector he was aware of the consequencies and must have appreciated that his international expectations were over.

Trinidad & Tobago went through a low period in the 1970s. Bernard Julien never quite made the mark which his considerable talents demanded. Perhaps he had been over-billed at the start of his career and, like some other allrounders, had not done quite enough to secure his position in either batting or bowling. Apart from long-serving wicketkeeper Deryck Murray the twin-island state had no regular regional representative to continue their tradition. The renaissance came from an unlikely, and thrice rejected, source.

Hilary Angelo 'Larry' Gomes from Queen's Park in Port of Spain made his first-class debut for Trinidad & Tobago against the New Zealanders in 1972, three years after his brother, Sheldon, had played his first match. Between 1973 and 1975 Larry played for Middlesex in England without achieving anything to suggest that he would sustain a lengthy international career. Yet within a year he made his Test Match debut, and it was at Lord's where the Middlesex home matches are played.

Gomes, a left-hander, was one of the few failures in England in 1976. Surprisingly, in view of his later stoicism, he was out too often while hooking before he had settled to the pace of the pitch and the bowling. The withdrawal of the World Series Cricketers in 1978 gave him a second chance. Larry had pressed for selection already by hitting a hundred for Trinidad & Tobago against the Australians. Recalled to the regional colours he reached three figures also in the Test Matches at Bourda and Sabina Park.

Because of his consistency in the following rubber in India, Gomes was one of only three members of Kallicharran's conventional West Indies side to be retained in the combined eleven when the World Series Cricketers returned. He commenced the series with three consecutive half-centuries and made 91 in the defeat at Madras. The fast bowlers on either side pitched intimidatorily short on a fast pitch conducive to bounce. Gomes struck thirteen fours as the West Indies collapsed to 151 all out. No other batsman scored more than 15.

The Trinidadian was left out of the side which went to England in 1980. Kallicharran's effective retirement and the failure of all prospective successors caused Gomes to be recalled for the home series against England in 1981 and for the following tour to Australia. In the abbreviated three-match rubber he scored centuries at Sydney and Adelaide, and scored 200 not out against Queensland at Brisbane. He steadied the innings at Adelaide after a jittery start and laid the foundation for the West Indies to win and square the series.

Larry's overall international record in the Caribbean is disappointing. He and Clive Lloyd rallied the side with a 237 runs partnership after the first three wickets had fallen for just a single against India at Queen's Park in 1982/83. The more attacking Logie and Richie Richardson pressed so strongly that within a year Gomes was considered to be lucky to be chosen to tour England in 1984. It was assumed that he owed his selection to his experience of that country and to the requirement of territorial balance.

Gomes was included as the statutory fifth bowler in the three limited-over matches which preceded the Test Matches. He seemed to be always in the game either chipping away at the opposing batting to take a vital wicket or affording a stubborn support to the more spectacular stroke-players. Nevertheless Lloyd's preference for the self-effacing Trinidadian to the brilliant Richardson for the First Test Match at Birmingham was not expected. It turned out to be an inspired choice.

Larry pushed, prodded, deflected and sometimes offdrove sweetly on his way to 143 on the same pitch on which the Englishmen had suffered humiliation, and even injury, and the West Indian opening batsmen had been dismissed cheaply. He and Viv Richards put on 206 runs for the third wicket. In the next match at Lord's he gave Gordon Greenidge as much strike as he needed in the unbroken match-winning second-wicket partnership of 287, of which his share was 92.

The value of Gomes' determination was most evident in the Third Test Match at Leeds. Conditions generally favoured the bowlers. In the final session of the second day the West Indies lost quick wickets as the total tumbled from 201-4 to 206-7. At that point the tourists were still 64 runs behind England. The Trinidadian played through the potential catastrophe and provided sound support for Holding's whirlwind counter-attack. He whittled his way to an undefeated century before his last partner was out with the tourists 32 runs ahead.

Gomes and wicketkeeper Dujon, both of whom scored centuries, rescued the tourists at Perth in late 1984 by putting on 147 runs for the sixth wicket after both Clive Lloyd and Richie Richardson had been dismissed without scoring. His batting was equally valuable at Adelaide where he followed 60 in the first innings by hitting an unbeaten 120 in the second and passed fifty again in his next innings at Melbourne.

Diminutive Gus Logie could provide with Larry the future fulcrum of the middle-order batting. He made his Shell Shield debut for Trinidad & Tobago in 1979 and moved swiftly towards representative recognition. After a disappointing start to his Test Match career he struck a spectacular, if somewhat fortuitous, 130 against India at Kensington in 1983. Then Gus faded from contention following a 'pair' at Ahmedabad in the return rubber. Richardson's arrival and the revival in Gomes' fortunes forced him temporarily into the background.

Logie, a spectacular fieldsman, especially in the covers, has been too inconsistent in batting to justify regular inclusion in the greatest team in the greatest game. He plays the ball unusually late, often taken as the sign of a very good batsman, and on form he is such a spectacular destroyer of the bowling that he could develop yet into a force of the late 1980s.

Trinidad & Tobago won the Shell Shield in early 1985 and, although the regions's leading players were in Australia, the restoration of their fortunes was most welcome. Opening batsmen Phil Simmonds maintained the promise he had shown with the West Indies Young Cricketers, and fast bowler Tony Gray indicated a revival in pace for the first time in almost two generations. Leg-spinner Ganesh Mahabir and middle-order batsman Prakash Moosai, both in their mid-twenties, contributed substantially to the success.

Ten

Queen's Park Oval,
Port of Spain

Trinidad is an island of contrasts and of character. The people are
positive in expressing an opinion, in criticising a fault and in encouraging a friend. The latter two attitudes are more often compatible
than exclusive. And so it is with their cricket. Matches played at the
Queen's Park Oval tend to contain both hope and despair for the West
Indies. Because of its pre-eminence in the erstwhile colonial administration and commerce in the Eastern Caribbean, the country became
a centre of early regional and international competition.

The substantial population, financial potential and the ground's
crowd capacity have made the Test Matches in Port of Spain integral
to the viability of tours to the Caribbean. Prior to the elevation of the
Recreation Ground at St. John's to similar status in 1981, the Oval
hosted two matches in a five-match series, except on those few occasions that the honour was accorded to Sabina Park, and twice took in
an extra fixture that could not be staged in neighbouring Guyana.
Consequently the attitude of Trinidad has been critical in determining
whether a possibly contraversial tour should go ahead.

In spite of its traditions and reputation the Oval holds some un-
happy memories for the West Indies. Too often things have gone
wrong just when they should not have done so. Two disastrous declarations come to mind particularly. In the late 1960s Gary Sobers
gambled from a strong position and lost the match and the rubber.
Several seasons later Clive Lloyd similarly under-estimated the Indian
batsmen who scored a record number of runs to win in the fourth
innings. On their previous visit the Indian slow bowlers brought down
the seemingly powerful West Indian batting.

Other matches here have been lost against the run of play, including
the first defeat sustained in a Test Match in the Caribbean. An inexplicable breakdown by a potentially powerful batting side led to a riot
in 1960, and apparent victory was thrown away against Australia in
1973. Even on occasions that the West Indies won the series decisively,
a shock defeat was suffered in the concluding contest in Trinidad.

The pitch at Port of Spain has been more conducive to spin than elsewhere in the region. This factor has aided the tourists more than the home slow bowlers. The most likely explanation of the disparity is that the West Indian batsmen have been less adept at countering the conditions. There have been nine wins, ten defeats, and sixteen drawn matches. High scoring has contributed significantly to the high proportion of inconclusive results.

Port of Spain, the capital city, is situated towards the north-eastern corner of Trinidad, an island which is geographically an extension of the South American continent. Venezuela is only seven miles away. The country is approximately rectangular with a peninsula projecting from each corner. Tropical forests cover half of the island, and low mountain ranges sweep from east to west. Trinidad is linked with Tobago to its north-east in a twin-island state. The latter is noted for its scenic beaches.

Independence Square and the adjoining streets in the centre of Port of Spain are a hub of activity. The population reflects the blending of cultures descended from Africa, Asia and Europe. Trinidad provided the earliest links between the cricket Caribbean and the outside. Port of Spain is still a thriving shipping centre and Piarco International Air-port, 16 miles away, has many direct international services. Unlike the tranquility of other West Indian islands, most notably Barbados, Trinidad's attraction lies in the excitement and activity of the urban population.

The Queen's Park Savannah covers 200 acres on Port of Spain's northern edge and includes a race course and numerous playing fields. It provides a haven for organised sport and casual recreation. Young female joggers attract their own male admirers. The standard of female pulchritude is higher here than anywhere else, at least in my present experience, and the popular saying that Trinidadians pass their time in talking politics, having sex and playing cricket ought to be true even if it is only wishful thinking. The inhabitants are prone to excessive self-criticism.

The Oval ground is dominated by the backdrop of the Northern Range of mountains, against which an approaching rainfall can be observed before it has arrived. The centre of the city is never far away. Spectators leave and enter the ground at will, nipping out for lunch-time food and refreshment at the excellent nearby restaurants. In spite of the tropical heat, which in Trinidad is different in texture to that of most islands in the region, the pavilion and stands seem always to be cool, perhaps due to the breezes wafted from the sea close-by.

Queen's Park Oval is an ideal place to visit on days when it is not being used for sport, just to browse around the photographs and exhibits from former years. The atmosphere of tradition lacks the formal frigidity of Lord's and, to the outsider at least, the sense of history is sharper than it is at Kensington. There appears always to be somebody on hand to guide you through the decades. The faded pictures evoke vividly the personalities, performances and even the atmosphere of a more successful past.

Perhaps it is wrong to dwell too much on this aspect, but whereas the average Barbadian follower, as opposed to the historian or administrator, is concerned chiefly with the heroes of today his Trinidadian counterpart has a greater living awareness of those who has gone before. George John, Clifford Roach, Learie Constantine, the Warners, and the pioneers beyond, are very much still part of the contemporary consciousness. From the 1930s to the 1950s the two Grants, Gerry Gomez and Jeffrey Stollmeyer captained the region, but there has been no other in the three subsequent decades.

Trinidad Cricket Club is described as being already 'of very long standing' in 1842 and twenty-seven years later the island played its first game against Guyana. E. Augustini and G. Wedekind put on 110 runs for the fifth wicket, the first century stand in the region, against the same opponents on the Parade Ground at Georgetown in 1876. Twenty years later the Queen's Park Cricket Club took occupation of the St Clair Oval and became the effective controlling authority of the country's cricket for the next 60 years.

In spite of having the better of a draw against Queen's Park, Lord Hawke's side suffered defeat in both games against Trinidad. The inclusion of the black bowlers, Woods and Cumberbatch, in contrast to some of the all-white teams which opposed the tourists elsewhere, was the deciding factor. Pelham Warner commented:

'The two black men showed themselves first class bowlers, and both of them would be good enough for any county team, especially as they are fine fielders and throwers'.

Although he played for the visitors the author had been born in Trinidad and his brother, Aucher, captained the island, making the highest individual score in the second game.

Warner was impressed with the ground:

'It proved upon inspection to be as good a ground as one could wish to see, with a most comfortable pavilion, excellent stands, scoring-cards, etc — in fact, everything that could be desired ....

The view from the ground is simply magnificent. A perfect amphitheatre of wooded hills swept round us from the Laventille hills to the mountains of the Maraval valley. In the foreground, at their feet, were several charming houses, surrounded by broad gardens bright with flowers of all the colours of the rainbow, and festooned with the gorgeous creepers that grow so luxuriantly in this part of the world. The Maraval hills were at the time a spectacle of much beauty'.

The writer had every reason to be pleased with the visit and in his book *Cricket in Many Climes* the relevant chapter is headed 'Good Times in Trinidad'. He explains how

'the day of my first match in my native island was one that I shall always look back upon with delight'

and describes how he went on to score a century against the Queen's Park Club. After the defeats against the island's full strength he trusted that Trinidad found the tourists to be more successful as friends than they had been as batsmen.

The ability to lose from an apparently winning position was illustrated in the first Test Match played at Port of Spain in February 1930. The West Indies led by 46 runs on the first innings after penetrative fast bowling by Herman Griffith and Learie Constantine. With defeat facing the visitors Patsy Hendren, the last recognised batsman, scored 205 not out in a substantial stand with wicketkeeper Leslie Ames. The home batting, then, collapsed to left-arm fast bowler Bill Voce, who took 7 wickets for 70 runs, and lost by 167 runs.

Nevertheless, the West Indies evened the score in winning by 217 runs five years later. Local hero Constantine played a prominent part in hitting a quick 90 and sharing the pace bowling success with Manny Martindale and Leslie Hylton. The victory, however, was won by a superior allround team performance. For a time England seemed to threaten to come back into the game as they had on the previous occasion. The tourists rallied from 28-5 to reach 258 in the first innings but failed to maintain the challenge.

The drawn match in 1948 was remarkable for two rare achievements. Billy Griffith, the English reserve wicketkeeper, went in first because the specialist openers were indisposed and scored 140, his maiden first-class century. Andy Ganteaume, the Trinidad opening batsman chosen to replace his injured compatriot, Jeff Stollmeyer, hit 112 in a first-wicket partnership of 173 with George Carew. As he did not bat in the second innings and was not picked again Ganteaume is the only batsman ever to hit a hundred the one time he has batted in a Test Match. The West Indies led by 135 runs on the first innings.

The next three matches, in all of which the West Indies were ahead on first innings, were drawn through high scoring. Everton Weekes, making 207, fought a fascinating duel with leg-spinner Subhash Gupte, who took 7 wickets for 162 runs, in the First Test Match against India in 1953. Although the same batsman hit 161 in the Third Test Match of the series on the same ground, the chief honour was achieved by Indian opening batsman Madhav Apte who saved his side with an unbeaten 163 after their first innings breakdown against fast bowler Frank King. Weekes scored another double-century, and Walcott and Worrell made single hundreds, against England the following year.

A third-wicket stand of 242 runs between Clyde Walcott and Everton Weekes comprised the bulk of the total against the Australians in 1955. Colin McDonald, Arthur Morris and Neil Harvey, the first three batsmen in the order, hit hundreds in the tourists' massive 600-9 dec reply. Walcott forced a draw by making his second century of the match and at the close Weekes, who had achieved three figures in each of four consecutive Test Matches at the Oval, was only 13 runs short of the same landmark.

The West Indies beat Pakistan by 120 runs in the Second Test Match in 1958 on the strength of their superior performance with both bat and ball, and the tourists were outclassed everywhere in the region. Yet when the teams returned to Trinidad for the Fifth Test Match, Pakistan sprang a surprise in winning by an innings and one run. The home batsmen faltered against medium-fast bowler Fazal Mahmood and and left-arm spinner Nasimul Ghani, each of whom took six wickets in an innings. Wazir Mohammad, who had been over-shadowed previously by his brother, Hanif, scored a decisive 189. Fast bowler Jaswick Taylor's feat in taking 5 wickets for 109 runs gave the home crowd some encouragement.

The Second Test Match against England in 1960, and with it the series, was lost in the batting breakdown on the third morning. Fast bowlers Freddie Trueman and Brian Statham ripped the heart out of the middle-order. The final stage of the innings, which reached only 122, was interrupted by the now celebrated riot on the run-out dismissal of Charan Singh. England, 270 runs ahead on the strength of centuries by Ken Barrington and Mike Smith, did not enforce the follow on and, in spite of Rohan Kanhai's determined defence for 110, won by 256 runs.

The Fifth Test Match, also at Queen's Park, was drawn inconclusively. Although, in an attempt to win, the West Indies declared 55 runs behind, they were frustrated by a seventh-wicket stand of 197 runs between Mike Smith and wicketkeeper Jim Parks. Ironically the latter had not been in the original party but, being on a private trip to the region, he had been drafted into the side due to injuries to key players.

Alan Ross described the Oval in his book *Through the Caribbean* as follows:

'The Port of Spain ground, in any case, must rank with

Newlands, Cape Town, and Adelaide as having one of the three most spectacular settings in the world. The enclosing mountains, densely wooded, of the Northern Range curve round ahead of the pavilion. The various stands are shaded by vast, scarlet-flowering tulip trees or overhung by the top-heavy filigree spread of samans, always, on account of their shallow roots and bulging superstructure, the first to be bowled over by heavy winds .... Towards close of play here, when the air sweetens, flocks of white pigeons endlessly circle behind the tulip trees, keeping perfect formation like an aircraft on display'.

The Indians were defeated twice in 1962, by 10 wickets and by 7 wickets. On the second occasion Polly Umrigar scored 56 and a rear-guard 172 not out as well as taking 5 wickets for 107 runs. Wesley Hall's blitz of 5 wickets for 20 runs in the first innings effectively settled the contest. Three years later the first encounter here against Australia resulted in a high-scoring draw but, though they had been bested throughout the rubber, the tourists won the Fifth Test Match by 10 wickets. Conrad Hunte carried his bat for 60, the only occurrance of this feat by a West Indian batsman in the Caribbean. Frank Worrell batted throughout the innings for 191 not out against England at Nottingham in 1957.

England came close to winning the First Test Match in 1968. With hundreds by Ken Barrington and Tom Graveney, the tourists took a first innings lead of 205 runs, in spite of young Clive Lloyd scoring 118. The West Indies, fighting against defeat all the way, struggled to 243-8 by the close. It had been touch and go. They were not so fortunate when the teams came back to Trinidad for the Fourth Test Match, and the series was still open.

The home batsmen began brilliantly. Rohan Kanhai, hitting his fourth century in as many series at Queen's Park — he had failed by only four runs to make a fifth in 1958, and Seymour Nurse added 273 runs for the third wicket. Colin Cowdrey, the visiting captain, steered his team into an apparently safe position, but the lower-order batted feebly, fumbling from 373-5 to 414 all out against Basil Butcher's occasional leg-spin. Although the West Indies seemed to be secure, there was insufficient time to achieve a victory.

Then Gary Sobers declared the second innings at 92-2, setting England to score 215 runs in 2¾ hours. It was a difficult decision to understand. He lacked the services of fast bowlers Charlie Griffith, injured in the early overs, and Wesley Hall, dropped from the team. Consequently he had to rely almost entirely on himself and Lance Gibbs. Cowdrey and Geoff Boycott batted positively to give England an unexpected victory by 7 wickets. In his publication *The Best of*

Cricket the Trinidadian writer Brunell Jones explained the decision: 'Sobers ... called a team meeting. He was, I was told, not happy about the growing spate of drawn matches. The team's decision was that the West Indies would set England a challenge'.

There was further disappointment on India's visit in 1971. In the Second Test Match the West Indian batsmen surrendered the initiative to spin bowlers Erapalli Prasanna and Srinivasan Venkataraghavan, and lost by 7 wickets. Again it was the only match in the rubber to be decided. In taking 9 wickets for 95 runs Jack Noreiga, the little-known slow bowler from Trinidad, established the best innings analysis returned for the West Indies in a Test Match. Local batsman Charlie Davis, who scored two undefeated half-centuries, could not be blamed for the breakdown.

The Fifth Test Match, also at the Oval, was made memorable by Sunil Gavaskar making 124 and 220 to complete an aggregate of 774 runs in his debut series. The little opening batsman, alone, stood between the West Indians, who led by 166 runs on the first innings, and a victory which would have evened the honours. And so, India won a rubber in the Caribbean for the only time to date. Sobers, like Gavaskar, reached his third century in consecutive Test Matches, and Davis, the other lynch-pin of the middle-order, achieved his own hundred.

The two matches against the New Zealanders a year later were both drawn. On the first occasion there was little between the teams, but in the Fifth Test Match the home side had its best chance that season of recording a win. The West Indies went ahead by 206 on the first innings after Alvin Kallicharran had scored a hundred and Inshan Ali, the Trinidadian left-arm spinner, had taken 5 wickets for 59 runs. The follow-on was not enforced and New Zealand finished the match 147 runs behind with just three wickets still in hand.

The Third Test Match against Australia in 1973 was lost in a few disastrous overs after a commendable fight-back. Although the tourists led by 52 runs off-spinner Lance Gibbs bowled the West Indies back into the contest, and they went into lunch on the last day at 268-4 with Alvin Kallicharran on 91 not out and only another 66 runs needed to win. The Guyanese left-hander was caught at the wicket immediately on the resumption and the remaining wickets tumbled so quickly that Australia won by 44 runs. The victors could claim the moral victory also in the drawn Fifth Test Match at the Oval, which their hosts finished 185 runs behind with only five wickets in hand.

The First Test Match against England the next year was full of incident. The visitors were unsettled by quick bowler Keith Boyce, so that the West Indies took a lead of 261 runs on the first innings.

Dennis Amiss and Geoff Boycott hit back by putting on 209 runs for the first wicket of the second innings, but when that partnership ended the rest of the batting surrendered to Gibbs, who took 6 wickets for 108 runs, and the West Indies won easily enough by 7 wickets. The preceding 21 Test Matches at Queen's Park had been either lost or drawn.

Subsequent proceedings were overshadowed by an incident right at the close of play in the West Indian first innings involving Alvin Kallicharran, then on 142. Brunnell Jones relates:

'When the (last) over was three balls old, left-handed Kallicharran had peeled off his right hand batting glove with his teeth and had rolled the left one off with his right hand. Now, as the final ball of the day comes to Julien, Julien plays forward, bat and pad; pushes the ball away from him, a yard or two from Greig's right hand.

The tension is broken ... even to Knott, a Test-tried warrior who breaks the stumps at the batsman's end and Julien, on 22, has turned on his heel and has begun his walk to the pavilion. All this is taking place behind Greig's back. His eyes are on the ball. He darts after it and, noting the non-striker is out of his crease ... that the bails at that end had not yet been lifted ... that the umpire had not informed the players that the day's entertainment had come to a close, Greig's direct throw sent the bails flying while he shouted "Howzatt!". The umpire informed a flabbergasted Kallicharran he was out'.

That evening the West Indies Board of Control issued a release confirming the decision to be strictly within the laws of cricket but added

'The English manager and captain have requested the appeal against the batsman be withdrawn. The umpires, bearing in mind the particular circumstances, have agreed to accept this and the batsman be allowed to continue'.

The next morning Kallicharran was bowled for 158.

The Englishmen, who had been outplayed throughout the series, squared the rubber by winning the Fifth Test Match at the Oval by 26 runs. They owed the victory to two men, Geoff Boycott and Tony Greig, and to a West Indian batting collapse after leading by 38 runs in a comparatively low-scoring match. There was nothing in the early stages to hint at such an outcome. After the tourists had been dismissed for 267 runs, Roy Fredericks and Lawrence Rowe put on over a hundred for the first wicket, and the West Indies went into the lead with only five wickets down.

Off-spinner Tony Greig, bringing the ball down from his great height and taking 8 wickets for 86 runs, ran through the lower-order. Batting was far from easy but when Boycott added 112 to his first innings 99 without effective support England seemed to be destined for defeat. However this time Greig spun through the middle-batting with another 5 wickets for 70 runs. This match ended the Test Match careers of Gary Sobers and Rohan Kanhai. It was time for a fresh start.

The Indians visited Trinidad twice in 1976, and each time had the better of the exchanges. Although Viv Richards made 130 in the Second Test Match his colleagues batted so badly against left-arm spinner Bishen Bedi that the total was only 241. Then Sunil Gavaskar, hitting his third century in consecutive innings at Port of Spain, and Brijesh Patel took the tourists ahead by 161 runs. The loss of the first day and a plague of missed chances when they were on top cost the Indians dearly, because the West Indies finished the match only 54 runs in front with just two wickets in hand.

The next Test Match was moved to Queen's Park from its scheduled site at Bourda due to the incessant rain in that country. The weather, thus, prevented Gibbs from making a farewell appearance on his home ground. The first innings became a personal duel between Richards, scoring 177, and Chandrasekhar, who took 6 wickets for 120 runs. The tourists fared even worse against Michael Holding's pace. The Jamaican took 6 wickets for 65 runs in bowling India to a 131 runs deficit. When Kallicharran scored an unbeaten hundred the Indians seemed to be out of contention, but the jinx of the Oval struck again.

Chasing a target of over four hundred runs the batsmen who had wilted previously to Holding played with unexpected confidence. The batting was sound rather than spectacular as Gavaskar made yet another hundred and added 108 runs in a second-wicket stand with Mohinder Amarnath which gave the tourists hope. Little Gundappa Viswanath took over with an inspired attack on some wayward bowling. Although he was run out in sight of victory, the Indians went on to win at 406-4. It is still the highest score made in the fourth innings to win a Test Match.

Colin Croft took 8 wickets for 29 runs, the best return ever by a fast bowler for the West Indies, in setting up the victory by 6 wickets over Pakistan in 1977. Roy Fredericks hit a hundred to give the West Indies a lead of 136 runs. Opening batsmen Majid Khan and Sadiq Mohammad all but wiped out the deficit before they were parted, but, apart from Wasim Raja's second spirited knock, the later batsmen were at sea against the fast bowlers. First-wicket pairing Fredericks and Greenidge scored almost half of the required total.

Mustaq Mohammad, the visiting captain, won the Fourth Test Match with a great solo allround performance. After scoring 121, the only century of the match, he took 5 wickets for 28 runs with his leg-breaks. The West Indies did not recover from their first innings batting failure and were outplayed by opponents who batted to greater depth. Mustaq Mohammad, maintaining his performance by hitting 56, and Wasim Raja ended any speculation on defeat by adding 116 runs for the sixth wicket, and the Pakistanis won by 266 runs, their only victory of the series.

The Australians went down twice in 1978. Their 90 runs total in the First Test Match could not have provided a more depressing start to the series. Raw batsmen, lacking the example and the experience of the missing World Series Cricketers, were overwhelmed by the West Indian fast bowlers. Kallicharran and Lloyd added 170 runs for the fourth wicket. Australia put up a better fight in the second innings and reached 194-3 before Andy Roberts punched through the rest of the innings for just another 15 runs. The margin of victory was an innings and 106 runs.

Because all of the World Series Cricketers had withdrawn by the Fourth Test Match the teams were better balanced and only two runs separated them on first innings. New captain Kallicharran made the match top-score of 92. Yet when the tourists started their last innings seeking to score 293 runs to win they were routed by spinners Parry and Jumadeen. The former dismissed the last five batsmen for six runs off 28 deliveries. The West Indies won the match by 198 runs and with it the series.

A one-sided victory by an innings and 79 runs was achieved over England in the First Test Match of 1981. Gordon Greenidge and Desmond Haynes saw the way to a strong total by adding 168 runs for the first wicket. Croft routed the visitors for a total of just 10 runs more, and they fared just as badly when they followed-on. The West Indians secured a complete psychological advantage. Damage to the pitch, which delayed the start of the match, was attributed to local annoyance that wicketkeeper Deryck Murray had been dropped from the side.

Two years later India lost quick wickets to Malcolm Marshall but seemed to have made more than amends by dismissing the first three home batsmen for just a single. Clive Lloyd and Larry Gomes, then, swung the balance in a 237 runs partnership for the fourth wicket. Facing a 219 runs deficit the Indians needed to bat through over 10 hours for a draw. They succeeded because Mohinder Amarnath batted with great confidence and Kapil Dev hit out for centuries.

The Australians made a similarly disastrous start to their innings the next year. Joel Garner dismissed the first three batsmen quickly and finished with 6 wickets for 60 runs. Stocky left-hander Allan Border held his side together by hitting 98 not out. Gus Logie, dismissed just short of his hundred, shared sparkling three-figure partnerships with Viv Richards and Jeff Dujon. The wicketkeeper batted brilliantly for 130 described by the *Benson & Hedges West Indies Cricket Annual* as

'a virtuoso performance ... dazzling the eye with his elegance and sense of timing'.

The tourists began their second innings 213 runs behind and were soon in further trouble. Half the side were out for 115 before Border found support in the lower-order. The ninth-wicket pair wiped off the deficit with defeat still seemingly inevitable. Eventually last man Terry Alderman stayed with Border, whose 100 not out followed his first innings defiance, to the close at 299-9. His combined innings lasted 10 hours 34 minutes and took in 535 deliveries.

The West Indies recovered well from losing their first two batsmen without scoring to fast bowler Richard Hadlee against New Zealand in 1985. Gordon Greenidge and Richie Richardson put on 185 runs for the third wicket. Playing for the first time under Viv Richards' leadership they led by 45 runs on the first innings and had the better of the draw. Unusually for the Oval the quick bowlers had the upper hand.

Eleven

Gordon Greenidge

Gordon Greenidge is to my mind the most exciting batsman in the world today, one of the very few to persuade a pass-carrying reporter to pay the admission fee at the turn-stile if there were no other way of watching him perform. He is prepared always to attack the bowling and, though he has been dismissed too often in a situation where patience would have taught him prudence, the Barbadian's array of strokes remain in the memory long after some longer and statistically more significant innings have faded.

If excitement is defined as a batsman's technical mastery of the opposing bowling, in the manner demonstrated so often by Viv Richards and Don Bradman, Greenidge would be only one among several. On the understanding that excitement conveys an expectation of the unexpected, he stands alone. While he is at the crease deliveries outside the off-stump may be forced to leg, and he has been known to cut the uncuttable or hook the unhookable. His form in the Prudential (World) Cup competition of 1979 was such that it seemed that only Gordon could get himself out. In the Final he obliged by attempting an impossible run. Nobody can be sure just what will happen.

Cuthbert Gordon Greenidge was born in Barbados on 1 May 1951 and lived in the island for the first fourteen years of his life. His move to England co-incided with the West Indies' home victory over Australia, the pinnacle of performance by the team forged by Frank Worrell and led by him and by Gary Sobers. The young Greenidge could not but have been touched by the euphoria. Like other Barbadians of his generation he would have exchanged news of the heroes of the day. Then he was taken away from that environment to the other side of the Atlantic, to his parents' new home at Reading and to Sutton Secondary School.

His progress there was swift. Within two years Gordon played for the Berkshire Bantams and for the South of England Schoolboys against the North and Midlands. Because Berkshire does not have first-class status aspiring county players have had to look elsewhere for a career in the game. Peter May, Ken Barrington and the Bedser twins went to Surrey. Greenidge accepted the offer of a trial with Hampshire, who had pursued an enlightened policy of engaging West Indian talent. Roy Marshall, the former Test Match opening batsman, was an established county folk-hero and Hampshire called regularly on Danny Livingstone.

Although he played for the county's second team in 1968 Gordon did not graduate to the first eleven until two years later. In that first season he and Barry Richards, the brilliant Springbok, shared a double-century first-wicket partnership. His impact was immediate. As he edged towards representative recognition there was doubt as to whether he should play for the West Indies, where he had been born, or for England, where he had perfected his cricket. The Caribbean had the stronger pull and he returned home for the 1972 season.

As Greenidge compiled century after century in 1976, and double-hundred after double-hundred in 1984, England's selectors must have contemplated how different their fate might have been if they had been quicker off the mark. Consequently when Roland Butcher, who had arrived in the country at about the same time as his compatriot, began to score runs in abundance he was guided towards his adopted country, perhaps a year prematurely. The orientation of later West Indians in England towards representing the latter derives mostly from the direction of policy in the Caribbean rather than from personal preference.

The year 1972 was not a happy time for West Indian cricket. The glory days of the 1960s were followed by seven fruitless series. The performance at home was particularly frustrating. The series in 1967/68 was lost to England on the over-optimistic declaration at Queen's Park, and batting failure on the same ground led to the loss of the rubber against India. Even lowly New Zealand managed to avoid defeat in all five Test Matches.

Although the West Indies won convincingly in England in 1973, the immediate return rubber caused further dissatisfaction. On top for most of the season, the West Indies could not force home their advantage. The loss of the final fixture in Trinidad split the decision at one victory each. Widespread changes were made to bring together a younger side for the tour to India and Pakistan in 1974/75. Gordon Greenidge came into the party as the latest in a lineage of world-class Barbadian opening batsmen.

The tradition stretches from the thresh-hold of international competition. P.J. Cox scored more runs than anybody other than Ollivierre on the first tour to England in 1900, including an innings of 142 in a 208 runs first-wicket partnership against Surrey at the Oval.

The opposing attack contained Tom Richardson, the outstanding fast bowler of the previous decade. Three years later G.B.Y. Cox and Harold Austin put on 263 for the second-wicket for Barbados against Trinidad.

George Challenor, described so often as the 'father' of West Indian batting, linked the pioneer period to the Test Match age. He toured England three times and would have gone more often but for the intervention of the First World War. He was a teenager on the first visit in 1906 and at 40 years-old on the third in 1928 he played a dashing innings of 46 against much-feared fast bowler Harold Larwood in the Third Test Match at the Oval. It has been argued that his batting in 1923, when he hit over a thousand first-class runs and carried his bat for 155 against Surrey, contributed more than anything else to the granting of Test Match status.

Nevertheless, his peak performances were achieved in the Caribbean, often in partnership with P.H. Tarilton. It would be impossible to catalogue all of their outstanding feats. In 1920 the latter scored 304 not out against Trinidad at the Kensington Oval and in their opening partnership of 292 seven years later the then veteran Challenor amassed 220 against the same opponents on the same ground. That season Barbados compiled 715-9 dec (v Guyana) and 726-7 dec (v Trinidad) in consecutive games. Challenor had retired from top-class competition by the time that Test Match cricket came to the region.

For a time Clifford Roach, a talented Trinidadian, seemed to be his natural successor. His attractive style previewed Greenidge's own exciting approach. Nevertheless he was too erratic to be consistent. Roach made the first century and double-century for the West Indies — respectively 122 at Kensington Oval and 209 at Bourda, both in 1929/30 — but was dismissed twice for a 'pair' in a comparatively brief career. The quick-scoring Roach and watchful Freddie Martin of Jamaica had the unfulfilled potential to blend a contrast of styles two decades before Rae and Stollmeyer realised the prospect.

George Carew was already a veteran when he scored 107 in his stand of 173 with Andy Ganteaume against England at Queen's Park in 1948. Their slow scoring was criticised subsequently for depriving the West Indies of sufficient time to convert a substantial first innings lead into victory. In the circumstances the criticism seems to be harsh. No charge of slouching could be attributed to the next Barbadian opening batsman to attain regional honours.

Barely 20 years-old, Roy Marshall scored 188 against Leicestershire, 143 against Surrey and 135 against Hampshire in 1950, but he was kept out of the Test Match team by the dependability of Stollmeyer and Rae. He had secured his selection to the tour by hitting a dashing 191 against Trinidad. Marshall played eventually for the West Indies against Australia and New Zealand in 1951/52 when more reputations were lost than were enhanced. He has a more particular connection with Greenidge than the brilliance of their stroke-play.

Marshall made his professional career with Hampshire in the English county championship in the late 1950s and the 1960s. At a time of restricted opportunities in the Caribbean it offered one of the few ways in which a West Indian could make a career in cricket. Roy's scintillating but sound batting was instrumental in the county winning the title for the first time ever in 1961. Due partially to his greater number of championship appearances Marshall has scored more first-class runs (35 725) than any other West Indian batsman.

Conrad Hunte was overlooked when he should have been selected for the tour to England in 1957. Those more favoured failed completely. He emphasised the error of that omission by scoring 142 on his international debut against Pakistan at Kensington Oval, and at Sabina Park two matches later he was run out on 260 in pursuit of the record individual score in a Test Match. Gary Sobers broke that record later in the same innings. As vice-captain to Frank Worrell, the Barbadian had a key part in building the successful side of the 1960s.

The lack of a regular partner caused him to adopt a more restrained approach than would have been the case otherwise. Cammie Smith, another Barbadian, tried to hit almost every delivery to the boundary, entertained the public, and passed soon from the selectors' consideration. Hunte was remarkably consistent in 1965 when the West Indies defeated Australia for the first time. His six halfcenturies included 60 not out amid the lone defeat at Queen's Park — the second of only two occasions on which a West Indian opening batsman has carried his bat throughout an innings. His retirement on the return from India a year later preceded immediately the disintegration of the victorious combination.

The choice of Gordon Greenidge to partner Roy Fredericks in 1974/75 was a gamble of hope rather than of faith. Since Hunte's departure so many specialists had been tried without long-term success, among them Steve Camacho, Joey Carew, Desmond Lewis, Ron Headley and Geoff Greenidge, and others, such as Seymour Nurse, had been moved up the order without producing the required result. The brittleness of the early batting had put a too great burden on the middle-order.

Greenidge set the selectors' minds at rest at the earliest opportunity. He was run out for 93 in his first Test Match innings at Bangalore, and achieved the hundred on debut at the second attempt. Under the impact of that barrage from the opening overs India went down to defeat by 267 runs. Gordon could not maintain the momentum for the remainder of the tour and, hindered by injury, was replaced by the more pedestrian Leonard Baichan for the two matches against Pakistan.

The Barbadian had a horrific time in Australia in 1975/76. He commenced the rubber with a 'pair' at Brisbane, was dropped, was recalled at Melbourne, failed to reach double figures in either innings, and was dropped again. Greenidge lost his position to Lawrence Rowe for every one of the home Test Matches against India, and owed his inclusion in the team to tour England chiefly to his experience of conditions in that country. Perhaps lucky to be preferred to the Jamaican he confirmed his credibility by hitting a spectacular 84 in the Second Test Match at Lord's, the only time that summer that the West Indies batting broke down.

When four wickets slumped for 26 runs on the first morning of the Third Test Match at Manchester, Greenidge countered the crisis with a range of boundary-strokes. Fortunate to be missed early in his innings he took the fight to the bowlers. By the time that he was ninth out he had scored 134 out of the eventual total of 211. The significance of his achievement in unfavourable conditions is emphasised by the fact that in the first innings of either side only three other batsmen reached double figures and only one scored more than 20 runs.

Greenidge was not finished yet with the England bowlers. He made another 101 to become the second West Indian opening batsman to register a hundred in each innings of a Test Match, in the course of which he shared three-figure partnerships with Fredericks and Richards. His 235 runs match aggregate was 38 more than the entire England team could manage. It was the beginning of a purple patch of extraordinary brilliance.

Fredericks and Greenidge commenced the Fourth Test Match at Leeds with a batting barrage of artillery proportions. By lunch they had scored 147-0 off 27 overs and went on to take their partnership to 192. Gordon hammered two sixes and fourteen fours in his 115, his third century in consecutive Test Match innings. Then he went on to plunder 123 from Middlesex (out of his side's 222 runs total) and 130 against Glamorgan before falling for a 'duck' in the run-spree of the Fifth Test Match at the Oval. Even genius is fallible!

Caribbean crowds saw Greenidge for the first time at international level against Pakistan in early 1977, and they were not disappointed. Consistent throughout the series he was dismissed in the 90s twice at Bourda and closed the series with exactly 100 at Sabina Park. In the second innings he and Fredericks added 182 runs in their last partnership. The winning margin of the match, and with it the rubber, was only 140 runs.

The matching of Greenidge, the brilliant Barbadian righthander, and Fredericks, a pugnacious Guyanese southpaw, was unusual in that neither had to play second fiddle. There was no need for the dourness of Rae or the reined-in Hunte. They assailed the bowlers with an array of strokes from the moment that they came to the crease. As a result, irrespective of the runs scored for themselves, the pair softened the bowling for the middle-order batsmen.

Fredericks came into the West Indies side in 1968/69 and is remembered especially for two innings of contrasting character. His dogged 150 at Birmingham in 1973 annoyed his opponents but ensured the draw that won the series. Just under three years later his whirlwind 169 at Perth was one of the fastest centuries ever hit in a Test Match. Although Fredericks was dismissed cheaply several times while hooking — nobody can forget his foot dislodging the bail as he hit the ball for six in the Prudential World Cup Final in 1975 — the stroke brought him a bushel of runs. After retiring from first-class cricket he became a minister in the government of Guyana.

There was time for Greenidge and new partner Desmond Haynes to share a century partnership at Kensington Oval in the two Test Matches against Australia in 1978 before international competition was rent by the World Series Cricket schism. The two Barbadians went with the majority of their colleagues and were lost to the conventional game for one-and-a-half series. Gordon's place was taken by name-sake Alvin Greenidge and by Basil Williams.

The full West Indies team came together again for the Prudential World Cup competition in 1979. Their ultimate victory owed much to Greenidge even though he was run out early in the Final at Lord's. Until then he had dominated the tournament with dynamic quick innings which had seized the immediate initiative and gave his own bowlers the security of a substantial total. He and Haynes shared century stands against both India and Pakistan.

The previous winter India had beaten the conventional West Indies side, from which the established 'Packer' players were missing, but they could not repeat the feat against the complete combination. Greenidge won the Man-of-the-Match award with an undefeated century. He scored 65 against New Zealand and set up the defeat of Pakistan in the semi-final by hitting 73. This second Man-of-the-Match honour had particular merit because there had been so many commendable performances on either side.

He disappointed on the successive tours to Australia, New Zealand and England. Apart from being dismissed twice in the 90s at

Christchurch, Greenidge was overshadowed generally by Haynes. After he had managed only one fifty in the exceptionally wet English summer of 1980, and that in the first innings of the series, there was inevitable speculation that his career was approaching its conclusion. That year had been disappointing for him in several ways. The batsman seemed to face a crisis of identity.

Greenidge was acknowledged as a good English batsman who until then had scored best only in his adopted country. Although he had erased that suspicion with halfcenturies at Queen's Park, St John's and Sabina Park, including participation in two century first-wicket stands, when England came to the Caribbean in early 1981, he was not considered as belonging to the region quite as much as Richards or Lloyd. Englishmen felt similarly about their own former captain Tony Greig.

Gordon's book *The Man in the Middle*, published during the tour to England, caused caustic comment. Some press reviews indicated that the cricketer did not endorse fully Clive Lloyd's captaincy and that he had a jaundiced opinion of West Indian cricket. Received contemporary opinion is that Greenidge, perhaps, was ill-advised in the timing of publication and ill-served by the attention of the reviewers primarily to this one issue. Either way he answered the criticism where he could do so best ... on the cricket pitch.

Gordon's contribution to the English domestic game has been considerable. Hampshire have never been one of the consistently strong counties. From its earliest days the team has depended on one or two exceptional players holding the side together. The Barbadian mastered the three-day championship game and at one time held the record highest individual score in each of the three national limited-overs competitions. He was indeed a batsman for all seasons.

Participation in the championship has done much to sharpen West Indian cricketers. In a matter of a few weeks' concentrated programme Greenidge could encounter at first-class level a majority of the world's leading bowlers, including Derek Underwood, Michael Holding, Richard Hadlee, Andy Roberts, Wayne Daniel, Phil Edmonds, Kapil Dev, Clive Rice, Sylvester Clarke, Joel Garner and Imran Khan. His fore-runners would have needed a life-time to acquire such experience, even if it had been available.

In his early years with the county Greenidge opened the innings with Barry Richards, considered by many to have been the best batsman of his generation. Without taking sides on the issue, it is sufficient to say that before he became bored with the enforced limits of his horizon the South African was very, very good. It is difficult to recall any other occasion on which two batsmen of such proven brilliance have shared first-wicket responsibilities for a team below representative standard.

If it had been true that in the 1970s Greenidge had been an England-trained batsman operating internationally in a West Indian dimension, in the 1980s he became identified more closely with Caribbean cricket. To some extent he was fortunate that world events, not least the desire to remove the leading players from the temptation to play in South Africa, caused an increase in tours to and from the region. These in turn stimulated the spread of competitive cricket within the West Indies.

The Indians suffered another drubbing in 1983. In the early part of the series Greenidge showed again his weakness of reaching fifty but failing to go to three figures. It all came good in the Fifth Test Match at St John's. Greenidge and Haynes scored 296 runs in a new first-wicket record for the West Indies against all countries. The former had to terminate his innings at 154 not out to fly to the bedside of his ailing daughter. It was his first Test Match hundred for six years and heralded a second blossoming of his career, if anything, more brilliant than the first.

In the opening engagement of the return rubber later in the year the Barbadian hit his then highest international score of 194. As in England in 1976 his runs were particularly valuable bacause they were scored while wickets tumbled at the other end. Conceivably without that innings the Indians would have tackled their task with greater confidence. The light of his performances in 1984 eclipsed everything that had gone before.

Greenidge and Haynes shared an unbeaten partnership of 250 runs in the closing moments of the First Test Match against Australia at Bourda. Two matches later they put on 132 runs at Kensington Oval. The reporter of *Wisden Cricket Monthly* described the achievement as 'something like their best form'. What would they have achieved at their best! The pair closed the series with a 162 runs stand at Sabina Park, where Gordon reached a century. No other batsman on either side even approached three figures.

Fame is so fickle that after Greenidge had failed to do himself justice in the opening weeks of the following tour of England some called for his replacement by the younger Richie Richardson. He was l.b.w. to Willis at Birmingham and caught cheaply in the first innings at Lord's. Consequently, in spite of his previous achievements, he was playing for his place when he commenced his second innings.

Shortly after the start of the final day Greenidge and Haynes went out to bat needing to score 342 runs to win. At first the target did not seem feasible. After his partner had been run out Gordon found in the defiant Larry Gomes a willing support. The Trinidadian gave him as much of the strike as possible. Greenidge's appetite was whetted by the wilting of the English bowling and fielding under the pressure he applied. He turned the closing stages into a romp in which the ball crashed repeatedly into or over the boundary pickets. Greenidge made 214 not out and the unbeaten partnership was worth 287 runs.

The subsequent double-century in the Fourth Test Match at Manchester was altogether different. Conditions of rain and bad light were not favourable to any cricket, let alone to batting. To make matters worse the West Indies lost early wickets. Eschewing the vigorous tactics with which he had met similar past situations Gordon battled to keep his stumps intact and to prolong the innings as long as possible. Any other approach would have been suicidal in the inclement climate.

His patience was rewarded. Wicketkeeper Jeffrey Dujon and fast bowler Winston Davis stayed with him in partnerships of 197 and 170 for the fifth and sixth wickets respectively. Eventually Greenidge was dimissed in grey mid-afternoon for 223, a victim as much of his own tiredness as of the catch to the 'keeper. He ended the series with an average way ahead of that of any of his colleagues — 30 points better than that of Lloyd and over 40 points that of Richards. Apart from himself few batsmen had prospered.

Greenidge is the master of a panorama of strokes. He is held to be the best cutter in the modern game, and, at the same time, the most potent hooker. The crispness of his cut devastates the offside field and his acute judgement of a swift single, a cause for concern in his earlier days, unsettles the opposition. The savagery of his stroke-play is incongruously compatible with a placid personality. All of the violence is directed into hitting the ball.

Not only the most spectacular strokes are etched into the memory. Gordon has achieved many boundaries in the direction of mid-wicket and square-leg by putting his weight onto the right leg and forcing the ball square past the raised left leg. A similar stroke in Ranjitsinhji's repertoire must have delighted late Victorian and Edwardian spectators. Because of the number of strokes at his command it is almost impossible to set a field for Greenidge in rampant mood.

Desmond Haynes is his ideal foil for both Barbados and the West Indies. Although the former is no slouch Greenidge is usually the dominant run-scorer. That may be deceptive in itself. Even when he is going well Haynes has a clinical quality which does not impress itself on the mind so sharply. He was overshadowed by the imperious Richards even during his innings of 184 at Lord's in 1980. As one of the few West Indians without a regular first-class career in England,

Haynes is essentially West Indian and has played his best innings in the Caribbean.

Misfortune continued to dog Greenidge in Australia, where he has yet to score a Test Match century. That target seemed to be well within his grasp when, just five runs short, he was caught off Geoff Lawson's bowling at Adelaide. On his return to the Caribbean he scored exactly 100 in the First Test Match at Queen's Park. Greenidge and Richardson put on 185 runs for the third wicket after Richard Hadlee had dismissed Haynes and Gomes before either had scored. Haynes' followed his hundred in the Fifth Test Match against England at The Oval with consistent, if not spectacular, batting in Australia. He and Richards prevented the New Zealanders from achieving success in the second innings at Port of Spain, and he put on 181 runs with Richardson for the second wicket at Bourda.

Throughout history the majority of successful opening batsmen have been linked in pairs: Jack Hobbs and Herbert Sutcliffe, Len Hutton and Cyril Washbrook, Victor Trumper and Reggie Duff, Bill Lawry and Bobby Simpson, Allan Rae and Jeff Stollmeyer, Vijay Merchant and Mustaq Ali. Few have been coupled more than once. Nevertheless Gordon Greenidge has formed effective partnerships with Roy Fredericks, Barry Richards and Desmond Haynes. It says much for his compatibility and capacity to blend.

The success of the West Indian fast bowlers has been assisted by the sharpness of the close-catching. Here, too, Greenidge and Haynes are in partnership on either side of the pitch. Desmond sits in the batsman's pocket, and since Roger Harper has come into the slips Gordon has moved to the gully. Both are adept at snapping up catches from the reflex action of batsmen surprised by the good-length flier.

In spite of a decade of service Gordon Greenidge has not been considered seriously as a potential West Indies captain. It is a tribute to his tenacity that his prospects are regarded at all. Perhaps he was seen to be too English when Viv Richards established his credentials as vice-captain in succession to Deryck Murray. When the Antiguan moves on Greenidge, too, will be too old. The office must devolve on younger men. It is intriguing, however, to speculate on what might have been if his candidacy had been promoted earlier.

He succeeded Albert Padmore as captain of Barbados in 1982/83 but the island's prospects had been blighted by the defection of several leading players to competition in South Africa. Even so Greenidge celebrated the appointment by hitting 237, his highest innings in the Caribbean, for Barbados against the Indian tourists. The following season he was with the regional side in Australia when Carlisle Best led Barbados to victory in the Shell Shield tournament.

Twelve

Barbadian Fast Bowlers

Barbados is the home of fast bowling. The tradition, which is without parallel anywhere else in the world, goes back to the origins of the game in the region. Barbadian fast bowlers do not come in ones: they are generated in clusters. Even the examples of previous eras have not prepared international cricket for the overflowing abundance of the late 1970s and early 1980s in which Joel Garner, Malcolm Marshall, Milton Small, Sylvester Clarke, Wayne Daniel and Vanburn Holder have played in Test Matches and others have come close to doing so.

The flat, tranquil island with its clearly defined coastal contours has produced a stable environment in which the cricketers are uncomplicated and lacking in guile. Sport competition lacks the edge of community rivalry or the social need for an individual to impress his personality on the status quo. Barbadians retain the basic instincts of wanting to score as many runs as quickly as possible and bowling with all the speed they can muster. There have been few Barbadian stone-wallers or spin bowlers.

Clifford Goodman, a member of the celebrated family in Barbadian cricket in the final decade of the nineteenth century, was the first West Indian fast bowler to impress teams touring the region. He bowled the island to victory against the pioneer party under R. Slade Lucas in 1895 and was 'wonderfully successful' against Priestley's side. Pelham Warner considered the big Barbadian's performances against Lord Hawke's team to have been 'practically nothing' in the first innings but 'remarkably well' in the second. Nevertheless he criticised the fast bowler for pitching short and too much on the leg stump. Warner was impressed even more by Woods and Cumberbatch of Trinidad. They were

'two black bowlers ... quite unplayable: the former bowls very fast with a rather low and slinging delivery, while Cumberbatch, who is perhaps the better of the two, bowls medium pace right-hand with a little work both ways'.

Woods was the bowling success of the first tour to England in 1900, even if he did like to feel the pitch with his toe, but his partner had to wait another six years for his chance, by which time he was past his best.

Trinidadians continued to dominate fast bowling until well into this century. George John was the outstanding character of Caribbean cricket in the decade overshadowed by the First World War, and immediately afterwards. His performances in territorial and club competition and anecdotes on his personality are legend: there is no better first-hand account than that of C.L.R. James in *Beyond a Boundary*. He steam-rollered through England in 1923 and the 4 wickets for 12 runs against the batting of the powerful H.D.G. Leveson-Gower's XI at Scarborough at the end of the tour snatched Test Match recognition in a spell.

His partner that summer, George Francis, had been taken on trust and the intuition of H.B.G. Austin, the captain, because he had no first-class background. The Barbadian took the honours in the victory over Sussex at Hove in the first game against a county, and he did not look back. Francis, though comparatively short for a fast bowler, had an intimidating leap at the end of his run, bowled a devastating yorker and moved the ball late towards the off. In 1923 the opening assault of John and Francis was supported well by the pace generated by the young Learie Constantine.

Francis bowled the first ball for the West Indies in a Test Match — at Lord's in June 1928. His first victim was dependable opening batsman Herbert Sutcliffe. George took 4 wickets for 40 runs in the first innings of the first West Indies victory at Bourda in February 1930. The English batsmen did not recover from the initial assault of Francis and Constantine, both of whom were among the earliest West Indians to play in the Lancashire League.

Herman Griffith, another Barbadian, who five years earlier had been left surprisingly at home in favour of his compatriot, was the most successful bowler in the first Test Match series, and again in the early part of the return rubber. He exercised great control and much variety but was well past the first flush of youth when international opportunity came his way. Francis and Griffith bowled so well in Barbados' shattering victory over Freddie Calthorpe's M.C.C. side in 1925/26 that their incisive penetration would have taxed severely the best in the world.

Although the veteran fast bowlers were then in the twilight of their careers, they combined to achieve the historic victory over Australia at Sydney on the first tour to that country in 1930/31. Griffith made his niche in history by bowling the incomparable Don Bradman for 'no score' in the second innings. The Australian, who then held the record for the highest individual Test Match innings, had not been dismissed without scoring before and his departure knocked the confidence out of his colleagues. Herman's serious approach to cricket and his physical fitness maintained him as a formidable bowler.

Manny Martindale relied on speed rather than guile. He was consistently fast, unlike Constantine who achieved even greater pace in bursts. Between them, and for a time with Hylton of Jamaica, they carried the West Indies' attack throughout the 1930s. Martindale's contribution to the bowling in 1933 was even more one-sidedly decisive than that of George Headley to the batting. He garnered 14 wickets in a three-match series in which England never batted more than once: the next most successful bowler, spinner Achong, achieved only five.

In the Second Test Match at Manchester, Martindale and Constantine subjected the English batsmen to a demonstration of bodyline such as their own bowlers had just inflicted on Australia. The Barbadian was the more successful in taking 5 wickets for 73 runs as the West Indies went ahead for the first time ever in England. Learie was not available again that summer so that the pressure could not be maintained. Manny, magnificent though he was, could not bowl from both ends at the same time.

The First Test Match against England at Kensington in 1935 was played on a rain-affected quagmire on which normal batting was impossible. The West Indies were shot out for 102. Then Martindale whipped out three Englishmen for 39 runs in an effective partnership with Hylton which caused visiting captain Wyatt to declare 21 runs behind to avoid the worst of the pitch. Jackie Grant, the home captain, repeated the ploy but though Manny took another 5 wickets for 22 runs he had little support as the tourists edged home by four wickets. The West Indies fought back subsequently and in the deciding Test Match at Sabina Park the Barbadian's burst of pace, in which he broke Wyatt's jaw, settled the series.

For the next two decades the island's well of fast bowling talent dried up as Johnson and Kentish of Jamaica, Trim of Guyana, and Jones and Pierre of Trinidad flitted onto and out of the regional team. Frank King seemed to herald a revival in the mid-1950s. He hustled the Indians, but his attempt to match bumper with bumper failed against the powerful English and Australian batting. King's stamina was considered to be suspect, and his failure to complete the tour of New Zealand in 1956 ended his international career.

The place which the Barbadian might have taken in the team visiting England the following year went to his fellow-countryman Wesley Hall. The youngster's inclusion, on speculation, was similar to that of

Francis a quarter of a century earlier, but initially it was less successful because he failed to play in any of the five Test Matches in even that disastrous and injury-hit year. Even so he had the physique, the personality and the potential to come again. His chance came with the decision to strengthen the pace bowling after Worrell's withdrawal from the side touring India and Pakistan in 1958/59.

At the start of the tour Hall overwhelmed Baroda, the domestic champions, and was preferred to Jaswick Taylor as Roy Gilchrist's regular partner throughout the series. Their names have passed into cricket mythology as one of the most feared and effective new-ball combinations in the history of the game. Wesley's greatest personal triumph was the achievement of matches figures of 11 wickets for 126 runs at Kanpur. When the Jamaican was sent home at the end of the Indian section of the tour, Hall was only West Indian bowler to prosper on the unaccustomed pitches in Pakistan.

His 'unflagging, agressive performance' in taking 7 wickets for 69 runs in the Third Test Match against England at Sabina Park in 1960, and a further 6 wickets in an innings in the following fixture at Bourda, marked him as a bowler of the highest world-class. He achieved great speed from a classical, almost poetic, side-on action with a long follow-through, and could maintain the pace for long spells. With the exception of Gilchrist's meteoric rise and fall, he was the first genuinely fast bowler to secure his place since the Second World War.

Johnny Moyes in his book *With the West Indies in Australia 1960-61* recalled with affection Hall's part in the historic tied Test Match at Brisbane:

'Hall was superb and I can picture him now bowling that final over, finding somewhere the strength and vitality to rise to his top in the closing stages after being on the field all day, taking five wickets, sinking to the depths as he dropped a catch, and then rising again to the heights, walking from the field with the evening sun gleaming down on his perspiring face, and with his golden cross dangling from his neck and showing through the open neck of his shirt'.

His review of the tour was similarly evocative:

'The personality player of the team was Wesley Hall, a young man in his very early twenties, a couple of inches over six feet, and blessed with tremendous speed and vitality. Whenever he was in action the crowd chortled and it was a strange thing that although he took a long time to bowl an over they rarely heckled him for it. They liked the look of this big chap with his lovely approach to the wicket; his readiness to chase the ball on either side of the wicket; his demeanour when he bowled a bouncer or got one to rise from a length. He was all action, something like Learie Constantine of an earlier generation'.

The Australians had further opportunity to appreciate his effectiveness. Hall was the match-winner when the West Indies won at Sabina Park five years later, the first victory over Australia in the Caribbean and the initial step in winning a rubber for the first time against these opponents. In a low-scoring contest he dismissed the first three batsmen and finished with 5 wickets for 60 runs in the first innings.

Charlie Griffith attracted regional attention first for his part in Barbados' win over the Englishmen in 1959/60. Two years later the selectors were looking for a new regular partner for Wesley Hall. Charlie came to their notice more forcefully than intended by delivering the ball which struck Indian captain Nariman Contractor on the side of the head, putting his life in danger. He pushed this controversy into the background by his performance on the victorious and happy tour to England under Frank Worrell in 1963.

Griffith, who was more successful in England than Hall, reaped a bushel of wickets with a lethal yorker, which was particularly effective against batsmen unnerved already by his steeply-rising bouncer. He took 5 wickets for 91 runs in the first innings at Lord's in possibly the most consistently enthralling and evenly contested Test Match of all time. Then he took 6 wickets in an innings at Leeds and again at The Oval. The latter performance enabled the West Indies to rally from a first innings deficit to win the match and the series.

The bowler's remaining years were clouded by controversy regarding his action and his allegedly hostile attitude towards opposing batsmen. As his legality in either aspect has not been found wanting his colleagues are convinced that Charlie was hounded unjustly by representatives of the public communications media and some opposing players. His captain Gary Sobers stated in *King Cricket*:

'I don't think any cricketer has been pushed so deep into the freeze since Harold Larwood invented bodyline bowling ....
These suggestions came at him sideways, like so many angry crabs, never straight so that we could face up to them'.

The insinuations did not harm his popularity, even in the country where they were most vociferous. On the afternoon of the day that the West Indies completed their 5-0 whitewash of England in 1984, a large number of the spectators made their way to the small club ground at Blackheath to see the long-retired Griffith bowling for the Desmond Haynes Cavaliers.

Hall and Griffith required no regular third fast bowler because Sobers served as an international-class seam bowler in addition to his many other capacities. He was so adept at making the most of the early advantages in the pitch that from time to time he took the new ball in preference to the specialists. The all-rounder's exploits extend beyond the scope of a particular chapter on Barbadian fast bowlers.

The island was extremely strong at this time and capable of taking on most Test Match countries on even terms. Against the Pakistanis in 1958 they fielded ten past, present or future international representatives — Conrad Hunte, Robin Bynoe, Gary Sobers, Everton Weekes, Eric and Denis Atkinson, Peter Lashley, John Goddard, Wesley Hall and David Allan. Only Holder was not so honoured. Frank Worrell and Clyde Walcott, both Barbados-born, were then playing respectively for Jamaica and British Guiana.

When they defeated the M.C.C. the next year the island brought in Seymour Nurse, Cammie Smith, Tony White and Charlie Griffith so that all eleven were Test Match class, and Teddy Griffith played for Jamaica. Even though Hall was missing, Barbados won decisively by 10 wickets. The final 58 runs were hit off in rain in 25 minutes. Nurse scored a double-hundred and shared a triple-century partnership with Sobers.

Hall and Griffith burned themselves out eventually on the Australasian tour of 1968/69. Richard Edwards, another Barbadian, was with them on that trip, bowled well in New Zealand, but was omitted from the following tour to England. Vanburn Holder, his compatriot, took his place. The speed of Holder and John Shepherd was appreciably slower than that of their immediate predecessors even in their declining years. Both were just as successful, if not more so, on English green-top pitches as at home.

Holder provided the backbone of the pace attack at the turn of the decade. He was already well over 20 years old on making his first-class debut for Barbados against Trinidad & Tobago, and graduated to the Test Match team two years later. His best achievements included 7 wickets for 44 runs against Jamaica at Kensington in 1972. Although he was particularly incisive in the early overs, and often bowled well without substantial support, Vanburn was even more effective when the arrival of even faster bowlers enabled him to be brought on later.

Andy Roberts stole the thunder in India in 1974/75, but the hosts fought back tenaciously to square the rubber at 2-2 so that everything depended on the outcome of the Fifth Test Match at Bombay. The Indians resisted well until Holder ran through the second innings with 6 wickets for 39 runs. A similar performance at Adelaide a year later could not prevent defeat there. The rise of a new generation of fast bowlers, welded into such a potent force in 1976, seemed to curtail his career for the West Indies.

The withdrawal of the World Series Cricketers in the rubber against Australia in 1978 led to Holder's recall as vice-captain — many observers assert that he should have been made captain. In the Fourth Test Match at Queen's Park, Australia reached a comfortable 254-5 in reply to the home side's total of 292. The last five wickets fell for 36 runs as Holder completed figures of 6 wickets for 28, his best analysis in a Test Match. The West Indies, thus, took first innings lead and went on to win the match and clinch the series.

Keith Boyce, who had developed essentially with Essex in the English county championship, enjoyed such spectacular allround success in 1973 that he was compared favourably to even Learie Constantine. His extra speed unsettled batsmen grown accustomed to the more gentle pace of the day — they could not have foreseen that Boyce had ushered in an era of even greater speed. In the First Test Match at The Oval he returned a match analysis of 11 wickets for 147 runs, and hit a dynamic 72. Then Keith took 4 wickets in each innings at Lord's.

His success continued deceptively at Queen's Park in the First Test Match of the return rubber. Kanhai won the toss and invited England to take first innings. Boyce bowled them out for 131 and the West Indies won easily. Nothing was ever quite the same after that. Within a year of his greatest success he was struggling to hold his place. His bowling was required less and, in spite of being stranded on 95 not out at Adelaide, he did not quite measure up to the standard of a batsman who could bowl.

Wayne Daniel, a strapping 20 year-old, was the third fast bowler to Roberts and Holding in England in 1976. Injury to the Jamaican led to his inclusion in the side for the First Test Match at Nottingham. Although he was wayward at first, Daniel took 4 wickets for 53 runs in the first innings including that of century-maker David Steele. He shared also in the assault which blasted England out for 71 and to defeat by 425 runs at Manchester. Here, seemingly, was yet another Barbadian fast bowler to join the giants of the past.

Yet history passed him by. Wayne sustained a back injury which kept him out of the home series against Pakistan and by the time that he was fit again Joel Garner and Colin Croft, and later Sylvester Clarke and Malcolm Marshall, had made any available place their own. It is unlikely, however, that any fast bowler in contemporary cricket has bowled as consistently well day-in and day-out over the past ten years. Daniel has been a main strike force for Barbados and for Middlesex and, unlike those who perform better in one environment than another, has been often near enough unplayable in both England and the West Indies.

Sylvester Clarke is in many ways the 'one that got away'. Because of the withdrawal of the World Series Cricketers he made his international debut against Australia in only his first year of first-class competition. He bowled with much fire in India in 1978/79, taking 5 wickets for 126 runs at Bangalore, but was probably too inexperienced to make full use of his opportunities. The selectors passed him over when the Packer players returned, until Holding's absence gave him the chance to head the averages of the specialist bowlers against Pakistan in 1980/81.

The Barbadian was probably at his peak at the time he agreed to participate in 'rand rebel' representative games in South Africa. His departure was possibly the greatest loss, together with that of Croft, in this venture. Sylvester is held in such awe in England, where playing for Surrey he thunders in against the background of leaden skies and the gasometer at The Oval, that any batsman performing well against him is accorded special merit. It is said that the hithero unconsidered Paul Terry owed his selection for England primarily to the manner in which he fared against Clarke.

Hartley Alleyne, also, was banned from participating in further cricket under the West Indies Cricket Board of Control because of his involvement with the 'rebels' in South Africa. He bowled well for Barbados and for Worcestershire and, though sometimes contraversial, he would have been worthy of regional representation in a time less well-endowed with talent. Milton Small, whose style resembles very much that of Colin Croft, advanced quickly, perhaps too quickly, in his first season. He took a wicket with his first ball in first-class cricket. Injury curtailed his tour to England in 1984.

Joel Garner is remarkable for more than his 6′ 8″ height. Even the harshest critics admit that for several years he has been the best bowler of his type in the world. He has crammed so much cricket into his career that he needed to rest from the tour to India in late 1983 to bring out the best in him yet again. The 'Big Bird' is easily the most recognisable, and certainly one of the most popular, members of the present side. On tour his walks through the crowd with the diminutive Gus Logie cause every head to turn.

The big man embodies much of the Barbadian tradition of cricket. At Foundation School he was coached by Seymour Nurse and Wesley Hall, and later by Wesley Hall and Charlie Griffith. In spite of his natural progress through the island's established strata of play, because competition was so stiff he did not make his first-class debut until he was 23 years-old. Then he was chosen primarily because Boyce and Holder were with the regional side in Australia. Nevertheless he was in the right place at the right time to take advantage of the international opportunities provided by the injuries to Daniel and Holding.

After bowling well for the President's XI against the Pakistanis at Castries, and devastatingly well for Barbados against Jamaica and Trinidad & Tobago, he was chosen for the First Test Match at Kensington. Garner took 4 wickets in the first innings and shared the new ball throughout the series with the seasoned Roberts and Croft of Guyana, another newcomer. He was consistent rather than spectacular so that his 25 wickets were spread evenly throughout the matches. Tony Cozier writing in Wisden described him as a 'virtual nonentity before the start of the season' and observed that he was somewhat slower in pace to Croft.

The latter achieved rare triumph in the Second Test Match at Queen's Park. His 8 wickets for 29 runs represent the best analysis by a fast bowler for the West Indies. Five of his victims were claimed for only 9 runs in a spell of 10.5 overs. Running in at a decidedly wide angle Croft was a regular spearhead of the attack until he joined the 'rebels' in South Africa. His absence was hardly noticed because there was always another world-class bowler to fill the place.

Garner's credentials deserve an almanack of their own. He established a record in the Final of the Prudential Cup at Lord's on 21 June 1979. England's openers Mike Brearley and Geoff Boycott began with a century stand in pursuit of the West Indies' 286 runs total. The end was sudden. As the evening darkened Joel in overall figures of 5 wickets for 38 runs dismissed five batsmen, four of them bowled, for four runs in eleven balls. With Croft bowling equally well from the other end England slumped from 183-2 to 194 all out. The shattering of wickets was awesome.

In Australia in 1979/80 Garner headed the bowling averages in an attack with Croft, Holding, Roberts, Collis King and himself, arguably the best that even the West Indies have produced. The second part of the tour to New Zealand was marred by bad temper and controversy. Perhaps Joel alone could claim satisfaction by taking 6 wickets for 56 runs at Auckland. Two years later his 5 wickets for 56 runs in the concluding Test Match at Adelaide enabled the tourists to share the rubber. His subsequent performances were less sharp until he took rest and recharged his batteries.

Revitalised Garner overwhelmed the Australians when they came to the Caribbean in early 1984. His 31 wickets in the rubber exceeded the next best by ten. Although he took 6 wickets in an innings at Bourda and 5 in an innings at the Recreation Ground, St. John's, his most destructive spell occurred in the opening overs of the Second Test Match at Queen's Park. Australia sagged at 16-3 and the Barbadian took all four wickets which fell before rain curtailed play at lunch.

The new purposeful approach was evident also in England later that year. While the fury of Marshall and Davis took the attention of the public communications media, Garner's added speed allied to his unusual bounce brought him more wickets than any other bowler. He was considered always to be the one most likely to dismiss the next batsman. The assault he launched with Marshall in the opening session of the First Test Match at Birmingham, and his match-clinching 5 wickets for 55 runs in the second, set the psychological tone for the rest of the summer.

Garner bowled well enough in Australia in 1984/85 without quite matching the impact of his compatriot Marshall. He wrecked the home side's first innings with 4 wickets for 67 runs at Brisbane, and took three wickets in 5 balls to send the Australian second innings toppling to 17-3 at Melbourne, from which position the hosts managed to hang on to draw the match.

Malcolm Marshall is yet another Barbadian fast bowler to step almost directly from obscurity into the international limelight. It happens so much more often in the Caribbean than anywhere else in the world. He is among the fast bowlers of shorter stature in the mould of Roy Gilchrist and Ray Lindwall, and, like them, has surprised press, public and opposing batsmen by his aggression. His rapid rise to the top came suddenly because he had been considered for several years to have been the third string to the established bowlers.

He was born in St Michael, Barbados and graduated from St Giles' Boys school. Malcolm had played in only one first-class match before he was taken to India in 1978/79 in the absence of the World Series Cricketers. Dicky Rutnagur observed in Wisden that he

'showed exceptional promise in the subsidiary games, but his Test performances suffered from want of experience'.

The selectors, too, had noted that exceptional promise and retained him in preference to either Clarke or Phillip when the rift was healed and the regular bowlers returned to conventional cricket.

A fitness enthusiast Marshall was inspired to excel by his desire to be the best and fastest bowler in Barbados and to exceed even the achievements of Andy Roberts whom he succeeded in the Hampshire county team. He learned well from colleagues and opponents, increased his speed which he maintains for unusually long stints, and, possibly because of his height, caused the ball to skid through to the batsman. The concentration on improving his bowling has probably prevented him from becoming a genuine allrounder.

It came as a surprise to batsmen still apprehensive of Holding and

Croft that by 1983 Marshall was the fastest bowler in the world. The Indians first felt the difference. He took 5 wickets for 37 runs on a rain-affected pitch in the Second Test Match at Queen's Park, and, as did Holding against the same opponents seven years earlier, bowled round the wicket for maximum effect. With his senior contemporaries jaded by too much cricket he brought a fresh wind of enthusiasm and hostility.

Garner's withdrawal from the tour to India gave Marshall and Holding the chance to recapture the spirit of the terror generated by Gilchrist and Hall a generation previously. The Barbadian blitzed the home batting with four wickets in each innings of the First Test Match at Kanpur, in which, for good measure, he also scored 92. In skittling the Indians for 90 in the second innings with 6 wickets for 37 runs at Calcutta he more than matched Gilchrist's massacre in the same city. His five wickets in the only innings at Madras included the dismissal of both opening batsmen before there was a run on the board.

Marshall played an increasingly decisive part in the home series against Australia. His hammer blows delivered at great speed in taking 5 wickets for 42 runs in the second innings at the Recreation Ground shot out the tourists for only 97. The last five wickets raised only 17 runs. His ability to come back powerfully in the second innings, and in a second spell in that innings, was emphasised again by his 5 wickets for 51 runs in the Fifth Test Match at Sabina Park in which he swept away the lower order.

Nothing in all that had happened could have forewarned the English batsmen of the tornado they ran into in the First Test Match at Birmingham in 1984. Contrary to expectation home captain David Gower elected to bat on winning the toss. England lost four wickets before lunch, and, although none of them fell to Marshall, his delivery which caused Andy Lloyd to retire hurt achieved an even greater impact. The unfortunate opener misjudged the length and the bounce. Disappointed home commentators criticised intimidatory tactics, but Malcolm is one of the few bowlers to seek always to take wickets rather than to bowl for containment.

Malcolm Marshall's name will be associated always with the Third Test Match at Leeds. Although he broke his hand in two places while fielding, he came to the crease with his arm in plaster on the fall of the ninth wicket to help Larry Gomes to reach his century. It was reminscent of Colin Cowdrey at Lord's in 1963, but Marshall hit a boundary. Then he destroyed England's second innings literally one-handed in taking 7 wickets for 53 runs off a shortened run. As Graeme Fowler, opening batsman and top-scorer, drove him back down the pitch Marshall clasped his injured hand to the good to complete the catch, then tossed the ball away as the pain hit him. Immediately afterwards he had Allan Lamb l.b.w. and sped through the remaining batsmen with little opposition. In the Fifth Test Match at The Oval the Barbadian humiliated the England batsmen again with 5 wickets for 35 runs after their bowlers had given them an open chance on the first day.

By now Marshall was the main striking-force of the West Indies attack. In Australia he took five wickets in an innings on four consecutive occasions. The home batsmen had seemingly no answer to his pace and pentration. In several instances, mesmerised by the possibility of a bodyline bouncer, they fell to the ball which moved across their body. Malcolm took ten wickets in the match at Adelaide. Significantly at Sydney, where he failed to break through for the only time in the series the West Indies were beaten for the first time in three years.

The New Zealanders experienced the full force of the whirlwind in early 1985. In the opening Test Match at Queen's Park he took three wickets for just 25 runs in 11 overs, but reached a crescendo in the Third Test Match at Kensington. There, after rain had delayed the start until well after lunch, he dismissed two batsmen before they had scored as the tourists tottered at 1-3, and he swept through the second innings with 7 wickets for 80 runs. In these two rubbers Marshall showed his greatest batting consistency to date.

Thirteen

Kensington Oval, Bridgetown

The Kensington Oval ground at Bridgetown in Barbados is a happy venue for the West Indies. They have won here nine times and suffered defeat only once, and that over half-a-century ago. The island reflects the spirit of Caribbean cricket for the several hundred tourists who come here rather than to any other Test Match ground in the region. Not surprisingly matches at the Oval have been marked more by outstanding individual feats of batting and, on occasion, fast bowling than by the excitement of close contests.

True to the Barbadian tradition of tranquility few controversies have shattered the pleasant image of this most pleasing sport. There have been no celebrated crowd disturbances to compare with those in Trinidad, Jamaica and Guyana, except in the World Series Cricket 'super-test' when other passions were at work. Declarations have not led to disaster, and mass walk-outs are unknown. Kensington has been the starting-point of ventures — the first Test Match in the Caribbean, the first after the Second World War, and various new beginnings after disappointing overseas tours.

Bridgetown, the capital city, is situated in the south-western corner of Barbados. The island is relatively flat and is composed mainly of coral. It rises gently in a series of terraces from the west coast to the central ridge. The principal centres of activity lie on the western and southern sides. Consequently Bridgetown is positioned ideally in the area of highest local population and at the axle of the two coasts frequented most by tourists. The Kensington Oval cricket ground is reached by going out of the city centre towards the western coast.

There are few more pleasant venues in the world at which to watch the game. The view is not interrupted by any mountain range or towering promontory, so that the eye can rove over the palm trees and gentle blue sea of the Caribbean. The ground can be found easily enough during a Test Match. It is necessary only to follow the throng outwards along the dusty road through Fontabelle, which contains the premises of the country's two principal daily newspapers, the Advocate and the Nation.

The celebrated Challoner Stand, named after the internationally-recognised father of Barbadian batting, to which the supporters of the visiting side are usually drawn, stands to the left of the pavilion. The new Sir Garfield Sobers Pavilion was opened by the cricketer, himself, on 19 April 1985 in a ceremony attended by the country's Prime Minister, Bernard St John, and by past and present Test Match players. The other principal edifice is the Three Ws Stand — there are no prizes for guessing after whom it takes its name. Apart from a rough-roofed structure on the seaward side, from which the young boys clambering on the ridge for a better view may be scattered by a well directed six, the rest of the ground is generally open to the sky. A vast crowd mills outside the gate, in addition to those seeking admission, either listening to the commentary on their radios or hearing the news of events shouted from those inside.

King Dyall is an intergral part of the layout. He is resplendent in his brightly coloured suits, sometimes changing often in the course of a day, and his arrival at the ground is greeted with such popular enthusiasm that the action on the pitch may be halted temporarily. King Dyall has become such a part of Barbadian contemporary culture that he is recognised as an 'unofficial ambassador' at Lord's and The Oval in London when the West Indians have been the visitors. Nothing illustrates the contrast in climate more than the sight of this splendidly-clad gentleman shivering in the English cold and damp.

The Grantley Adams International Airport, the most modern in the English-speaking Caribbean with its wide range of facilities, is only 11 miles to the south-east. Aircraft from far afield hang in the air unhindered by the natural obstacles which make the minutes before landing so interesting at Piarco in Trinidad. They are a poignant reminder that the Test Match played in this near paradise, isolated from almost every other sign of the outside world, is part of a regional series and when the last delivery has been bowled the players, the press and some of the spectators will be off to the next stop.

Although taxi-drivers seem to materialise out of thin air all over the island, the inability of find a cab as the hundreds stream from the ground at the end of the day's play is a blessing. The walk from Kensington into the centre of Bridgetown by way of Cheapside and Broad Street is rich in character and interest. The extended rows of street-sellers, their produce either spread in front of them or on make-shift stalls, are never less than colourful. At Trafalgar Square the main body of the home-wending crowd breaks off into its different directions.

Kensington has been touched by tragedy. Ken Barrington, the England assistant manager, who had scored a hundred here in 1959, returned to his hotel after the second day's play in March 1981, seemingly well and cheerful, and died of a heart-attack that evening. The sudden bereavement cast a sombre shadow over the rest of the Test Match. The fight seemed to go out of the tourists, but opening batsman Graham Gooch is reported to have dedicated his second innings century to Barrington's memory.

When he visited with Lord Hawke's team just before the end of the last century Pelham Warner was suitably impressed by the ground, even though it was three miles away from his hotel at Hastings, by the crowd's sporting attitude and by the hospitality.

'The black men are thoroughly good sportsmen, and given good cricket, they don't seem to mind which side wins .... The Kensington ground, though perhaps a little small on one side, is in every way an excellent one .... We found the colonials much better against fast bowling than slow .... We had a splendid time in Barbados; the hospitality of every one was of the greatest'.

Every subsequent visitor must have echoed those sentiments.

Pickwick C.C. was founded in 1882 and took occupancy of the Kensington ground the same year. Many significant and interesting events occurred here in the pioneering years. In 1895 Barbados totalled over 500 runs against the first English touring side, led by R. Slade Lucas, and two years later G.B.T. Cox and H.B.G. Austin scored 263 for the second wicket for the island against Trinidad, the first double-century partnership in first-class cricket in the West Indies. Challendor and Tarilton plundered many runs against the same opposition in the 1920s, and, although the Barbadian fast bowlers overwhelmed the M.C.C. tourists in 1925/26, Walter Hammond scored 238 not out to give the visitors the better of the drawn representative match.

The first Test Match ever staged in the West Indies took place at Kensington in January 1930. The home batsmen, who had been so much at sea against the English slow bowlers on the tour there in 1928, scored freely on the firmer pitch. Clifford Roach, the opening batsman from Trinidad, made 122, the first century recorded for the region in a Test Match, and Derek Sealy, at 17 years 122 days still the youngest man to play for the West Indies, scored 58. Even so opener Andy Sandham saw the tourists to a lead of 98 runs.

The later stages of the match were made memorable by George Headley, the young Jamaican, hitting 176 on his international debut and making the game safe in a substantial second-wicket stand with Roach. Eventually England were set to score 287 runs in just under three hours and were a comfortable 167-3 at close. In view of Roach's success the Barbadian crowd would have forgiven his selection instead of local hero Tarilton who had put on 261 runs with Teddy Hoad for the first wicket in the preceding colony game.

The next Test Match here in 1935 was one of the most bizarre ever played. Survival, let along scoring, was almost impossible on a rain-affected pitch. The West Indies, put in to bat, lost opener George Carew before he had scored and wilted to 15-5 against fast bowler Ken Farnes. Headley stemmed the slide by making 44, the highest individual score of the match, before he was run out. Only one other batsman reached double figures in the 102 runs total. It was only a foretaste of what was to come.

England fared just as badly. Wally Hammond, alone, whose 43 in such unfavourable conditions stood comparison with the undefeated 281 he had registered against Barbados, was able to counter the bowling of Manny Martindale and Leslie Hylton. With the pitch playing, if anything, worse after a further fall of rain visiting captain Bob Wyatt closed the innings at 81-7 to trap the West Indies again before conditions improved. Jackie Grant, his opposite number, responded to the challenge by reversing his batting order. The move might have succeeded, in spite of Jim Smith 'mopping up the rabbits' offered, had not further rain delayed the start on the final day.

The dismissal of even Headley for a duck convinced Grant that batting was becoming even more difficult. At tea he declared at 51-6 setting England to make only 72 runs to win. When Wyatt reversed his own batting order Martindale scythed through the innings with 5 wickets for 22 runs. His fine bowling came close to justifying his captain's gamble. Hammond, however kept his head in the crisis, and, with Hylton being more expensive than the situation required, hit England to victory by 4 wickets.

Rain forced a draw in the first post-war Test Match in 1948. In spite of offspinner Jim Laker taking seven wickets West Indies led by 44 runs on the first innings. The home side was rescued from some faltering in the second innings by Robert Christiani, adjudged l.b.w. just one run short of a century, and by spectacular hitting from Foffie Williams. The tourists faced a target of just under four hundred runs, and with the intervention of the weather struggled to 86-4 at the close.

India, the first visitors other than England, went down by 142 runs in 1953. There was little between the teams in the early exchanges. Although the West Indies led by 43 runs on the first innings they were soon unsettled by pace bowler Dattu Phadkar. Rain, which had hovered around the match, made the outcome difficult to predict. The final target of 272 runs did not seem to be too imposing for the Indian batsmen accustomed to playing spin bowling, on which the attack was based. Sonny Ramadhin, however, caused a complete breakdown.

Clyde Walcott dominated the match against England one year later. Stollmeyer and Worrell failed to score as the first three wickets fell for 26 runs on a pitch enlivened by rain. Coming in at a crisis Walcott hammered 220, many more than the other ten batsmen put together. England trailed by 202 runs so that when J.K. Holt hit a spectacular 166 the issue was all but over. The early batsmen struggled to come back into contention but a collapse of the lower-order left them stranded by 181 runs.

Denis Atkinson could not have chosen a more appropriate time or place to set his record than the Fourth Test Match against Australia in May 1955. The tourists steamrollered their way through the Caribbean and with regular captain Stollmeyer injured Atkinson, a Barbadian, was appointed to the position. He was fair-skinned and hardly assured of selection as batsman or bowler compared to the experienced Walcott, Weekes and Worrell. To make matters worse for him the Australians helped themselves to another 668 runs total.

The West Indies at 146-6 were in imminent danger of the follow-on and defeat when Atkinson was joined by wicketkeeper Clairmonte Depeiza. The bowling of fast bowlers Ray Lindwall, Keith Miller and Ron Archer and the wiles of Richie Benaud and Ian Johnson were able, varied and hostile, but the two Barbadians put on 347 runs in establishing a new world record partnership for the seventh-wicket in all first-class cricket. Although the follow-on was not necessarily saved the bowlers were too tired to make it a viable option. Encouraged by his success in forcing a draw Atkinson, whose contribution to the stand as 219, took five wickets in the tourists' second innings.

Further records were set up on Pakistan's visit in January 1958. The First Test Match at Kensington was played immediately after the disastrous tour to England. The regional team was under reconstruction, in which the younger players needed the confidence of a good performance. Opening batsman Conrad Hunte, a surprise omission from the team which went to England, and Everton Weekes, who played there below his best, punished the bowlers in a 579-9 runs total.

Roy Gilchrist's pace troubled the Pakistani batsmen. He disciplined his speed with direction against opponents who had spent the previous two days in the field. Left-arm spinner Nasimul Ghani was at 16 years 248 days the then youngest player to participate in a Test Match. No batsman scored more than twenty as Pakistan followed on 473 runs in arrears. It seemed to be all over bar the shouting, but by this time the West Indian bowlers were tired and the opposing batsmen determined. First-wicket pair Hanif Mohammad and wicketkeeper Imtiaz Ahmed scored 152 before the latter was dismissed. His partner, diminutive and defiant, kept going, and going. He was still there on the fall of the fourth wicket at 539, edging ever nearer to the world record individual score held then by Len Hutton. At last he was caught at the wicket by Alexander off Denis Atkinson for 337, just 27 runs short of the target. Hanif shared in four three-figure stands and batted for 16 hours 13 minutes, still the longest innings played in any first-class match.

The First Test Match against England in 1960 was less exciting. The tourists gained an early grip through centuries by Barrington and Ted Dexter, and, then, Easton McMorris, the Jamaican opening batsman, was run out backing up before he had scored and, indeed, before he had faced a ball. Gary Sobers and Frank Worrell, seeking to re-establish himself after an absence of two years for study, ground the match to a draw with a 399 runs fourth-wicket partnership. Whatever honours the game held were even.

The preceding territorial game against Barbados had been more eventful. The home batsmen revelled in the conditions to reach 533-5 dec, none more so than Seymour Nurse, who made a double-century, and Sobers. The English batsmen failed initially against the speed of the then unknown Charlie Griffith and, more surprisingly, were teased out by occasional bowler Everton Weekes just when they seemed to have the match saved. In drizzle and poor light Cameron Smith hit out to bring victory by 10 wickets against the clock.

In *Through the Caribbean* Alan Ross described the ground:

'Kensington Oval ... is not among the most decorative of grounds, though it has a certain local appeal. The pavilion, with its green balconies and white beaded back, is latched on to various stands that are both gimcrack in appearance and of contrasting and undistinguished design ... The Challenor Stand, where the gentry sit on the first floor, is under cover, the lower part forming a cream-coloured cement sight-screen. There are two other covered stands, also an uncovered one, but over half the ground is simply grass, wired off from the field of play so that the spectators there appear to be prisoners in a cage. There are no seats here, so people either squat on their haunches in front, or stand behind with faces peering through the wire. Down here are the fried flying-fish booths, the negroes in fabulous garish shirts, cowboy-style hats and pants, and their women in cinnamon, scarlet or turquoise dresses. Elsewhere, higher in the social scale, sit the coloured Barbadians, magnificently dressed, the lithe women moving to and from their seats with affecting and regal grace. Tall palms curve round to the south, studded here and there with flamboyants and tamarinds, and in several of these rickety private pavilions, howdah-like in opulence of decoration, had been constructed. At moments of excitement these swayed alarmingly in the north-east Trades'.

In 1962 the Indians came and were conquered, as they were elsewhere in the region that year. Although they trailed by over two hundred runs on the first innings Dilip Sardesai and Vijay Manjrekar seemed to be taking them to the safety of a draw. It was then that offspinner Lance Gibbs struck decisively. From 158-2 at lunch on the last day India collapsed to 187 all out. The batsmen went on to the defensive and snicked catches to the eager fieldsmen. Gibbs took 8 wickets for 6 runs and had only 38 scored against him in the entire innings.

There had been drama in the tourists game against Barbados. Nariman Contractor, India's slightly-built captain and left-handed opening batsman, ducked into a delivery from Griffith. Substantial transfusions of blood were required to save his life. Contractor's international career was ended and Griffith's probably blighted before it had really begun. Thereafter opposing batsmen regarded the Barbadian with fear even before they faced up to him.

High-scoring ruined the competitive interest in the drawn Test Match against Australia in 1965. Both visiting opening batsmen, Bill Lawry and Bobby Simpson, scored double-hundreds, and when Nurse replied with another one for the West Indies any chance of a keen contest was over. There were also two single hundreds and eight half-centuries, even Charlie Griffith managed one.

The Third Test Match against England in 1968 petered out similarly after batsmen had gained the upper-hand, and further high-scoring precluded the possibility of a result on the visit of the Indians three years later. On the latter occasion both Gary Sobers and Sunil Gavaskar made hundreds in their respective sequences of three centuries in as many innings. The West Indies were ahead on points at the close without the capacity to convert advantage to victory.

The next year New Zealand forced a similar draw, but this time it was not inevitable. Quick bowler Bruce Taylor destroyed the home batting with 7 wickets for 74 runs on the first day in the only spell of the whole series in which a result seemed to be possible. Bevan Congdon and Brian Hastings hit centuries as the tourists led by almost three hundred runs. Charle Davis smothered the danger in a marathon second innings battle of attrition in which he scored 183 and was supported well by Sobers after the fall of three early wickets.

Australia achieved the fifth consecutive draw at Kensington in early 1973. Once again the bat seemed to be impervious to the ball. The Chappell brothers, Ian and Greg, both made a hundred, to which

Rohan Kanhai, the newly-appointed home captain, replied in kind. Batting became even easier during the match and the West Indies' first innings lead of 67 runs was not sufficient to influence the result.

Lawrence Rowe's magnificent 302, in which he shared a second-wicket stand of 249 with Alvin Kallicharran, made memorable yet another draw in the Third Test Match against England in 1974. The Jamaican was at the brilliant best which caused commentators to compare him favourably to the great batsmen of history. The tourists finished the match well under a hundred runs ahead with only three wickets in hand. Keith Fletcher's rearguard unbeaten hundred came between the West Indies and success.

Tony Cozier observed in *West Indies: Fifty Years of Test Cricket*:
'That was soon being dwarfed by the majesty of Rowe, whose magnetism swelled the stands to bursting point on the Saturday when he moved from one century to another. On the Sunday, he passed his third hundred and, finally, after 10½ hours with a six and 34 fours, he was caught in the deep for 302, the first Test triple-century on the ground, and his own first first-class century outside Jamaica'.

He had written earlier in the same section:
'Rowe, classic in style and ravenous in appetite for runs, was the dominant West Indian'.

In a supplement for the Nation newspaper to mark a subsequent tour the same writer elaborated on Rowe's crowd-drawing appeal:
'The whole of Barbados, it seemed, was there to see him bat. The authorities did not foresee the response and there was no control on the crowds thronging to get into Kensington. Gates were broken, walls were scaled and even high-tension electric cables were used as means to enter. Rowe himself and the other players had to be escorted through the mass to enter the ground through a fence'.

Yet Wisden described the crowd as 'splendidly behaved despite their real discomfort'.

As they had done on some previous occasions the West Indies recovered from the disappointments of a tour to Australia by thrashing the Indians is 1976. It was good for morale and for individual reputations. After the damage done by the fast bowlers in earlier series it was surprisingly leg-spinner David Holford who undid the Indians in their first innings. Bridgetown has no real tradition of helping slow bowlers, and the visitors would have been disappointed.

Viv Richards, moved back to first-wicket down, continued the run of success he had achieved in Australia as an opener. He and Lloyd made hundreds, Kallicharran also just failing, in preventing the experienced Indian spinners from getting into their stride. The West Indies led by 311 runs on the first innings and won the match convincingly by an innings and 97 runs.

Although the Pakistanis were involved in yet another draw in 1977 the match was full of incident from the start to finish. Clive Lloyd's century picked up the West Indies from a disappointing start and took them to within 14 runs of the tourists' total. The recovery looked even better as fast bowlers Colin Croft and Andy Roberts reduced Pakistan to 158-9. Then the tide turned again. Left-hander Wasim Raja, dropped several times, and wicketkeeper Wasim Bari, a better batsman than the number eleven position would suggest, put on 133 runs for the last wicket. The total included 68 extras, a record number for a Test Match innings.

The West Indians started the quest for victory confidently. Roy Fredericks and Viv Richards added 130 runs for the second wicket. The bowlers gave away a further 31 no-balls to complete a rare match aggregate of 103. Wickets tumbled suddenly as the batsmen tried to force the pace against the quick bowlers. Eventually the West Indies were forced to struggle to save the game. When the ninth wicket went down at 217 tail-enders Roberts and Croft hung on to achieve a draw over fifty runs behind.

In 1978, the Australians, weakened by the absence of their World Series Cricketers, were no match for the West Indian fast bowlers. Nevertheless it was the Barbadian first-wicket pairing of Gordon Greenidge and Desmond Haynes that clinched the victory by 9 wickets. Although fast bowler Jeff Thomson posed problems in the first innings, he lacked effective support. This was the last Test Match in which the region was at full strength before the schism.

The Third Test Match in 1981, which the West Indies won by 298 runs, was marked more by individual achievement than by the excitement of the contest. The action was welcomed after the scheduled previous match at Bourda had been cancelled in the light of the 'Jackman affair' but was tinged with sorrow on Barrington's death. By that time, however, the home side was well on top. Lloyd and Larry Gomes pulled them through an akward patch on the first morning in which wickets fell quickly to England's pace bowlers. A modest first innings total was made to look comfortable by Michael Holding's memorable assault on Geoff Boycott and by England's complete batting collapse.

With a 143 runs lead Viv Richards recovered from his lean spell to hammer a majestic 182 not out, in which he received firm backing from Lloyd and from nightwatchman Croft who made 33. Although England's fighting spirit had been dampened by the overwhelming deficit and by the bereavement, Graham Gooch and David Gower scored exactly 100 runs for the third wicket. The former fought a lone though foredoomed battle after his partner, having defied the thunderbolts of the fast bowlers, was bowled by offspinner Richards.

India succumbed by 10 wickets in 1983. Apart from Mohinder Amarnath, who made a half-century in each innings, the batsmen had no answer to the fast bowlers on a lively pitch from which early morning rain caused the ball to lift. Gus Logie, prospering from a dropped catch soon after he came to the crease, scored his maiden Test Match century and four other West Indians reached fifty. India saved the innings defeat, but their hosts needed to score only a single to win. As it was achieved off the first delivery, a no-ball, the analysis showed no legitimate delivery for the innings.

The Australians went down by the same margin the next year. There was little in the early action to indicate such a one-sided result. The visitors batted soundly with wicketkeeper Wayne Phillips making a hundred to reach 429. The West Indies hit back at full charge. Greenidge was run out after he had helped Haynes put on 132 runs for the first wicket, and then his partner and Richie Richardson took the score to 277 before the next man was out. Fast bowler Rodney Hogg swung the game dramatically by breaking through the middle-order in taking 6 wickets for 77 runs.

Lloyd counter-attacked so well, however, that the West Indies finished 80 runs ahead. As only a day and a session remained to play, a draw seemed to be inevitable. Malcolm Marshall and Michael Holding unleashed a furious assault and the match was over shortly before lunch on the last day. Only two Australians reached double-figures as the tourists were skittled out for just 97 runs. It was the lowest total ever recorded by any team in a Test Match at Kensington, and it demoralised the Australians for the rest of the rubber.

Marshall was even more devastating in bringing about the victory by 10 wickets over New Zealand in 1985, the first time that these opponents had been beaten in the Caribbean. After rain had delayed the start of play until 70 minutes after lunch on the opening day, the Barbadian fast bowler reduced the tourists to 1-3 by dismissing Jon Wright and Rutherford before either had scored. New Zealand were bowled out for a mere 94. Richards set up the first West Indies' victory under his own captaincy by hitting 105, in which he was supported well by half-centuries from Roger Harper and Marshall. The latter, bowling at pace around the wicket, was then irresistible in taking 7 wickets for 80 runs. The visitors' complaint of intimidation echoed that of the Indians after similar defeat in the face of Michael Holding's fast bowling at Sabina Park in 1976.

Fourteen

Festival Cricket

Cricket is still played for fun in the West Indies. Test Matches are no less tense and the presssure of instant cricket no less keen, but that is not the whole picture. There is a natural balance between formal competition and informal enjoyment so that the game, itself, is indivisible. The urban urchin and rustic youth chasing ball in the backstreets and country glades are as integral part of Caribbean cricket as the international celebrity. Indeed, they are essentially the same. Stars who have represented the region from Birmingham to Brisbane, from Kanpur to Christchurch, trundle their arms over and flex their wrists in impromptu neighbourhood knockabouts.

The social scene and geographical features which make the West Indies vulnerable economically and administratively as a centre for international competition are favourable for festival cricket. Barbados leads the world in attracting tourists to make a holiday playing cricket in the island. In addition to the climate and hospitality, the opportunity to bat and bowl with/against wellknown local cricketers of today and the immediate past is a potent incentive. Results do not matter over much. Playing the game, taking part, is still the main motivation.

The pioneer English tourists were festival cricketers. Pelham Warner was on the thresh-hold of his career, and, apart from Andrew Stoddart, who was in Arthur Priestley's side, none were regular Test Match representatives and few had consistent county experience. They were generally good club players with the occasional specialist on whom success depended. In that it was not much different to some of today's parties of adventurers. The visitors were victorious against home sides of similar standing but were defeated when professionals were included.

A personal rapport developed between some of the Englishmen and the West Indians. Pelham Warner, whose brother, Aucher, was the touring captain, and Lord Hawke hosted the welcoming party for the first team from the region on their arrival in England in 1900. H.D.G. Leveson-Gower, scorer of a memorable 136 for Lord Hawke's pioneers against British Guiana, organised regular festival games against visiting sides at Scarborough in Yorkshire at the end of the English season. The encounter in 1923 is considered to have done more than any other single factor to win Test Match recognition for the West Indies.

Leveson-Gower paid the tourists the compliment of selecting an exceptionally strong side, more powerful than those which represented England officially in the West Indies over the next thirty years, including Jack Hobbs, his country's greatest ever batsman, Ernest Tydesley, J.W.H.T. Douglas, Wilfred Rhodes, Percy Chapman, Frank Mann, Percy Fender, Cecil Parkin and Greville Stevens. It seemed to be too strong for the West Indians, leading by 108 runs on the first innings and needing to make only a token 28 runs to win in the fourth.

George Francis had Hobbs l.b.w. with only three runs scored. Then he and George John, the new-ball attack which had been so effective against the counties throughout the season, made the batsmen struggle for every run. When six men were out for 19 runs the game could have gone either way. Although Leveson-Gower's XI rallied to win by 4 wickets, the shock to England's pride was remembered for years to come. Few festival games have had such significant repercussions for cricket's development.

Much of the overseas tour programme of former years was less formal than it is today. The public delighted in seeing the West Indians play against sides brought together for the purpose rather than in more serious encounters with established teams. The first West Indians to visit India in 1948/49 took on the Cricket Club of India, the State Governor's XI at Nagpur, the State Governor's XI at Calcutta, the Governor of Bihar's XI and a States XI as well as the more powerful zones and provinces. The results were not really in doubt, but the local people had the chance of being entertained by cricketers, home and visiting, whom, otherwise, they might not have seen.

Individual excellence is remembered more than any contrived result. For years afterwards a particular innings or spell of bowling is recalled by spectators who saw it for themselves. Often it is merely the presence of a celebrity fielding on the boundary near to them. Some memories are more easy to understand than others. A Jamaican left his homeland many years ago on marrying a girl of different nationality and moving to her country. Yet nothing moves him to poetic expression as the memory of Everton Weekes batting at Sabina Park in 1948.

It is more difficult to sympathise with the judgement of a Barbadian, living now in London, who claims Tommy Greenhough to have been England's greatest ever bowler, even though he bases his assessment on having seen the Lancashire slow bowler on the 1959/60 tour. Greenhough took only one wicket for 125 runs against Barbados — admittedly his victim was Gary Sobers — and was not chosen for any of the Test Matches. At least he made a very good impression on one of the spectators then present. Alan Ross in *Through the Caribbean* saw it differently:

'Barrington bowled his leg-spinners rather more reliably than Greenhough, getting greater bounce out of the pitch and ... keeping Greenhough out of the first Test'.

Pre-tour trial games are neither festivals nor competitive fixtures. Performances are less important in themselves than for the manner in which they are achieved. So much talent was available in 1950 that, in spite of their success, opening batsmen Bruce Pairaudeau, Nyron Asgarali and Andy Ganteaume could not displace Allan Rae, Jeffrey Stollmeyer and Roy Marshall in the team that went to England. The effect on the selectors was only delayed because they were taken seven years later when their trial performances were no more impressive.

Hammond Furlonge was the casualty in 1957. He had shown much promise on the previous tour to New Zealand and scored well in the trials, but for once the selectors preferred experience to potential — the reverse of their attitude in the choice of wicketkeepers. Young Wesley Hall made the team by hitting 77, and, thereafter, played solely as a fast bowler. The development of regular regional competitions removed the need to present special trials to evaluate form and ability.

In early 1956 writer E.W. Swanton arranged a visit to Barbados and Trinidad by a side of leading English county cricketers to erase some of the bad feeling generated in the Test Match series two years earlier. Wisden confirmed that 'they created an excellent impression with the West Indies public'. Barbados won the first game by an innings and the second was drawn with the honours even. Trinidad lost by only 24 runs after being dismissed for just 94 in their first innings by whirlwind fast bowler Frank Tyson and legspinner Gamini Goonesena.

A selected West Indies XI won easily by 8 wickets at Port of Spain. Spinners Sonny Ramadhin and Gary Sobers were too good for the visiting batsmen. Everton Weekes made top score of 89, and was well supported by half-centuries from opening batsman Conrad Hunte, who had made 151 and 95 in the two games for Barbados, and Sobers. The opportunity was taken wisely to blend the best youngsters with some of the established players.

The Duke of Norfolk's team went to Jamaica a year later in the foot-steps of Lord Tennyson's sides half-a-century earlier. They were undefeated in three games against the island, two of which they won, and six in the country districts. In spite of the defeats Jamaica could take credit for some enterprising individual performances. Collie Smith hit two hundreds, Easton McMorris and L.N. Bonitto one each, and J.K. Holt passed fifty in all three games. Fast bowlers Roy Gilchrist, Esmond Kentish and Tom Dewdney each had one match of devastating effectiveness.

Trinidadian writer Brunell Jones took several teams to Bermuda between 1952 and 1965. They did much to entertain the public and to provide a platform on which the unknown and the famous could play together. The first side, which was entirely Trinidadian, included Rupert Tang Choon, Nyron Asgarali, Bunny Butler, Syd Jackbir, Clarence Skeete, Donald Ramsamooj and Simpson Guillen. The last two went to live in England and New Zealand respectively. Three years later he persuaded Gary Sobers, Collie Smith, Alfred Valentine and Clairmonte Depeiza to join, and on the last trip selected Basil Butcher, Richard Edwards, Peter Lashley, Hammond and Carl Furlonge, Charlie Griffith and Steve Camacho.

In the late 1960s the same writer's party stopped off in Antigua and St Kitts on their way home from a goodwill visit to the U.S.A. The side included the international experience of Wesley Hall, Everton Weekes, Cammie Smith, Alfred Valentine, Easton McMorris and Andy Ganteaume, and respected territorial players Bunny Butler, Teddy Griffith and Clarence Skeete who did not quite make it to permanent regional recognition — Butler played for the West Indies once against Australia in 1955 but it was not a year for making a reputation. Such sides kept the life-blood of Caribbean cricket flowing.

The hazard of contemporary conditions is that the star players may become too tied up in the seemingly endless international competitions to take part in these such enjoyable jaunts. What shall it profit any team if it should rule the whole world, and, yet, lose that soul which is the essence of cricket. The gap between amateur and professional is already too wide, and for that festival games provide a ready antidote.

Barbados apart, the islands are not geared to make cricket an integral part of their tourism strategy. The emphasis of Jamacia is to attract overseas visitors to the hotels and beaches of the north coast, from Ocho Rios to Montego Bay, and the so-publicised hedonist resorts around the western tip. Many of those coming into the island do not enter Kingston. The Government's exhortation for greater attention to be given to promoting the capital city's prominent houses, landmarks and cultural centres has met with only partial success.

Jamaicans returning to the island from their new homes overseas have hardly enough time to meet all the friends and relations, and to see again the old places of fond recollection, let alone to play cricket. Various attempts to bring down West Indian clubs from England and North America have stumbled on this factor. The majority Jamaican membership do not want to tour the Eastern Caribbean islands if there is a chance of going 'home', but once there cricket has a low priority.

The island has not won the Shell Shield since 1968/69 and the so-called festival matches have been usually exhibition games which the public attend to watch teams of professionals play against each other, rather than events in which they, themselves, participate. These promotions have had much good cricket to commend them. Eddie Hemmings, the England offspinner, took all 10 wickets in an innings for 175 runs for an International XI against a West Indies XI at Kingston in September 1982.

The following year there were four one-day games, including one under floodlight at the National Stadium. The West Indies XI beat the International XI easily in the three meetings that were not curtailed seriously by rain. In the night knockabout Gordon Greenidge and Desmond Haynes flayed the bowlers for 230-0 to win by 10 wickets in 25.3 overs. Later that same week Greenidge's own benefit match at the National Stadium in Bridgetown was subjected to controversy for the inclusion of Chris Smith, a South African with whom the Barbadian plays in Hampshire, who was on holiday in the island at the time.

Jamaica is associated more readily with music than with cricket. Bob Marley is probably the country's best-known citizen, and reggae music has permeated parts of the globe in which cricket is still unknown. The Sunsplash festival, from which Yellowman, among several house-hold names, achieved his initial international recognition, attracts more native Jamaicans and visitors from the cities of the neighbouring U.S.A. and Canada than any Test Match at Sabina Park. Cricket is not unimportant, but it is only one factor in the overall picture.

The island enjoys the legacy of a rich and varied history which was hardly ever free of incident and was the homeland of Marcus Garvey, a pioneer in projecting a sense of black identity. There is good racing at Caymanas Park and intellectual stimulation among the staff and students of the university at Mona. Yes, there was George Headley, Collie Smith and Alfred Valentine, but Carole Joan Crawford and Cindy Breakespeare won the Miss World title and beauty queens are given as much prominence as cricketers in the country's tourist-conscious press. With so many things to see and do, it is difficult to get sufficient visitors together, available and ready to play cricket at the same time.

Just under a century ago Pelham Warner, who did not visit Jamaica, noted in *Cricket in Many Climes* that

'Cricket seemed to me to be established on a firmer basis in Trinidad than in any other part of the West Indies. There is more money in the island than in some of the others, and the inhabitants of all classes loyally support the game'.

Much of that remains true today. Although there is some exchange of teams, the operation is hardly on a scale to merit comparison with that in Barbados.

While undoubtedly Trinidad & Tobago, like Jamaica, has not made the playing of cricket a principal plank in their plan for tourism, there are extenuating circumstances. The country's administration takes pride in providing sport facilities primarily for the enjoyment of its own citizens than for the benefit of visitors. There is more than the two hundred miles of sea between the attitudes of the compliant Barbadians and the independent-minded Trinidadians. It is an inheritance of culture and history.

Tourists, especially Trinidadians living overseas, come mainly for Carnival. It is too much to expect them to travel down again at considerable cost for a separate cricket festival, and when Carnival is on the streets few find the opportunity for cricket. The island has much to offer. The images which come quickest to mind involve steelbands, calypso/soca, the oil industry, the natural beauty and the vitality of the people. Sparrow stands comparison to the legend of Learie Constantine, more so because he and his music are alive today, and other calypsonians take preference over the island's Shell Shield cricketers in the values of a substantial section of the community.

Trinidad has much natural beauty, which is overshadowed too often by that of neighbouring Barbados, St Lucia and Grenada, as well as that of Tobago, its twin-island partner, as Alan Ross related in *Through the Caribbean*:

'Another Sunday I drove over ... to Maracas, that most vaunted of Trinidadian beaches. The road there, through the steep cedar woods and mahogany forests, rivals any part of the southern French corniches. The thick tangle of coffee, cocoa and nutmeg hedges the winding road in, and as you climb into the cool sweet air you can look back on the rust-pink patches of the immortelles — heralds of the dry season — shading the green hillsides of cocoa, and the sudden glitter of sea below.

Maracas — a racing expanse of sand between thickly forested headlands — is a surf beach, with fawn-coloured rollers running up to where the long pirogues of the fishermen lie under a continuous overhang of coconut. At one end the shacks of the fishermen cluster among bamboos and tropical scrub. At the other, far out of earshot, steel bands throb among the parked cars and picknicking bathers ... The white sand glistens; the orange sellers slump in the shade of the coconuts, the sun dips, and then the lines of traffic wind back into Port-of-Spain'.

Cricket is one of many subjects which Trinidadians debate with vehemence or listen to on car radios in the long traffic jams leading into, out of and through the capital. Few communities are so politically conscious. Jamaicans may shoot each other during an election campaign, but Trinidadians inhale current affairs and, if it is in order for an outsider to say so, make political many of the things that other people would not consider to be so. Yet Trinidad & Tobago took no active part either way in the greatest regional crisis in recent history, namely the overthrow of the Bishop government and the American/Caribbean intervention in Grenada, in October 1983. Debate is an art in itself.

Tourism is more important to Tobago where it is the island's major employer and the mainstay of the community. For the country as a whole, however, tourism accounts for less than 1 per cent of the Gross Domestic Product, but it continues to be a major earner of foreign exchange. Trinidadians are the most hospitable of people but are reluctant to give their country the public relations image which has made Barbados and Antigua, for example, identified more easily as magnets for tourists.

Everything has come together to make Barbados the ideal setting for festival cricket. The tourist attractions, beaches and the landmarks of Bridgetown, are in the vicinity of the cricket venues. The country is so compact that it is not only possible but almost imperative to play cricket, shop and swim in the same day. After an exhausting session in the field, there is no long journey over mountains or through wooded hillsides to reach the hotel, the stores and the innumerable beach-bars.

Nothing rivals cricket for attention, no Sunsplash or Carnival, neither Marley nor Sparrow. Political history has been tranquil and present politics are conducted at low key. Trees, sand, buildings, people — and probably also the lizards — are so steeped in the spirit of cricket that to promote Barbados is to promote the game. It is but natural, therefore, that cricket and the requirements of the tourist trade go hand in hand. Even visitors from Western Europe and North America expect to see the bat against the ball in Barbados — it is part of the atmosphere of the place.

The Test Match at Kensington has acquired special affection for

English visitors. Wives and girlfriends are permitted to join the team here. As well as many former cricketers who had played previously at the Oval, celebrities such as singer Mick Jagger and television presenter Michael Parkinson come down for the occasion. It has the ideal holiday setting and is inevitably chosen by those press commentators and visitors who have the time, and funds, to attend only one match of a series in the West Indies.

Jamaican-born John Hanson, the best West Indian club cricketer in England, explained that the highlight of his career was to be included in a side playing at the Kensington Oval when he was visiting Barbados. It is the ultimate ambition of any cricketer coming into the island from outside. Alas, this time there was no happy ending. Rain washed out the entire game. Hanson is not certain whether he can afford to take the time from work to repeat the journey. Many amateur cricketers are more fortunate in realising this chance of a life-time.

David Gower, the England captain and keen participant in festival cricket, summed up the spirit of the game in the island:

'West Indies cricket is just not about those all too familiar names and faces that keep occupying both the crease and our television screens, but about the base of their game back home ... Barbados, of course, has long had a reputation for being capable of producing a side of Test Match standard all by itself, and it does not take long, when you visit the island, to find out why. Everywhere people are playing cricket, from the dusty lanes through the sugar cane fields, through the many rough and ready grounds dotted round the island, plus of course the more elegant and historical clubs such as Wanderers, to the beaches that we all know so well from the travel brochures. This is the heart of Caribbean cricket, the origin of all the talent that springs from the region.

I have often been across to play some supposedly friendly cricket in that part of the world, where the fellow who has poured you a beer the night before, as often as not turns up on the field beside you the next day and is either trying to let the ball go at the speed of light or disperse it to some far corner of the ground. It is a place where cricket is to be enjoyed as much or more so as anywhere in the world and in an atmosphere vastly removed from either Lord's or the traditional village green!'

The tour operators offer a blend of cricket, sunshine, beaches and parties for those who wish to play, score, umpire or watch the cricket. It is an occasion for bringing together friends and families with the incentive also to engage in scuba diving, water ski-ing, para-sailing, fishing, sailing and just lying in the sun. There is an extra attraction in the opportunity to converse with celebrities from different aspects of the world of entertainment, as well as from the game itself.

In the longest-established and best-known festival, any cricketer of any standard can play under the guidance of a former or current Test Match representative. The teams are balanced by selection once the information given on the booking form has been evaluated. Then the selected teams stay together throughout the tournament. The captains are drawn usually from current England players and Barbadians who have played for the West Indies.

The festival competition is played on five or six separate days on a league basis with rules similar to those used in the John Player League, the leading Sunday afternoon limited-overs tournament in England. Each team from one group plays all teams in the other. Finals day decides the winner by a play-off between the league leaders and runners-up. All equipment is provided by commercial sponsors and is distributed afterwards to relevant causes in the island.

Most tourists stay for an extra week after the fortnight's festival. Accommodation is situated usually in St James parish on the west coast. Facilities are available for sports other than cricket and swimming, and include a golf competition organised by former England allrounder Trevor Bailey at the Sandy Lane Golf Club. The stoical, dry-humoured Bailey is reported to have received the news of Ken Barrington's sudden death while he was writing his copy and uttered the curt comment: 'Damn, now I shall have to re-write my intro'. Maybe it is apocryphal but it would have been in character.

The celebrated Pro/Am Cricket Festival is presented usually in November. At that time England is shivering in the damp fogs of the first onset of winter. The amateur cricketers who hurried to the sun and beaches in the autumn of 1983 encountered unexpected excitement ... the American/Caribbean military intervention in close-by Grenada. In spite of the build-up of soldiers and the outside possibility of the conflict spreading, the game went on.

Three to four months earlier the same operators presented a Youth and Schoolboy Cricket Festival in the island. The format was basically the same as that for the adults. Although mothers, fathers, brothers and sisters were welcome to join the holiday, boys who wished to attend on their own were looked after by a selection of guardians all of whom were experienced in the care of young people. Even so the organisers hoped that an adequate number of fathers would come along to umpire and to keep score.

The talk in the bar with well-known cricketers, or just listening to their stories, is as important as any batting, bowling or fielding exploits. Many of them have a good tale to tell. Fred Rumsey, the principal organiser, must find arranging the festival to be less arduous than his debut as a fast bowler for England when Bobby Simpson, the Australian captain, hit 311 at Manchester in 1964. Admittedly he followed his 2 wickets for 99 runs there by taking four wickets in an innings against New Zealand at Lord's the following year.

Richard Edwards, one of his representatives in Barbados, was also a Test Match fast bowler. He was understudy to Wesley Hall and Charlie Griffith on the disappointing tour to Australia in 1968/69 and by taking 5 wickets for 84 runs against New Zealand at Wellington immediately afterwards seemed to have secured the succession. The selectors, however, had decided already on a clean sweep in the pace department and Edwards was left out of the side which went to England. He did not get back.

The other representative, Tony Cozier, is the authorative voice of West Indian cricket to the millions who listen to his commentaries throughout the world. He is also a foremost writer on the game, cricket historian and author. By participating in the arrangement of festival cricket he is following the tradition of other scribe-impressarios such as E.W. Swanton, Brunell Jones and Ron Roberts. The standard of cricket journalism in the West Indies is exceptionally high, in respect of comment, content, observation, analysis and balance — much higher than it is in the national press of some countries with greater experience in such things.

There has been tragedy in the press. Jack Anderson, Jamaica's best-known writer on cricket, was shot fatally by assailants at his home in Kingston shortly after he had returned from viewing the third day's play in the Fifth Test Match against Australia at Sabina Park in April 1978. Apparently the assailants had intended to eliminate a potential witness in an impending court case, but were mistaken in the address of two neighbouring and close-sounding streets.

David Holford, regular captain of one of the festival teams, is a legspinner remembered best for an outstanding batting feat. At Lord's in 1966 he and Gary Sobers, his cousin, shared an unbroken sixth-wicket stand of 274 runs to take the West Indies from the brink of almost certain defeat to the verge of an improbable victory. He was tipped as an outside candidate for the regional captaincy when it was given first to Rohan Kanhai and then to Clive Lloyd. Holford bowled the West Indies to victory over India by taking 5 wickets for 23 runs at Kensington in 1976.

Barbados festival cricket came to England in the autumn of 1982. The Barbados Tourist Board hired The Oval in London for a match between an international side and another drawn from the island's outstanding cricketers of the immediate past. Everyone with any significant connection with the game was flown in from Barbados. The hospitality was generous to the point of being almost self-defeating, because many of the reporters and commentators dallied so long in the restaurant/bar that they saw hardly a ball delivered.

The occasion was blessed with tropical weather. Thousands of spectators from the Barbadian community, other West Indians and English, flocked to see Hall and Griffith bowl at the scene of their triumph two decades earlier. Barbadian veterans have an excellent record at The Oval. Bertie Clarke, who bowled there for the West Indies in 1939, still turned his legbreaks successfully in a veterans' match when he was well in his sixties.

The smaller islands are still too small individually and too disparate geographically to present their own major festival. Nevertheless the situation can change, The Organisation of Eastern Caribbean States has appointed a head of the sports desk — the first being the celebrated cricket commentator 'Reds' Perreira — to stimulate the development of sport in the member states, to seek the necessary finance and technology, and to heed the advice of successful entrepreneurs who have overcome similar handicaps in other spheres of activity.

Fifteen

St Vincent and the Windward Islands

St Vincent — and the Windward Islands generally — had been so neglected by the administrators, the selectors and the press that when Wilfred Slack hit a purple patch for Middlesex a few seasons ago the correspondent of the Guardian, one of England's better-informed daily newspapers, claimed that he was the first batsman of repute from the island. Yet the first West Indian star batsman in international competition, C.A. Ollivierre, had been Vincentian. Such is the passing glory of sporting fame.

Until the last 25 years the islands seemed to lay beyond the confines of regional and inter-continental travel, including visits by the principal touring teams, and outside the vision of the administrators of Caribbean cricket and selectors of the West Indies team. Ironically the Windward and Leeward Islands were integrated within the region's sporting entity at about the same time that the experiment of political Federation expired.

St Vincent won the first match played against St Lucia in 1894. As that same year their opponents defeated Dominica, the Vincentians could claim fairly the championship of the Windward Islands, and they gave a better account of themselves than their neighbours against early touring sides. Neither St Lucia, who had been reputed to be a good batting side, nor Grenada could get anywhere near raising a hundred total against Lord Hawke's touring team in 1897/98.

In contrast St Vincent provided strong opposition in leading on the first innings before admitting to final defeat. The tourists were not happy with their stay in the island. The sea-crossing through the Grenadines was rough, the hotel accommodation was so restricted that they had to sleep two to a bed, and the mosquitoes proved that their bite was worse than their buzz. The visitors, too, were unused to the only matting wicket they encountered on the tour. Excuses, though sometimes valid enough, are common-place whenever and wherever the game has been played.

The Englishmen batted unevenly against F. Layne, described as being the best all-rounder, and R. Ollivierre. The latter bowled Lord Hawke before he had scored, which caused the several thousand spectators to throw their hats into the air, beat the ground with their sticks, and shake hands with one another. There was a keen struggle for the lead. St Vincent went ahead thanks to opener Ivan's half-century. Even so the margin was only 13 runs, but the visitors lost two further wickets in clearing the arrears.

With the game in the balance Pelham Warner and Lord Hawke counter-attacked in a devastating manner. The former, who was born in Trinidad but went on to captain England and to become one of cricket's greatest administrators, hit a magnificent 156, the highest individual innings of the tour, and Hawke just reached his fifty. Warner has described in his book *Cricket in Many Climes* the danger which the avalanche of shots posed for the by-standers, many of whom were women attired in bright costumes.

'Hawke hit two colossal sixes, one of which nearly killed a lady who was watching the game from the balcony of her house. The ball struck the woodwork about a foot from her face ... I made one drive straight over the bowler's head, which knocked a tray full of cakes clean off the head of a black woman who was standing near the ropes. The ground, I may say, is rather short in the drive, but broad enough for all purposes'.

The assault knocked the spirit out of the local side. Although Layne passed fifty, he could find no regular partner. Yet the innings was not without incident. Warner's account reflected the kind of controversy which would beset future matches of even greater competitive interest:

'One or two of their batsmen seemed rather disinclined to go when they were given out by the umpire ... John refused to leave his wicket albeit palpably caught and bowled ... and this was not the only batsman on the home side who evinced the greatest reluctance to leave the crease unless the centre ash was absolutely felled'.

Passions ran high at even this early age.

Charles Augustus Ollivierre, a Vincentian, was the star batsman of the first tour to England in 1900. He finished the season with 883 runs, the highest aggregate, at an average well above that of Lebrun Constantine, Percy Goodman and P.J. Cox. Ollivierre shared in two double-century partnerships for the first wicket: 238 against Leicestershire with Pelham Warner, playing in his only game for the visiting side captained by his brother, and 208 with Cox against Surrey at The Oval.

After the tour Ollivierre was invited to stay on and to represent Derbyshire in the county championship. He became the first of the now many West Indians who have made their cricketing home in England. The Vincentian emphasised the point by hitting 64 not out in the county's victory over the next West Indian touring team in 1906. Yet his greatest achievement for Derbyshire was probably in the remarkable match against Essex at Chesterfield two years earlier.

Essex reached a seemingly impregnable 597 runs total in which P.A. Perrin made a record 68 boundaries in his undefeated 343, but Ollivierre kept Derbyshire in the contest by scoring 229 out of 548. Essex collapsed suddenly in their second innings and were dismissed for just 97. The West Indian made a further 92 not out as his side came from behind to win by 9 wickets. No other team has rallied so successfully after facing such a large score in the first innings of a three-day match.

Three years later Ollivierre retired from first-class competition on account of eye trouble. He continued to play in club cricket in Yorkshire, where he passed his later years, and for sixteen years, until the outbreak of the Second World War, he coached schoolboys in the Netherlands. Ollivierre's expert batting, together with that of S.G. Smith, the talented Trinidadian all-rounder who joined Northamptonshire shortly afterwards, put West Indian cricket on the international map at a time when Test Matches were limited to Australia, England and South Africa.

Richard Ollivierre, his brother, destroyed the batting might of Yorkshire in the famous victory by 262 runs at Harrogate in 1906. The northern county seemed to be almost invincible in English domestic cricket and four years previously had dismissed the powerful Australians for only 23 runs. This time the boot was on the other foot. Ollivierre ripped through their first innings in taking 7 wickets for 23 runs. The touring captain did not enforce the follow-on as Yorkshire failed to recover from a mere 50 runs total.

W.H. Mignon bowled 'uncommonly well' for St. George's C.C. and 'excellently' for Grenada against Lord Hawke's tourists, but the home batting could not match the quality of his bowling. Warner observed that 'the combined island team included three or four black men', one of whom, Straker, held a couple of very good catches. Much was expected of Mignon when he went to England in 1900, but, although he finished third to Woods and Burton in wicket aggregate, his performance was somewhat disappointing.

Even at this time the Windward and the Leeward Islands tended to be over-looked in the selection of regional sides to play against the early tourists. The situation deteriorated as Barbados and Trinidad dominated cricket in the Eastern Caribbean into the present century. Yet some administrative efforts were made to encourage the development of the game throughout the region. Hon Philip Clark Cork, the British administrator, presented the Cork Cup in 1910 for competition among the Windward Islands and the Hesketh Bell Shield, donated by a Governor of the Leeward Islands of that name, was instituted in 1914.

Nevertheless the cricketers of the smaller islands continued to be neglected for the important tours and matches. Winston Lloyd has pointed out in *The West Indies Cricket Annual* that

'The minutes of the first meeting of the West Indies Cricket Board of Control, held in Port of Spain on 17 and 18 June 1927 noted that the Board felt that it would be impracticable for a visiting official side to play in any of the islands of the Leewards and Windwards group.

It was, therefore, decided that every effort should be made to arrange matches (one against Leeward Islands and one against Windward Islands) at either Barbados and/or Trinidad. In such event, the expenses of the Islands' team to be for their account subject to a payment of such proportion of the gate receipts as may be arranged by the Barbados with the Barbados and/or Trinidad cricket authorities'.

So much for resolution, no games were scheduled for the islands against a visiting team until the visit of England in 1954.

Ironically the islands bristled with talent in the 1950s, at a time when the West Indies were in decline as an international force. F.O. Mason, a Vincentian fast bowler, would have come into more serious regional reckoning in a later age, and Ferrell Charles of St Lucia shook the Australians in 1955 by taking 7 wickets for 45 runs in bowling the Windward Islands to a 46 runs first innings lead. Not many West Indian bowlers could do that as the powerful batting battery moved through the Caribbean.

Reid, the Dominican wicketkeeper, must have come close to inclusion in the team which toured England in 1957. He kept impressively in the pre-tour trials, but strange things happened that year, not least in the choice of wicketkeepers. Seasoned specialists Depeiza and Binns were left at home while the selectors put their faith in the inexperienced Gerry Alexander and part-timer Rohan Kanhai. Neither had a successful season behind the stumps, and Reid's selection would not have weakened the side.

Ian Neverson, the opening batsman who scored a half-century against the Australians in 1955, sustained an injury which terminated his career. However Alfie Roberts, the teenage Vincentian, showed sufficient progress to go with the comparatively young team to New Zealand the following year. He made his debut in the Fourth Test

Match at Auckland, the first representative of the smaller islands to play for the West Indies. The occasion was hardly auspicious because New Zealand, too, made history by achieving their first ever Test Match victory.

At first Roberts batted well enough for 28, second highest to only Hammond Furlonge, but in the second innings he was bowled by Beard without scoring. At any other time he might have been given another chance, especially as he made 53 against the New Zealand Colts at Palmerston North immediately afterwards. Unfortunately there were no further Test matches on that tour and by the time the team met again Frank Worrell and Clyde Walcott, as well as Everton Weekes, were available once more to shut out any opportunity in the middle-order.

The revival of the region's fortunes in the early 1960s owed so much to the allround excellence of Barbados that the island challenged the Rest of the World to a special match staged at Kensington Oval in March 1967 to celebrate the recently acquired political independence. There was speculation at the time, only half-joking, that if Barbados had been successful their team would have seceded from the regional side and would have competed in Test Matches on their own account. Events made such speculation unnecessary.

Spinners Lance Gibbs and Mustaq Mohammed routed Barbados for just 84 runs in their first innings and set up the visitors' victory by 262 runs. It was the high-point of their mastery. Although the island continued to be the strongest individual territory it was henceforth only the first among equals. Within two years of this game West Indian cricket was in such decline that the selectors cast their net further afield. For the first time since the pioneer age their choice for a full overseas tour included representatives of the Windward Islands.

Wicketkeeper Mike Findlay of St Vincent was understudy to Jackie Hendriks in Australia and New Zealand in 1968/69. He used his experience well and on the following tour to England he succeeded the Jamaican in two out of the three Test Matches. Findlay was in and out of the regional team for several years while the selectors experimented with a batsman who could keep wicket, Desmond Lewis, and made up their mind whether or not to stick with Deryck Murray, the precocious Trinidadian. Although the latter eventually secured the position, Findlay pressed him all the way on the triumphant tour to England in 1976.

Fast bowler Grayson Shillingford came from a family with a long cricket pedigree in Dominica. He was one of the new generation chosen to replace Wesley Hall and Charlie Griffith in England in 1969. Grayson's initial impression was favourable, but in the subsequent home series against India and New Zealand he did not show sufficient penetration or consistency to withstand the later challenge of Keith Boyce and Bernard Julien to share the new ball with the dependable Vanburn Holder.

Irving Shillingford had been around a long time — he was over 30 years old — when as a result of some exceptionally high and consistent scoring in domestic competition — he was chosen to play in the Second Test Match against Pakistan at Queen's Park in 1977. The Dominican's aggression in scoring 120, in which he was especially severe on Imran Khan, put the West Indies 254 runs ahead in the following drawn match at Bourda. His experience was needed again after the walk-out of the World Series Cricketers on the same ground a year later, but it was his last Test Match appearance.

The schism in the late 1970s should have opened more opportunities for the Windward Islanders. That promise did not then materialise. Viv Richards and Andy Roberts by then had made the Leeward Islands a force in the region. Jim Allen and Derek Parry of Montserrat and Nevis respectively also were coming along well. Yet few newcomers had come forward in the Windward Islands to take the place of Findlay and Irving Shillingford, upon whom so much still depended.

Opening bowler Norbert Phillip of Dominica, who had been playing at first-class level for almost a decade, shared the new ball with Sylvester Clarke against Australia at Georgetown in 1978. He took two quick wickets and finished with 4 victims for 75 runs. His contribution with the bat was just as significant in the next match at Port of Spain. There was little between the teams on first innings, but a hard-struck 46 in the second by Phillip, the last man out, turned the contest in favour of the West Indies.

In spite of suffering from many dropped catches Phillip and Clarke provided an incisive initial thrust in India in 1978/79. Norbert's best match was at Calcutta. He took 4 wickets for 64 runs, which would have had more effect if Sunil Gavaskar had not hit the first of his two hundreds in the match, and scored 47 to put the tourists ahead after Venkataraghavan had spun through the middle-order. After this tour, however, the promising but hitherto untested Malcolm Marshall was chosen for the one fast bowling place when the World Series Cricketers returned to conventional competition.

The Combined Islands, competing then as a joint team, were by now a good match for Barbados and Guyana even at full strength, and usually more than a match for Jamaica and Trinidad & Tobago. Their success realised a prophecy voiced by Frank Worrell several years previously. He had said that the nucleus of future West Indian teams would be provided by the Leeward and Windward Islands. Unfortunately he did not live long enough to see that, given their chance at last, the islands have more than repaid that confidence.

The splitting of the successful Combined Islands into the Leeward Islands and the Windward Islands for the Shell Shield competition in 1981/82 was expected to favour the former. The Leewards were endowed richly with star cricketers. Even so the under-estimated Windwards produced such a competent team performance that they finished second in the tournament behind the powerful Barbadians. Each side won thrice and drew once, but Barbados picked up more bonus points.

Indeed, the Windward Islands inflicted the only defeat sustained by the ultimate champions. Lockhart Sebastien, Wilfred Slack and Norbert Phillip each made sixties in a fight back from a first innings deficit to win by 4 wickets at Kensington. They repeated the result by the same margin the next year, in which they were again runners-up (this time to Guyana). Nevertheless the victory by a single run over the Leeward Islands must have brought greater satisfaction, because their neighbours to the north had handed them the defeat which had deprived them of the title in 1981/82.

Phillip had considerable influence on his side's fortune. In the first year in which they participated as a separate entity he took 21 wickets in the Shell Shield to finish second to only Joel Garner in the averages. He took 7 wickets for 33 runs in the defeat of the Leeward Islands at Roseau, and returned a further 6 wickets for 41 runs in the sweeping victory over Jamaica. As if to confirm his sustained international potential Norbert had another five wickets in an innings against the touring Indians.

Wilfred Slack, though born at Troumaca in St Vincent, has built his first-class career substantially in England. The left-hander's flood of runs in club cricket for High Wycombe, the town with the highest concentration of Vincentians, brought him to the attention of Middlesex. The county was unusually strong in batting at the time so that first-class opportunities were initially few and far between. His stoical competence against pace won him preference as opening batsman on Mike Brearley's retirement.

In July 1981 he and Graham Barlow put on an undefeated 367 for the first-wicket against Kent at Lord's, a county record, and in the next championship match on the same ground Slack plundered 248 not out from the Worcestershire bowling. The dependable Vincentian is considered in some quarters to lack the necessary flair and imagination to achieve the selection for England which he deserves. Yet in the humiliations inflicted on them in 1984 his courage and consistency would have served England better than any amount of flair.

At home Wilfred plays primarily in the middle-order. It is unfortunate that he could have not returned earlier to Caribbean competition. He would have challenged strongly for international honours, perhaps to the exclusion of either Basil Williams or Alvin Greenidge during the schism. Slack is a useful allround cricketer who has many of the right attributes and has been generally at the right place but usually at the wrong time to take full advantage.

Neil Williams from Hope Well in St Vincent also has made his professional career with Middlesex. Experienced observers of the English game consider that he could be a better international cricketer than county colleague Norman Cowans. He was on the fringe of being drafted into the England team when it was beset by injury in New Zealand a couple of years ago. Neil's prospects have been hampered by the strength of fast bowling at Middlesex and by a lack of consistent selection that would have been possible at a county less well endowed.

Middlesex have been unusually rich in bowling resources. In order to play two match-winning spinners the side has room for only one other quick bowler to supplement Cowans and Wayne Daniel. On several important occasions Williams has been stood down in favour of Simon Hughes, in contrast to the single-minded faith and recognition by which Eldine Baptiste has been noted and developed by the West Indies' selectors. Many consider the Vincentian to have the better potential. To his disadvantage he has been considered to be an England rather that West Indies prospect.

Winston Davis, another Vincentian, forced his way into the exceptionally strong regional fast bowling battery by taking a record number of 33 wickets in the Shell Shield competition in 1983. He returned five wickets in an innings against Guyana, Jamaica and the Leeward Islands. When the last-named seemed to be home and dry at 185-6 in pursuit of 204 runs to win Winston hustled out the tail to finish with 4 wickets for 57 runs and snatch the decision by a single.

Davis established his international credentials by taking another five wickets in an innings against the Indians at St George's in Grenada, and made his debut for the West Indies at St John's in the Fifth Test Match. He took a couple of wickets in each innings which ensured his selection for the Prudential Cup competition in England later that summer. Perhaps surprisingly in view of his modest batting record Winston was sent in as nightwatchman after Haynes and Greenidge had scored 296 for the first wicket. This time he did little, but a precedent had been set.

The Vincentian made a record-breaking initial appearance in the competition against Australia at Leeds. The West Indians batted patchily to reach 252-9 on an uneven pitch affected by the wet weather which caused the innings to overlap into Sunday. Although opening batsman Wood retired after being hit on the side of the head by a delivery from Holding, the Australians, advanced tentatively to 114-2. The West Indians, who had lost the preceding fixture against India, seemed to be on their way out of the competition.

Australia were skittled out for 151. Davis finished with 7 wickets for 51 runs. It is the best innings analysis in the competition. His last six wickets cost only 14 runs. All bar the last fell to catches. The West Indian fast bowlers discovered that, not for the last time, the Australian batsmen could be blasted into submission. Winston could not repeat the performance in the remaining matches and lost his place in the team before the disappointing Final at Lord's, but he had demonstrated that on his day he could be almost unplayable at even the highest level.

Davis, who had been omitted from the original touring party, was called into the Fourth Test Match at Manchester in 1984 following injuries to Malcolm Marshall and Milton Small. He came to the crease late on the first day with Gordon Greenidge in full command and the score at 267-4, and stayed there as nightwatchman until the next rain-seaped afternoon. They put on 170 runs before Winston was bowled for 77. John Thicknesse wrote in *Wisden Cricket Monthly*:

'Botham tried to dislodge nightwatchman Davis with bouncers round the wicket. Davis, built like an elongated stick of rhubarb, played them as though he had one in his hand, hooking, pulling, and once helping one over the slips, with intent, off the middle of the bat. Even Greenidge was over-shadowed for a time'.

The Vincentian subjected the England batsmen to a torrid ordeal of fast bowling off a short run. One delivery cracked Fowler on the back of his helmet and another broke Paul Terry's arm and ended his international career, temporarily at least. Christopher Martin Jenkins of the *Cricketer International* magazine wrote:

'It was Davis whose fire and pace caught the eye and unsettled the batsmen, but Baptiste whose accuracy took most of the wickets .... Terry took his eyes off a ball which bounced less than he expected and was hit on the left forearm. The result was a clean break'.

Wicketkeeper Ignatius Cadette of St Lucia might well have played for the West Indies if he had been a more prolific batsman. He seems to have been always the one left behind. Cadette was considered to be the next in line to the two Murrays, but was passed over in favour of near veteran Milton Pydanna for the tour to Pakistan in 1980/81. By the time that the St Lucian was back into consideration, Dujon, a higher run-scorer, had moved ahead of him. Since then the selectors have preferred another batsman/wicketkeeper, Thelston Payne, to a specialist, even as deputy.

In spite of the great progress of recent years the Windward Islands have still a long way to go to catch up with the rest of the region in amenities and prestige. In a world which values runs more than wickets no Dominican, Vincentian, Grenadian or St Lucian can compare with the fame of Richards and Richardson from the Leewards, and the lack of a Test Match venue cannot be compensated by the granting of token one-day limited-over matches against touring teams. Playing conditions are comparatively primitive, especially in St Vincent from which the principal contemporary cricketers come.

Winston Davis, Wilfred Slack, Neil Williams and to some extent Norbert Phillip have depended on their service in the English county championship for their day-in and day-out playing experience. Nevertheless coaching schemes involving distinguished former players including Gary Sobers and Wesley Hall have done much to encourage development at the roots of the community. It is not enough — nothing is ever enough — but it is a start upon which the Windward Islanders have capitalised.

Mike Gatting, the England batsman, noted the enthusiasm to overcome disadvantage during his tour with the England Young Cricketers in 1976. He wrote in the programme for the Agatha Christie under-19 Test Series 1982:

'All West Indians are fanatical about cricket, and whilst we were in Dominica a man walked 10 miles to reach us during a rest day. We had an impromptu game of cricket on the beach with him — not an amazing story until you know he walked the 10 miles on crutches as he had only one leg'.

Much has happened since Lord Hawke's band of English amateurs rolled over the island cricketers: much of it has happened in the last decade. In early 1984 Lance John, the Vincentian opening batsman, scored over two hundred runs in his two combined innings against the Australians. He proved to be as difficult to get out as his name-sake almost a century ago, but his persistence at the crease was more legitimate. This echo from the past was also a pointer to the future.

Sixteen

Viv Richards and the
Leeward Islands

Viv Richards is the personification of Antigua to the outside world, and to many people inside the island itself. Several sportsmen have become identified with their country to the exclusion of their contemporaries, but none so transcended all other spheres of life. The Leeward Islands, the last part of the region to be developed to international standard, experienced a rapid rise in performance and reputation co-incident with the career of Richards. The Recreation Ground at St John's is the most recent in the Caribbean to achieve Test Match status.

There is no doubting the loyalty which Antiguans feel for their folk-hero. During intervals or periods of dull play, outside journalists goad their Antiguan colleagues by comparing Richards unfavourably to Gordon Greenidge, Lawrence Rowe or even George Headley. The joke is rarely appreciated. No Leeward Islander played for the West Indies before 1973, and now Antigua, alone, holds its own with Barbados and Guyana in the number of its representatives in the regional team. The island's standing in the world generally has risen with its exploits on the cricket field.

Pelham Warner considered Antigua's wicket to have been 'one of the best we played on in the West Indies' when he visited the islands with Lord Hawke's side, and the local bowlers had the visitors in early trouble. Unfortunately the exceptionally weak home batting, sound in defence but lacking in strokes, could not reach a hundred in either innings. It was here that an exceptionally deaf batsman was given out stumped, but the umpire summoned him back to the crease because he had called 'over' before giving the decision. The batsman was found weeping in the pavilion and was so unnerved by the experience that on the resumption of his innings he ran out two of his colleagues.

St Kitts were overwhelmed even more decisively. One home batsman, not named by Warner but understood from the score-card to have been Donowa, antagonised the bowlers by looking round at the field after each delivery as if convinced that their positions were being altered constantly. After a contretemps with the bowler over the issue he rushed out of his ground and was stumped. Then, apart from the institution of the Hesketh Bell Trophy just before the outbreak of the First World War, the Leeward Islands were effectively ignored for another half a century.

Bermuda, even further to the north, has not been considered usually to be within the Caribbean region. Even so opening batsman Alma Hunte came close to selection for the West Indies team which went to England in 1933. The island reached the semi-final of the inaugural International Cricket Conference Trophy in 1979 and progressed to the final three years later. The batting of Gladstone Brown, Winston Reid and Colin Blades was consistent, but the bowling lacked penetration.

After the Second World War the Leeward Islanders fared well against first-class opposition when they were given the chance. Sydney Walling of Antigua hit a century for the combined Wind-wards/Leewards against British Guiana at Georgetown in 1948 and in the next decade opening batsman Oscar Williams made a hundred against Jamaica. Although the lack of a stable first-wicket partnership was then the chief weakness in the West Indies team, he was not given a representative chance. Nevertheless the islands generally were seemingly bursting with talent in the 1950s.

Hubert Anthonyson was the best of several fine fast bowlers at the time. In this department, too, the region was below standard. Yet in spite of the toll of runs exacted by the Australians, in particular, against the depleted pace attack, he was not included. Malcolm Richards, the famous father of an even more famous son, Winston Soanes and Mel Roach were other fast bowlers of that era, and Eustace Matthew, a spinner, shattered the visiting Pakistanis by taking 7 wickets for 89 runs in 1958. Even so the Leeward Islands did not come into consideration from the fringe of the Caribbean until the last fifteen years, even after Findlay and Grayson Shillingford of the Windward Islands had made their mark in the late 1960s.

Then Antigua exploded onto the centre of the international sporting stage. Anderson Montgomery Everton Roberts, born at Urling Village on 29 January 1951, should take the pride of place. Unlike his compatriot, Viv Richards, who grew up within a cricket environment, the future fast bowler did not play his first game until he had left school at 16, and his parents were not keen for him to pursue the sport as a career. The Antigua Volunteers Cricket Committee sponsored him and Richards for coaching to Alf Gover's indoor school in London and Hampshire invited him for a trial. He was retained as the county's one permitted overseas player only on balance over New

Zealand spinner David O'Sullivan.

Roberts took 4 wickets for 75 runs for the Leeward Islands against the touring Englishmen in 1973/74. When he returned 5 wickets for 62 runs against Trinidad & Tobago in the Shell Shield competition the Antiguan was chosen to replace Keith Boyce when the latter had to drop out of the Third Test Match at Kensington. In the English domestic season of 1974 he unleashed the whirlwind which established his reputation and, though it was not necessarily appreciated at the time, initiated a new era of fast bowling. Wisden stated that Andy's bowling 'stirs the blood'.

He made history on the following tour to India and Pakistan when the West Indians moved decisively out of the lethargy of recent rubbers. The region was delighted that after six years of gentle pace a bowler of genuine speed and hostility had been found to fill the position vacated by Wesley Hall and Charlie Griffith. His 5 wickets for 30 runs at Calcutta, 7 wickets for 64 runs and 5 wickets for 57 runs at Madras, and 5 wickets for 66 runs at Lahore confirmed him as the principal challenger to the supremacy then enjoyed by the Australian fast bowlers Dennis Lillee, Jeff Thomson and Jeff Hammond.

Roberts' pace unsettled especially Mansur Ali Khan, the former Nawab of Pataudi, whose return to the Indian side as captain coincided with the hosts levelling the series from 2-0 down. He was just as successful against the seasoned middle-order as against the brittle first-wicket batting. If he had been joined by a bowler of similar pace the Indians, surely, would have fared as disastrously as they had against Gilchrist and Hall and would do so later against Marshall and Holding. He received some of the support he needed on the following tour to Australia.

The Antiguan beat the Australians at their own game by taking 7 wickets for 54 runs at Perth, where he was partnered in triumph by the youthful Michael Holding. He had bowled well in dismissing both openers on the first morning, but the main onslaught came in the second innings. Andy's victims, the first seven in the batting order, included both Alan Turner and Ian Redpath out without scoring. The injury to Holding deprived him of similar support throughout the rest of the rubber when the Australian batsmen were very much on top.

Injury restricted him to only a minor role in the home victory over the Indians, but Roberts returned quickly to the fore on the tour to England in 1976. The attack of Roberts, Holding and Holder unsettled the young M.C.C. batsmen so much in the early season game at Lord's that the shadow hung over them for the remainder of the summer. On the same ground he took five wickets in each innings of the drawn Second Test Match, the only time in the series that the West

Indians' batting broke down, and they trailed by 68 runs on the first innings.

Character differentiates the great from the good cricketer. Andy showed character in abundance in the Third Test Match at Manchester. In the second innings he twice took two wickets with consecutive deliveries but was denied the hat-trick. On the second occasion, in which a drinks interval intervened, Gordon Greenidge dropped what seemed to be a simple chance from Mike Selvey. Roberts looked to the sky in anguish, thought to himself, turned, walked back and bowled again.

The same coolness and even temperament stood him in good stead in probably the most memorable moment of his batting life. The previous year Roberts, specialist bowler and the last man in, came to the crease in the Prudential Cup preliminary round match against Pakistan at Birmingham with his team still 63 runs behind and defeat an apparent formality. The manner in which he and Deryck Murray eked out those runs and stole victory by one wicket in the last possible over has passed into cricket legend. The two West Indians showed rare judgement while the panicky Pakistanis were lulled into indiscretion.

Andy is one of the few cricketers to be remembered solely for his cricket. There have been no controversies on the field of play, and no rumours of violent temper, bad faith or boisterousness away from the pitch. Roberts has been unusually laconic in a team and a sport for extroverts. He has shown dedication and commitment, zipping in with the vitality of youth or taking the old ball long after the shine has departed and keeping the batsmen in check with patience and persistence. Even when bowling less well than usual he has been hardly ever mastered.

His bowling had been too much for the weakened Australians in the two matches before the schism in 1978, and five years later the Antiguan set up the victory over the Indians. There was only three runs between the teams on the first innings of the First Test Match at Sabina Park. The tourists seemed to have achieved at least a draw when rain intervened. In the first over after the resumption Roberts dismissed Kirmani, Sandhu and Venkataraghavan to finish with 5 wickets for 39 runs and save enough time for the West Indies to win by 4 wickets.

In his later years he added two dimensions to his art through experience. Andy was adept at breaking through the early batting and exposing the middle-order to his more forceful colleagues, and he could come back from a rest in the outfield to break a persistent partnership and turn the game again in his side's favour. His international career came to an end only when the similarly skilfull

Holding cut down his own run and filled the same role. Nevertheless he was still sufficiently effective for the omission to be disputed.

The legacy of Andy Roberts is apparent at two levels. He introduced in 1974 an era of outstanding West Indian fast bowling which has not ended yet, and through its success has induced all other countries to trust their fortune to speed. Roberts was also the first Antiguan fast bowler to achieve international acclaim. Through his inspiration George Ferris, who broke Roland Butcher's jaw in a match in England, and medium-fast Eldine Baptiste are well on the way to emulating that achievement. Roberts, Richards and world light-middleweight boxing champion Maurice Hope brought national pride and confidence to Antigua.

Isaac Vivian Alexander Richards, born on 7 March 1952, kept pace with his compatriot's early achievements. He is the son of Antigua's leading fast bowler of the preceding generation, Malcolm Richards, and excelled at both cricket and soccer. Three years after the celebrated incident in 1969 when partisan spectators forced officials to change an umpiring decision which had been given against him, he was chosen for the Combined Islands and took a half-century from the New Zealanders.

In early 1973 he accompanied Andy Roberts on public subscription to Alf Gover's cricket school in London and the following season began to play for Somerset in the English county championship. He was one of the new wave of talent, which included also Ian Botham, encouraged by then county captain Brian Close, that developed the West Country side from traditional wooden-spoonists to one of the powers in the country. Within a couple of seasons he was the only rival to namesake Barry Richards, the South African, as the best batsman in the world.

Richards was the surprise choice for the tour to India and Pakistan in 1974/75. He took the place that many expected should have gone to Rohan Kanhai, but once the selectors had decided to appoint a younger captain they were right to gamble on youth. Although he was still erratic at this stage in his career, Viv gave a foretaste of what was to come by scoring a match-winning 191 not out in the Second Test Match at New Delhi. His success was sufficient to force the incomparable but injury-prone Lawrence Rowe out of the No 3 position.

The Antiguan did not score as many runs as had been expected in the first Prudential Cup competition in 1975. Yet his electrifying fielding close to the wicket caught the eye and shattered the opposition. It was nowhere more clear than in the Final against Australia at Lord's. Richards, sharp at short-leg, or anywhere, ran out three batsmen while the Australians still had the chance of getting on top. At that stage, in which they had played the bowling with surprisingly little difficulty, it seemed to be the only way in which they could be dismissed.

As with so many of his colleagues Viv found the following tour to Australia to be testing. In spite of making a majestic 175 against Western Australia he failed almost totally in the first four Test Matches and might have been passed over completely if other batsmen had been more successful. Then going in first he scored a hundred in each innings against Tasmania at Hobart. Clive Lloyd tried him in the same position for the last two Test matches. He responded by hitting 30 and 101 at Adelaide and 50 and 98 at Melbourne, innings which Wisden described as being 'brilliant', 'splendid' and 'marvellous'.

Richards demonstrated his renewed confidence against the touring Indians. He took 142 in the innings victory at Kensington, 130 in the draw and 177 in the defeat in two consecutive matches at Queen's Park, and was satisfied with a mere 64 at Sabina Park. In the Trinidad Tests his contributions exceeded the combined scores of the other ten batsmen. That season, apart from Lloyd's own century in Barbados, no other West Indian batsman reached three figures against the formidable spin quartet.

Although he missed one match through injury Richards plundered an awe-inspiring 829 runs from England in the exceptionally hot summer of 1976. He set the pattern by scoring 232 in the First Test Match at Nottingham, a pitch traditionally suited to high scoring on which Frank Worrell had played his memorable innings in 1950 and 1957 and Basil Butcher had ground out a double-century in 1966. Kallicharran shared with him a triple-hundred stand for the third wicket. Viv took a single century at Manchester and was limited to a mere 66 at Leeds.

In the Fifth Test Match at The Oval he took England apart in substantial partnerships with Fredericks, Rowe and Lloyd. This 'majestic exhibition' ended in sight of the record individual Test Match score. Immediately after hitting one towering six from Tony Greig he tried to repeat the stroke but, perhaps tired by his exertions, got only the faintest of touches and edged it into his stumps. Only Sobers and Rowe have bettered his score of 291. His dismissal shortly after the adjournment was missed by those returning late from lunch.

Wisden was enthusiastic in praise of Richard's performance that summer: 'Richards was exceptionally brilliant and must be ranked among the finest West Indian batsmen of all time, worthy to be coupled with the great George Headley of pre-war fame, even if

perhaps he did not have to deal with the same class of bowling . . . .
Mere figures cannot convey his perfect style and stroke play. His cover
driving was superb and with his feet always in the right position the
way he flicked the ball on his leg stump to square leg had to be seen to
be believed'.

Viv excelled at Lord's. He scored centuries there for the West Indies
in Test Match and the Prudential Cup, and for Somerset in the Gillette
Cup Final. The game's international headquarters was the big place
for the big occasion. His undefeated 138 against England in the
Prudential Cup Final on 23 June 1979 was overshadowed only by the
whirlwind, yet controlled, hitting of Collis King with whom he joined
in a match-winning and impressive stand for the fifth wicket.

A year later the Antiguan scored 145 for the West Indies against
England on the same ground. His powerful allround stroke-play
eclipsed that of even Desmond Haynes who made a higher score. Rain
ruined the match with the tourists very much in command. Late on the
second evening Richards launched a vigorous attack on left-armer
Derek Underwood in gathering gloom. Immediately the umpires
called the players off . . . presumably because the fieldsmen were in
danger of injury! There was no similar respite when he hammered fast
bowler Bob Willis in the rain at Manchester one match later.

To that point in his career Viv had not fared so consistently well in
the Caribbean. His failure to score in the first innings of the Third
Test Match against England at Kensington in 1981 seemed to put his
place in jeopardy: there was local speculation that Emerson Trotman
should have been called up. At his second attempt Richards was
faultless in scoring 182 not out. The demoralised visitors went down to
defeat by 298 runs. The scene could not have been set more
appropriately for his coronation at the Recreation Ground, St John's
in the next Test Match.

The Antiguan ground had been added to the international venues in
recognition of the advance of the Leeward Islands generally and the
impact of Richards and Roberts in particular. King Richards did not
miss his cue. The *Pelham Cricket Year* edited by David Lemmon
commented:

'Then came Richards. That the man would hit a Test century on
his own ground to mark its use as an international arena for the
first time was one of cricket's more predictable happenings. He
began in dominant mood, rested a while, then flourished again
before easing off to his hundred. It was his first week of married
life, his home ground and his fourteenth Test hundred'.

The Australians, too, had experienced the tough side of his bat. Viv
averaged almost a hundred runs per innings in the successful three-

match rubber in 1979/80, the first series won by the West Indies in that country. He commenced by hitting 140 at Brisbane, followed by 96 at Melbourne and concluded by scoring 76 and 74 at Adelaide. Many of those who have followed the team most closely in recent years are convinced that it reached its peak performance in this season.

The Antiguan has achieved so much that in this age of concentrated competition he may have lost a little of his edge. Recently he has contented himself with one century per series. At Bourda in 1983 he finished the first day against India on 97 not out. He had to wait through the next day, Good Friday, the rained off Saturday and the first session on Sunday before he could complete the hundred. On balance he could not have been entirely satisfied with the outcome of his various struggles against the Indians that year.

Twelve months later the Australians were in the Caribbean. By his own high standards Richards began modestly. Yet he was back to his brilliant best for the Fourth Test Match at the Recreation Ground. The bowlers held the upper hand until he joined young Richie Richardson. The two Antiguans laid about them with a bushel of boundaries in their third-wicket partnership of 308 runs. Viv seemed to be set for another double-century but was caught at the wicket off a gloved hook with his score on 178. The West Indies won here by an innings and 36 runs.

Richards' attitude has been questioned by some. He has been described as arrogant and casual. Perhaps he has been just bored. Undoubtedly he does lack the constant run-acquisitiveness of Don Bradman, to whom he has been compared so often, but that great Australian did not have to play up to three Test Match rubbers and seemingly innumerable limited-overs series each year. It would be difficult for any batsman to be 'fired' for each and every innings. Consequently he has saved his best for the big occasions and increasingly, to the chagrin of traditionalists, the big occasions have occurred in one-day competition.

There was some doubt about Richards taking over the captaincy from Lloyd. As vice-captain for five years he had led well enough the few times that opportunity had come his way. Nevertheless the seemingly petulant attitude displayed at a bad umpiring decision, though he did win an apology at Lord's in 1984, did not fit easily the office of a diplomat. He gave little advance evidence that he had the breadth of vision to unite the team and their aspirations. That, too, could have been said about all his predecessors before their appointment.

Richards began quietly in Australia and was caught for no score by wicketkeeper Rixon at Adelaide. That failure spurred him to one of his greatest achievements. Viv hit 208 at Melbourne, the highest individual score by a West Indian in that country. Surprisingly in view of his many memorable performances it was only his third Test Match double-century. He and Clive Lloyd, alone, batted with any confidence on Sydney's treacherous wicket.

The Antiguan assumed the reins of captaincy for the home series against New Zealand which he commenced by scoring a half-century in each innings at Queen's Park. His 105 at Kensington, where the rain-affected pitch did not favour batting, set up victory in the match and in the rubber. By winning the first series in which he was captain Richards achieved a landmark which, in spite of all his honours, had eluded Lloyd, victory over New Zealand.

Elquemedo Willett, a slow left-arm bowler from Nevis, preceded Roberts and Richards as the first regional representative from the Leeward Islands. He made his debut against Australia at Kensington in 1973. In spite of some impressive performances outside Test Matches he was unfortunate to bowl at a time when there was little consistency in the choice of spinners. Offspinner Derek Parry, also from Nevis, was treated similarly at the end of the decade. Perhaps they were unlucky in their time or they did not have that extra quality which lifts a cricketer to regular world-class.

Jim Allen of Montserrat, a middle-order batsman, was pressing closely for representative honours at the time of the World Series Cricket schism. When harmony was restored he remained a candidate for selection for several seasons without securing his claim. Three Kittitians — allrounder Victor Eddy, offspinner Noel Guishard and opening batsman Luther Kelly — have been discussed frequently as having regional potential but that promise has not been translated into reality. Antiguan Ralston Otto achieved the highest aggregate recorded in a single Shell Shield season when the established batsmen, and bowlers, were away in India and Australia in 1984.

Richard Benjamin Richardson, born in Five Islands village on 12 January 1962, is probably the most exciting batsman to develop in the West Indies exclusively in the 1980s. He comes from a family equally skilled at football and cricket, and was directed to the latter as a career after he visited England with an Antiguan schools team in 1979. He progressed quickly to the West Indies representative youth side the next year and made his first-class debut for the Leeward Islands against Barbados at St Kitts in 1982. His subsequent rise to the top was rapid.

Centuries against both Barbados in Bridgetown and Jamaica in Montserrat, in which he encountered the pace of Wayne Daniel, Malcolm Marshall and Michael Holding, convinced the selectors that he should be taken to India at the end of 1983. There was a parallel with the similar faith placed in Viv Richards nine years earlier. This time however, the move seemed to have been premature. Richardson, who had failed to score in his first first-class innings, was dismissed again without scoring in his first tour innings against the President's XI at Nagpur and on his international debut in the Fourth Test Match at Bombay.

The Antiguan and Gus Logie, a young batsman of similar promise and vulnerability, were in direct competition for the same place with the Trinidadian having the advantage in experience. Richie was considered fortunate to be retained after making yet another duck for the Leeward Islands against the Australians in 1984. He seized the opportunity of Logie's absence to come good by scoring 131 not out in the Third Test Match at Kensington, in which he and Desmond Haynes put on 155 runs for the second wicket.

Then Richardson went one better by joining Richards in a record 308 runs stand for the third wicket in the following Test Match at the Recreation Ground. The youngster's contribution was 154 before he was out driving. He showed mature caution and concentration, as well as some exciting stroke-play, in both centuries. As if to prove that he had not eradicated indiscretion completely he was caught again at the wicket, hooking before he had scored, in his next innings at Sabina Park.

The Antiguan lost his place, surprisingly at the time, to Larry Gomes at the start of the series in England in 1984 and, in view of the Trinidadian's success, did not win it back that summer. Nevertheless he was brought into the side again in Australia, with his accustomed frailty and brilliance. Richardson was bowled without scoring at Perth, but, enjoying the confidence of the selectors, stroked 138 in the next match at Brisbane. The pattern continued when the New Zealanders came to the Caribbean early in the next year. Richie was dropped early in his innings at Bourda but went on to hit the top-score of 185.

Eldine Ashworth Elderfield Baptiste, born on 12 March 1960, was an unlikely recruit to the regional team. He was 21 years-old on his first-class debut for Kent against Oxford University and made his first appearance in the Shell Shield against the Windward Islands the following year. At the end of 1983 he was a surprise selection for the tour to India, where he was run out cheaply in his first Test Match at Bombay. A competent allround performance for the Leeward Islands against the visiting Australians led to his retention for the West Indies.

Baptiste's role was vital in the 5-0 'whitewash' of England in 1984. As a fourth seam bowler who could bat well enough to support the specialists, he permitted the selection of an extra player and allowed front-line bowlers to rest without surrendering the initiative. The regional selectors had shown great perspicacity in selecting him initially towards the end of a year which he had started in the Kent 2nd XI. His recognition, contrasted with England's continued overlooking of Neil Williams and other youngsters, underlines the difference in approach, and consequent fortune, of the two teams.

One piece of fielding in the Second Test Match at Lord's was unforgettable. Eldine gathered a long shot at fine-leg. The batsman running towards him saw the danger and dived for the crease. Geoff Miller running towards the farther end was less aware. Baptiste's throw took everyone by surprise. It was so much off course for the near wicket that bowler Malcolm Marshall attempted to catch it in mid-flight. Only when the ball plucked the stump cleanly out of the ground with the unsuspecting Miller still clearly short did anyone realise that it had been directed towards the far wicket.

Seventeen

The South African Question

South Africa, even after almost two decades of isolation, will not disappear from the considerations of international sport. Like an unknown planet whose existence can be demonstrated by its effect on the orbits of the other bodies with whom it shares the solar system, that country's presence is made obvious by the manner in which the recognised countries react to it. That presence has come close to destroying the integrity of the West Indies. South African influence is essentially strong because those outside consider it to be strong. Yet there are signs that the presumption may be over-stated and reality could be leading the Springboks adrift.

It is impossible to estimate the potential strength of South African cricket, as a team. They were undoubtedly the most powerful side in the world at the time of their alienation at the end of the 1960s. Present evidence indicates, however, that, starved of international experience for so long, that standard has declined. Links are maintained through individual South Africans pursuing their career overseas, visits by miscellaneous sides, and the importation of coaches from outside. The longer the present pattern remains, the harder it will be to fit in the South Africans at a later date. Yet it is by no means certain that the pattern can continue.

The story goes back a long way. It is impossible to know how the relationship between South Africa and the West Indies would have developed if there had been any tradition of competition before apartheid became such a major issue. Over the years English and Australian cricketers have found personal bonds of friendship with their South African counterparts which have transcended political inclinations. Many otherwise liberal-minded players have participated in that country because they have identified with individual friends rather than with a system. Significantly some of the Englishmen who have resisted the lure of the rand have cited the friendship of a specific West Indian as being the deciding factor. Ian Botham, for example, has been quoted as saying that if he had accepted the South African offer he would not have been able to look Viv Richards in the eye again.

No such ties were established between West Indians and Springboks, even at the time that both were part of the same colonial Commonwealth and Empire. For many decades England, Australia and South Africa, alone, had Test Match status. The West Indies, India and New Zealand were elevated at the end of the 1920s, and for at least another twenty years the newcomers were very much junior members of the world cricket structure.

Before the outbreak of the Second World War the West Indies made three Test Match tours to England and received two. They went also to Australia. There was no similar inter-action with South Africa. The administrative difficulties would have been considerable. Yet they could not have been any greater than those involved in arranging an English tour through the scattered territories of the Caribbean or by the Australians in putting together a detailed tour of that vast country. As the senior country South Africa introduced the negative aspect of politics into sport by not supporting the newcomers.

West Indian cricketers had found their way to South Africa, but not to play cricket. Harold Austin, the father of the game in the region and captain of two of the three pioneer sides to England, missed the first when he was one of several West Indians serving the British Empire in the Boer War of 1899-1902. By 1910 South Africa had been accorded independent Dominion status and for years enjoyed a special relationship with Britain. The veneer of racial values, limited though it was then, was not reciprocated.

Post-independence South African political history has been dominated by the former Boer adversaries and their descendants, even those who have been most loyal to the British ideal. Racial attitudes have been always out of step with those of other countries. England's selectors had to take South African sensitivities into account in deciding whether star batsman K.S. Duleepsinhji should play against them.

The National Party's electoral victory in the late 1940s led directly to the internal adoption of enforced apartheid and externally to the move away from Britain and to the withdrawal from the Commonwealth. By then it was already too late to build bridges, because the West Indies had completed their inaugural representative matches also in India, Pakistan and New Zealand. The framework of contemporary competition had been concluded, and by choice South Africa was on the fringe.

The Springboks occupied the centre of attention in the 1950s and 1960s on the strength of their team. Under the leadership of Pieter van der Merwe and Ali Bacher they humbled both Australia and England. Yet even these achievements were overshadowed by the victories of the West Indies. South Africa became the victim of its own restricted vision. They had ignored the West Indies when the positions had been reversed and could not complain that they had lost their own place in the sun.

The 'white' Commonwealth hesitated still to suspend relations with the republic. The South African Government broke the impasse by bringing politics into the forefront of cricket. At first the England selectors seemed to go some way to meeting their sensitivities. In spite of heading the batting averages against Australia the previous summer Basil d'Oliveira, a coloured South African playing for England, was left out of the original party to tour his homeland in 1968/69. When he was added to the team on Tom Cartwright's withdrawal Prime Minister Vorster declared him to be unwelcome. It is ironic that South Africa's apologists should now accuse the non-white countries of seeking to influence the selection of the England team.

Individual West Indians became involved in the politics of southern Africa by participating in Rhodesia, now Zimbabwe. The colony, though permitting some integrated competition, was racially exclusive socially and was in rebellion to the Crown. No cricketer was above the disdain felt throughout the Caribbean for that territory's political system. Even the incomparable Gary Sobers was taken to task officially for playing there, and he suffered substantial, but thankfully temporary, loss of popular respect.

It was a sign of things to come. Miscellaneous international sides were brought together to fill the need for world-class competition in South Africa and Rhodesia, which for cricket administration had been part of the same entity, and to encourage the rising aspirations of the countries to the immediate north. A combined East Africa team competed in the first Prudential Cup tournament in 1975. At a time of limited opportunities elsewhere the professional cricketer, including West Indians, was tempted to accept the offer of winter employment.

Caribbean governments became increasingly radical in the early 1970s and were less inclined to treat the South African question with indulgence. Jamaica and Guyana were seen to lead the way. The smaller islands, which came to prominence in that decade, shared this attitude. The conservative reaction which stemmed the radical tide by the early 1980s did not lessen significantly the official, and then popular, opposition to any links with South Africa.

The England team which arrived in the region in the early weeks of 1981 had little premonition of the trouble ahead. Problems soon sprouted like shoots in the springtime sun. The tourists were beset by injury almost immediately. Batsman Brian Rose and fast bowler Bob Willis had to return home after the First Test Match in Trinidad. The latter was replaced by Robin Jackman, a competent though hardly spectacular fast-medium bowler, who was married to a South African and had played in that country.

The next Test Match was scheduled for Guyana, perhaps the most uncompromising in its attitude. After much dispute and behind-the-scenes activity the match was cancelled and the teams moved on to Barbados, where the political and social environment was considered to be more accommodating. For days the future of the tour was in the balance. The tourists did not agree to their selection being amended on a matter not related directly to cricketing merit. Eventually Jackman, to whom there was no personal animosity, took the field for England in the Third Test Match at Kensington and the rest of the tour was saved.

Some English writers seemed unable to understand the West Indian point of view or to accept even that world cricket could exist without the participation of their country. Unbalanced reports of unfavourable conditions and attitudes in the region inflamed opinion on both sides of the Atlantic. The *Pelham Cricket Year* commented:

'The fact that several of the West Indian players had played with South Africans, and that the great Gary Sobers, among others, had played in Rhodesia ... did not seem to trouble the authorities who seemed unable to understand the freedom of the individual as practised in England. The ministers were meeting not simply to discuss whether the tour would continue with England playing those men whom they chose to play, but, in effect, to decide if Test cricket was to be continued in the West Indies. This was not the first threat to Test cricket in the Caribbean. The riots which had developed over the years when the home side seemed in danger of defeat on occasions was a factor which did not make the lot of the tourist an easy one, nor was the fact that in Guyana, after dark, and in Jamaica, all day, it was unwise to leave one's hotel alone'.

The same publication was more pertinent in observing:

'The cricket authorities were helped by the good sense of the politicians who allowed the tour to go ahead without provisos. The politicians were motivated in no small measure by their own economic considerations for to deny tourism was to deny an important contributor to the economy of the islands'.

Even so it is hard to imagine that the tourist industry is dependent on the few hundred visiting cricket fans.

The issue loomed even larger a year later. The South Africans had been unable to persuade the Test Match countries to re-admit them to conventional international competition and, perhaps inspired by the example of World Series Cricket, sought to attract the world's leading players to their own alternative representative competition. The move met with much initial success. Some prominent Sri Lankans and one or two leading English players, more from the secondary level, took up the offer.

The administrators acted swiftly to nip the threat in the bud. The Sri Lankans, and the West Indians, were banned from international competition for life, and the Englishmen for three years. Although the latter was comparatively mild, it effectively ended the careers of the majority of those involved. The 'rand rebels' knew well enough that they were acting against the conventional game to which they owed their livelihood. To that degree, the issue of race conditions in South Africa was immaterial. The cricketers were penalised for participating in a pirate competition rather than for playing in South Africa as individuals. All parties seem to have learned lessons from World Series Cricket.

The defection of several well-known West Indians caused the biggest surprise. Alvin Kallicharran had drifted so far away from the mainstream of Caribbean opinion that, following his earlier participation in the Currie Cup, the South African domestic competition, his involvement in the 'rebel' matches was not unexpected. Others were past their best, but there were still sufficient defectors who could have expected further regional honours for the threat to have been realistic. The life ban was essential to discourage the others.

The Springbok initiative failed at this time because, after the initial defections, few, if any, current world-class cricketers joined the circus. Thus far the ban was effective. In spite of the many predictions to the contrary, no Australians joined the 'rebels' at that time. English observers, in particular, had taken for granted a link between the two white powers in the southern hemisphere based on a common colonial and Commonwealth heritage and the fact that Australia was the last country to sever cricket ties with South Africa.

Race had blinded them to reality. The World Series Cricket schism wrested traditional administrative power from England, and from Lord's, in particular. International competition in the new structure revolved around the axis of Australian media sponsorship and West Indian success on the field. The former would not throw away lightly what they had gained either to link themselves with a country still beyond the general pale or for a re-alignment in which the South Africans would be dominant. The scoop of Australians in 1985, some of whom had been left out of the team for the approaching tour to

England, after a surfeit of cricket had dulled public interest, demonstrated, nevertheless, that the danger is ever present.

England's administrators lost further tricks by failing to appreciate how the world had moved on. The first three (Prudential) World Cup competitions were presented in England with the final at Lord's. It was the most appropriate setting, but not the only one. When the host country wanted a bigger share in the revenue, the tournament went overseas. The substantial crowds of the Indian sub-continent are the third fact of contemporary cricket to be taken into the calculation.

The best South African cricketers have voted with their feet against their own country's long-term prospects. While second-line West Indians and Englishmen were attracted to South Africa, Allan Lamb and Chris Smith qualified by residence for England and Kepler Wessels for Australia. The England team of the early 1980s, which included also Phil Edmonds, Ian Greig and Derek Pringle, owed much to the African continent.

Even the most successful codes of instant cricket have failed to make a long-term impression. Although World Series Cricket attracted much larger crowds than comparable conventional matches and the players' careers hardly suffered, performances in that artificial environment are not remembered as well as a century or a good bowling return in a Test Match, however devalued. The entrepreneurs of the many limited-overs festivals appreciate that the strategical purpose of the enterprise has been to gain a grip on the conventional game. To that extent the South African venture had only passing interest.

Lawrence Rowe, captain of the West Indian rebels, was a popular hero in his homeland. Few batsmen have made such a commanding initial impact. He made his first-class debut for Jamaica against the Windward Islands in 1969 and three years later hit a record 214 and 100 not out in his first Test Match against New Zealand at Sabina Park. Rowe's 302 against England at Kensington in 1974 is the second highest score ever achieved for the West Indies: it is bettered only by Gary Sobers' world record 365 not out against Pakistan at Kingston.

Thereafter, however, his career, and many shrewd judges consider him to have been a better batsman and stroke-player than either Gordon Greenidge or Viv Richards, was beset by illness, injury and the difficulties of temperament. His century on a turning pitch at Queen's Park in 1974 rates as highly as many record-breaking innings. Rowe's best performances were attained as an opening batsman, but the effective partnership of Fredericks and Greenidge forced him into the middle-order. While on form he was a batsman of rare quality, those occasions became fewer and far between.

At home the Jamaican stood behind only George Headley in popular acclaim, and even after his 'defection' to South Africa many remained loyal to him rather than to conventional opinion. Nevertheless in spite of his achievements, which are many, Rowe is the 'lost genius' of contemporary Caribbean cricket. Idolised in his own country he has not always been given overseas the credit which his undoubted talents have deserved. Given the circumstances Lawrence was the jewel in the pirates' crown.

Opening batsmen Richard Austin and Alvin Greenidge, and Everton Mattis, Emerson Trotman and Collis King in the middle-order had been passed by in conventional competition. Austin, a Jamaican, made his Test Match debut against Australia immediately prior to the schism in 1978. He was one of the few World Series Cricketers that did not come back into regional contention. Ironically Greenidge, the third Barbadian of that name to open for the West Indies in the 1970s, received his chance when Austin withdrew but was omitted later in favour of Desmond Haynes when harmony was restored.

Mattis, a Jamaican, was not without expectation of recall to the regional side. Just two years previously he had played for the West Indies against England. He, Trotman of Barbados, Kallicharran, Collis King the Barbadian six-hitter and allrounder, and, more surprisingly, Faoud Bacchus, recent captain of the West Indies 'B' side in Zimbabwe, seemed to have given up hope that they could find a permanent place in the existing middle-order dominated by Viv Richards, Clive Lloyd. Larry Gomes and wicketkeeper-batsman Jeffrey Dujon. Yet if any of these had failed the 'rebels' would have been among the obvious candidates to fill the vacancy.

Fast bowlers Sylvester Clarke, Colin Croft, Ezra Moseley, Hartley Alleyne and Franklyn Stephenson would have been automatic Test Match selections anywhere other than in the pace-rich West Indies. Clarke and Croft, then at their prime, were the outstanding loss to the official regional team. Batsmen who wilted under the attack of Michael Holding, Malcolm Marshall and Joel Garner were more fortunate than they realised, in that Clarke and Croft, by their own choice, were not added to their troubles.

Allrounder Stephenson had been expected to play a prominent part in the rebuilding of the mid-1980s. He had performed well for Barbados, Gloucestershire and Tasmania. David Murray was another surprising recruit to the rebels. The Barbadian had understudied name-sake Deryck Murray since the tour to England in 1973 and, still only just over 30 years old, could have looked forward to several more years as an international wicketkeeper. However veteran Bernard

Julien and offspinner Derek Parry were genuinely at the end of their careers.

The problem will not go away just because the South Africans have been rebuffed. Those West Indians staying with the conventional team will be replaced in time by a new generation. Then they might be attracted by a final fling. It remains to be seen whether the prestige of their name will weigh more heavily in the balance than the excitement generated by their successors. The failure to secure the services of Viv Richards, and more specifically Malcolm Marshall and/or Desmond Haynes, whose defection had been announced in some newspapers, rang the knell for Rowe's rebels.

The tide of cricket's currents is not static. The concept of nation teams will not endure for ever, and probably not beyond the next ten years. The pattern of overseas tours has changed appreciably. The traditional itinerary of a sequence of first-class games leading up to, and interspersed with, Test Matches has been replaced by a shorter schedule containing a high proportion of one-day engagements. Teams are more compact and their tours encompass a series of countries in the course of a season. Cricket programmes depend considerably on air travel. It is likely that the pattern of soccer may be repeated, in which a side flies in for one international match and then out again.

The traditional practice of the West Indies playing five Test Matches in a series against one opponent is already a thing of the past. Triangular tournaments have been favoured in Australia since the turn of the decade. It may be the blue-print for the future. Alternatively, the very teams Australia, England, India, Pakistan and New Zealand could cease to exist. Future cricket matches will be contested at the highest level either by regional composites or by smaller units taken out of those national teams.

Sri Lanka's admission to Test Match status points towards the latter pattern. The island cannot match its competitors in social, playing or financial amenities. It sustains a home Test Match only if it is part of a more extended itinerary. The level of viable competition for a country of that size could apply similarly to Barbados, Jamaica, Guyana and Trinidad & Tobago. The potential for the undertaking and receiving of tours by individual territories lies only just below the recognition of regional reality.

Conversely, the trend could be towards more extensive units. At first club games and inter-territorial matches provided the highest level of competition, until they were superseded by Test Matches between countries. A progression towards a regional dimension may seem to be logical, especially if one team continued to dominate the others. Australia and New Zealand would comprise one region, India, Pakistan, Sir Lanka and Bangladesh another, and England and the West Indies would remain as they are.

Although the latter scenario is the less likely, it affords the best opportunity for South Africa to return to the conventional fold. The continental option could be that country's only chance, whether or not the rest of the world adopted a regional structure. South Africa, Zimbabwe (which is close to Test Match recognition on its own account) and the other countries of Central and East Africa would form the regional unit. Cricketers within that compass, including South Africans of all ethnic variations, would compete for selection on merit. The inevitable obstacles, though considerable, are no more impenetrable than some of the hurdles which the progress of the game has encountered elsewhere.

The All India XI of the 1930s contained Hindus, Muslims, Sikhs, Parsees and Christians in comparative harmony at a time when communal and social disturbances were prevalent in the sub-continent. There were clashes of personal temperament, but rarely based directly on race or religion. The West Indies is a region comprised of territories with different geographical, social and cultural backgrounds.

The outstanding objection is that any selection on merit would restrict the initial choice to white South Africans, because they, alone, have the facilities and the experience. It is likely but not certain. The Springboks have been out of touch for a long time, and the Zimbabweans, at least, would challenge that presumption. Even if true in the short term the situation would not endure for long. Whatever its shortcomings the concept of an integrated African team would be no further away than it is today after years of contending bans and appeasement.

Test Match status would be invested in the African regional authority, who would have the responsibility to negotiate tours and to invest resources as and where they were needed most. As a result the standard of facilities and coaching would be raised especially in those sectors which are presently deprived. Although opposition can be expected from the South African politicians and administrators, they hold few of the important cards.

Because the opportunity to play in Test Matches is the most impelling incentive for all cricketers, white South Africans, even if they were discouraged from participating at home, would need to travel only to nearby Zimbabwe to pursue their career. The journey is much shorter than that to Australia or England today. The introduction of regulations to limit international qualification to the region in which they had learned their cricket should ensure that African Test

Match cricketers remained in the continent, and, thus, by example raised the standards of those who played with them.

Although South African domestic competition would be stronger initially than the regional entity, it would not lead anywhere. In contrast Test Matches played in the continent would provide the chance to play against the highest possible competition, including the West Indians. The imbalance, therefore, would not last too long. The cream of the cricketers should be drawn to the higher standard. It is not necessarily that easy. There would be political problems but at least cricket would attempt its own initiative.

Such speculation is important to understanding the troubles which will affect West Indian cricket in the medium term. Success has obscured the differences which exist in any team. The West Indies have not known failure in the modern age since World Series Cricket and the South African connection intensified issues. Cricket is no longer the same game that it was when Clive Lloyd took over the reins of leadership for the tour to India and Pakistan in 1974/75. It is difficult to estimate the direction or the extent of any reaction to failure.

Political events within the region itself cast their shadow over sport. In this time the territories of the Caribbean have come more within the American sphere of influence. In the 1970s they were fragmented and fragmenting. It was conceivable too, that West Indian cricket would be levered apart by the same forces. Now at least political tensions seem to be pulling in the same, rather than contradictory, directions. It may not be enough, and only a surface impression, but it is something.

The effect on world cricket could be similarly drastic if the West Indies keep winning. There must be a limit to the number of times that England and Australia can be beaten and keep on being beaten. Somewhere along the line the rules would be amended. Opponents have mooted already the possibility of restricting the run-up of the fast bowlers, the number of short-pitched deliveries and the quota of overs bowled in a day. The next changes could be more structural. If the West Indies continued to dominate conventional competition, experimentation would be made in other types of tournament.

Future generations will look back on the late 1970s and early 1980s as one of the game's 'golden ages'. The last decade has been exceptionally rich in excellence: Viv Richards and Barry Richards, Greenidge and Gavaskar, Lloyd and Zaheer Abbas, Kallicharran and Viswanath, Rowe, Fredericks and the Chappell brothers, Haynes and Glenn Turner, Holding and Lillee, Marshall and Thomson, Garner and Hadlee, Roberts and Kapil Dev, Ian Botham and Imran Khan. On the law of averages there should be an anti-climax.

Nature abhors a void. If cricket should dine too freely on a surfeit of Test Matches, limited-overs knockabouts and personality, the doldrums of the 1950s and the late 1960s/early 1970s could yet return and the players and public seek solace in other diversions. Where would they turn? Whatever the shortcomings, however many intiatives have failed in the meantime, South Africa remains the only centre of cricket outside the accepted circle.

Changes are enforced only from positions of strength. Sri Lanka and New Zealand are hardly likely to change the structure of the international game. The West Indies have that advantage. They are the team that the world wants to see. The prospect of the withdrawal of that popular spectacle, provided that it is handled adroitly and not as a bluff that could be called, would make the administrators think seriously.

The Achilles' heel of Caribbean cricket is the region's lack of finance, small populations by world standards, and, by dint of geography, a fragile administrative structure. West Indians have had to go overseas for a full-time career. Most play in England or Australia, and others in New Zealand. South Africa, which is still very rich though perhaps not so much as hitherto, continues to be an attraction to those with reputations to sell or potential futures to mortgage.

West Indians will not be so welcome in South Africa if the region ceases to be the world's most powerful team. That advantage is more dubious than it seems at first sight. Any overture to the rising stars, whether English or Australian, could be on a more official level. In decline the West Indian connection will have less appeal to the Australians who would need then another team to balance their own contribution in administration and media coverage.

For the moment, however, West Indian playing expertise, Australian money, English tradition, and Indian/Pakistani popular support determine the course of world cricket. It is important that the South African question should be solved in that context on favourable terms rather than to wait until the pattern is disturbed to the advantage of South Africa or until individual Springboks form almost the entire backbone of the England side.

Eighteen

Professional Cricketers

For many years professional cricketers had to leave the region to pursue their careers overseas. By regular practice against top quality opposition they developed their own allround skills, but the sides played with little team cohesion. Running between wickets, team tactics, leadership and some aspects of their out-cricket left much to be desired. Only too often the West Indies broke down from a position of seeming superiority, because they did not know the extent of their own strength and ability, or how to attain it. Confidence came with experience.

Today's professionals are involved in first-class competition around the world and around the calendar. The result of this changed attitude is shown most clearly in the 5-0 'whitewash' of England in 1984. More often than not the West Indies recovered from a disappointing start to demonstrate a greater determination and grasp of strategy. The evolution from talented amateurs, entertaining but fragile, to fully-fledged professionals, going for a win by the shortest and most direct route, has been gradual but inevitable. The difference was reflected in the games in the 1970s against the Pakistanis, who played like the West Indian sides of the past.

Even before the end of the nineteenth century professionals were engaged to bowl and field at club members in the nets. Blacks, who, otherwise, could not expect election to membership, earned their presence there by toil. Pelham Warner observed in *Cricket in many Climes* that, even apart from the renowned Cumberbatch and Woods:

'The fielding of the side is brilliant, the black men, of whom there were five in the Trinidad eleven, being especially fine throws'

and from neat, trim Barbados

'a thoroughly good practice on the Pickwick ground at Kensington, where we found that more than one of the black men bowled uncommonly well'.

Woods went to England in 1900, where he and Burton took 150

wickets between them — the other six bowlers shared only another eighty. Cumberbatch did not go there until six years later when he was past his best, coming a long way behind Smith, Morrison, Layne and Ollivierre in the averages. Woods, it is recalled, bowled best without shoes, his sole tapping the earth, and begged his captain for permission to remove his boots during Gilbert Jessop's assault in hitting the tourists for 157 in an hour in their game against Gloucestershire. At home, professionals were required to ease down against batsmen of higher social status.

The patronal attitude of the age, in which the gentlemen took care of their professionals in exchange for their services on the pitch, is illustrated also in the story of the Hon. Vincent Brown, Attorney-General of Trinidad, offering Cumberbatch five dollars if he bowled out Lord Hawke. The bowler complied by knocking back the nobleman's middle-stump before he had scored. It was duelling at one step removed. For all their skill professionals were omitted from the early official territorial competition.

Even then the professionals were expected to master more than one skill. Lebrun Constantine, recognised by the pioneer visitors as a competent stumper, was also a leading batsman and bowler. On that first overseas tour he scored 113 against the M.C.C. at Lord's. He was in good company because the host side contained three of the game's natural aristocrats, Lord Harris, Dr W.G. Grace and Andrew Stoddart. The Trinidadian returned there in 1906 and came close to a third trip in 1923, but his son took his place.

From the earliest years West Indians could make a career in cricket in the English leagues. This code of competiton is common throughout the northern and midland counties but is associated most usually with Lancashire. Teams comprised ten amateurs, usually from the professional and commercial classes with alternative employment rather than from the social elite, and one professional, who was expected to win the match by his own effort. Consequently the latter was called upon to bat in various moods and styles depending on the state of the game, and to bowl throughout the innings with new ball and old.

Because of their league commitments several leading bowlers could not play in every Test Match in England. Learie Constantine played only at Manchester in 1933, and George Francis at Lord's. Manny Martindale bowled so well that season that the presence of a regular partner could have turned the balance. Yet in the long term West Indian cricket gained much from the education in the leagues. The professionals tightened their game by experience, and passed on the knowledge to their successors.

In one summer of afternoon matches they played against the varied best batting and bowling from Australia, the West Indies, New Zealand, India and South Africa, as well as the many Englishmen who for one reason or another had fallen out of the county championship system. That extent of competition would have taken more than a lifetime to acquire in Test Matches. Until the scope of opportunity was expanded in the 1960s the leagues provided the only substantial professional outlet.

The ties between the community and its professional were considerable. Learie Contantine, the league cricketer par excellence, took the name of 'Nelson', as well as that of 'Maraval' in his native land, into his title when he was ennobled. On Frank Worrell's death in 1967 the flags flew at half-mast on official buildings at Radcliffe. Fourteen years later local residents Cecil and Jessica Lockwood, who stayed at the Windsor Hotel in Hastings at the same time as myself, travelled to Barbados to pay tribute at his grave. They have similar affection for Clive Lloyd, another Lancastrian by adoption and grace.

Clashes of loyalty to contending codes were inevitable. The authorities wanted George Headley to go to England in 1939 as an amateur, even though his skills commanded a professional contract in the leagues. The incentive of a career in cricket attracted many territorial representatives of the late 1940s, 1950s and early 1960s to England. There they were able to play every week of the season instead of the two or three occasional appearances each year for their island. When the regional selectors could not find them at the time of picking the 1957 touring team, Conrad Hunte and Clairemont Depeiza were available readily for an English club.

At home Depeiza was a wicketkeeper who could bat, as he showed only too well in his world record partnership with Denis Atkinson against Australia at Kensington in 1955. In England he achieved success as a bowler. Because of that master-of-all-trades experience few West Indians could not turn their arm over when it was needed. Test Matches played by the West Indies at Old Trafford in Manchester, in the heart of the leagues, are attended by more front-line cricketers of that period, some forgotten too easily by the younger generation, than those at any venue outside the Caribbean.

A Commonwealth XI drawn extensively, but not exclusively, from league professionals played regular games against an England XI in festivals at the end of the summer. In 1953, taken as a random example, Frank Worrell, Clyde Walcott and Sonny Ramadhin were included in the same team as the Australian spinners George Tribe and Bruce Dooland, Indian allrounder G.S. Ramchand and the outstanding New Zealander John Reid. Commonwealth sides of similar composition undertook a number of tours to the Indian sub-continent.

A migrant people, West Indians have travelled abroad for many years. Sam Morris, who played for Australia against England in 1884, had West Indian descent. Although those who went to the non-cricket countries of North America faded prematurely from the game, some who made their way to England, Australia and New Zealand enjoyed a second career. The contribution of some of those who played in the English championship in the 1950s and 1960s in examined later.

Simpson Guillen of Trinidad, wicketkeeper on the tour to New Zealand in 1952, settled so easily into that country that he went to live there, representing his new home country against the West Indies three times in the next series four years later. Bruce Pairaudeau, who played for the region between 1953 and 1957, was the only visiting batsman other than Everton Weekes to make a century on the tour. He, too, settled there, became one of the first overseas players to captain a provincial side, and played for the Northern and Central Districts against the Englishmen in 1959. The tradition has deep roots. S.G. Smith, the Trinidadian allrounder who later represented Northamptonshire, went on to play for Auckland in the years immediately after the First World War.

The strength of Australian cricket, as well as the distance and difficulty of travelling, prevented for many years the importation of West Indian professionals. Such transactions were unknown at the time of the first tour in 1930/31, and in view of the home country's superiority in 1951/52, there was little call to offer the leading tourists competitive terms, even if the opportunities had been there. The situation was changed by the impact of Frank Worrell's team in 1960/61. The Australian public could not get enough of those West Indians.

Wesley Hall in Queensland, Gary Sobers in South Australia and Rohan Kanhai in Victoria were among the leading overseas players in the Sheffield Shield domestic first-class competition in the 1960s. Knowledge of the conditions, however, did not prevent the one-sided defeat of the next touring side. Sobers, in particular, became at home in Australia, where in 1972 he hit a double-century for the Rest of the World which has been described as the most brilliant innings of the modern era. More recent West Indians have competed in Shield and grade tournaments.

The standard of club cricket in Scotland and Ireland is higher than is often realised. The former attracted a range of professionals from Rohan Kanhai and those of similar international renown to Irvine Iffla of Jamaica and others whose celebrity did not extend far beyond their homeland. Everton Mattis played in Ireland the same year in which he was selected for the West Indies. It should not be overlooked that the emerald isle cricketers defeated the West Indian tourists to England in 1969.

Other links have been established with the Netherlands, especially through player-coaches from Barbados. C.A. Ollivierre took school-boy sides to that country in the years leading up to the outbreak of the Second World War. Alvin Greenidge was summoned from his Dutch club to field for the injury-hit West Indies in the Fourth Test Match against England at The Oval in London in 1980.

Ollivierre and S.G. Smith pioneered West Indian involvement in the English county championship. Early participation was restricted generally to the socially privileged and to graduates from the principal schools and colleges. John Cameron, vice-captain of the West Indies in 1939, represented both Cambridge University, as did Jackie and Rolph Grant, and Somerset. Thus he laid down the path followed by Viv Richards and Joel Garner. He and a few others apart, Common-wealth cricketers took part in the championship only after they had given up Test Match aspirations.

Roy Marshall, heir apparent to the Rae-Stollmeyer partnership, and Danny Livingstone, the first Antiguan batsman to make his name in regular first-class competition, made Hampshire a power in the 1960s. In the 1950s Peter Wight of Guyana was a leading run-maker for Somerset, when the county was not as fashionable as it is today, and became later a leading umpire. Carlton Forbes, the Jamaican all-rounder with Nottinghamshire, was one of the most effective, and under-rated, county players of the same era. Middlesex, led two gen-erations earlier by Pelham Warner, picked Jamaican legspinner Harry Latchman and fast bowler R.W. Stewart as the precursors of a side in the early 1980s containing Roland Butcher, Norman Cowans, Neil Williams, Wilfred Slack and Wayne Daniel.

Warwickshire, set around the substantial West Indian community in Birmingham, included fast bowler S.S. Griffiths against John Goddard's second side in 1957, and their attack was spearheaded by Rudi Webster of Barbados in the early 1960s. In the next decade, when most of the then current Test Match team were involved in the championship, the county called on at the same time Rohan Kanhai, Deryck Murray, Alvin Kallicharran and Lance Gibbs, as well as Bill Bourne, a Barbadian from the local community.

The rebuilding of the pace attack for the tour to England in 1969, following the retirement of Wesley Hall and Charlie Griffith, and in the years immediately afterwards drew heavily on those with experi-ence of that country's conditions, particularly John Shepherd, Vanburn Holder and, later, Keith Boyce. In the runaway success of 1973, Boyce opened the bowling with Bernard Julien, another quick bowler with regular English experience. In that rubber every West Indian who scored over fifty or took four wickets in an innings played in the county championship.

Gary Sobers brought new life to Nottinghamshire, title-holders frequently in the nineteenth century but fallen on recent hard times. In 1968 the Barbadian left-hander became the first, and for a long time the only, batsman to hit every delivery of a six-ball over for six. It happened at Swansea and Glamorgan's Malcolm Nash was the unfortunate bowler. Sobers' service for the county, as well as his many other commitments, contributed to the apparent staleness which affected his international performance towards the end of his career.

West Indians have prospered from their participation in the English county championship. Since the defeat in 1969, when the side was depleted substantially, the four subsequent Test Match series were won decisively. The region, also, won two out of the three Prudential Cup limited-overs tournaments and reached the final of the other. It is interesting to speculate how earlier teams would have fared with a similar depth of experience of the country.

It was inevitable that the increased international activity of the 1970s should cause the players to seek a corporate representative voice in their conditions. Deryck Murray, the wicketkeeper and long-serving regional vice-captain, became their spokesman. Nevertheless his position was made superfluous by the intervention of Australian television magnate Kerry Packer's World Series Cricket which gave the front-line players an unexpected opportunity to demonstrate their earning power to the embarrassment of the conventional administrators.

The schism sundered international cricket between the end of 1977 and early 1979. Repercussions were different in each country. England, beaten decisively by the West Indies in 1976, were already improving and, through losing comparatively few established cricketers to World Series Cricket, became one of the strongest sides, challenged only by New Zealand, who were untouched by the trouble. India, similarly intact, were exceptionally weak but took the chance to beat the reserve-strength West Indians.

The mercurial Pakistanis were disorientated and, not unexpectedly, the Australians suffered severely. A poor replica replaced the strong team of the mid-1970s. The wound was mortal. Even since that country has been united again, Australia has not regained its traditional position of power. Whereas their principal opponents were weakened by the dissension, the West Indies went into the crisis almost united. As a result the region failed in conventional Test Matches, but returned easily to their former pre-eminence on the restoration of harmony.

Instant action provided the appeal of World Series Cricket. The statistics are not usually stored and savoured as the cognoscenti do for traditional competition. Most of the so-called 'super tests' were presented in Australia, but the circus came to the Caribbean in early 1979. The five-game rubber was drawn at one victory each. In spite of the devalued status of the home series against the same opponents a year earlier, these contests between the best cricketers in the world failed to make a permanent impact.

The West Indies won by 369 runs at Sabina Park. Clive Lloyd caned 197 from the formidable attack of Dennis Lillee, Jeff Thomson and Gary Gilmour, which had caused his own tourists such damage three years earlier. Australia squared accounts in winning by 24 runs at Queen's Park, a success they owed to centuries by Bruce Laird and Greg Chappell as Michael Holding's pace and Albert Padmore's offspin almost turned the tables. There were draws in the riot-disturbed game at Kensington, in the rain at Bourda where Collis King and Greg Chappell hit hundreds, and at St John's. In Antigua the tourists, for whom in the first innings Greg Chappell reached three figures for the third time in the series, were rescued by century-maker Rodney Marsh and by Lillee's incisive bowling after Lawrence Rowe had taken the West Indies to a lead of over two hundred runs.

The pace of modern international cricket is considerable. Between 1928 and 1939 the West Indies made three tours to England and one to Australia, and received two England teams, in a total of 21 Test Matches. Manny Martindale, for example, played in only 10 Test Matches in his seven-year career. His successors play as many in one calendar year. The problems, as well as the opportunities, of the two generations are correspondingly different.

Malcolm Marshall came into the regional side for the tour of India in 1978/79 with the experience of only one previous first-class match. He claims that with his commitments for the West Indies, for Barbados and for Hampshire he had only two months rest from top-level competition in the next seven years. His experience is unusual only in that he has avoided any long-term injury or indisposition which would have given him some respite from continuous action.

In the early months of 1983 the West Indies were hosts to the Indians, followed immediately with a visit to England for the Prudential Cup competition, undertook an extended tour of India and Australia at the end of the year and the beginning of the next, hurried home for the visit of the Australians, returned to England in the summer for a full Test Match series, went straight away again to Australia for conventional Test Matches and two limited-overs tournaments, and came back to the Caribbean just in time to take on the New Zealanders.

It is small wonder that the West Indians have become such competent cricketers in all conditions, and the only team in the last decade to
win consistently away from home. In the twelve months from early
1983 they had to cope with the varying conditions of three overseas
countries and to the different pace of pitches in their own component
territories. From the inception of Test Match cricket in 1928 their
predecessors had to wait two decades before the first visit to India.
There was a gap of over twenty years between the first and second
tours to Australia, but the event is now almost annual.

English critics, in particular, argue that the poor performance of
their own team has been due to the influence of instant cricket in that
the players are confused as to which tactics and pace of game should
be adopted. The West Indians have not had that difficulty, even
though they have engaged in an even wider range of codes of competition. The region has dominated Test Matches and won the principal
limited-over tournaments. Even the defeat in the final of the Prudential Cup competition in 1983 derived from causes other than
unfamiliarity with the conditions of play.

The informal West Indian nature is conducive to assessing each
situation on its own merit rather than in the light of some precon-
ceived plan or strategy. A bad ball deserves to be punished whether it
is the first ball of a timeless Test Match or the last in a backyard
thrash-around. Runs have to be taken quickly. Sharp fielding is
essential. Bowling directed positively takes wickets and prevents the
batsmen from getting the upper hand. Let others confuse themselves
with theory.

Hitherto there has been one important difference between an
English professional and his West Indian counterpart. For years the
former's experience was confined to the three-day game. The West
Indian's professional background is rooted in the leagues where he
was required to perform with bat and ball as the situation demanded.
The league legacy has been a key factor in the ability to adapt to the
changing conditions of contemporary cricket in four, or even five,
continents.

A modern cricketer does not stop travelling. The pioneers took
several weeks to reach England by sea, amusing themselves with
games aboard ship. They watched the tropical sunshine fade by
degrees into the mist and rain. Interest in a forthcoming tour was built
up from inverviews at ports of call or cabled conversation. On arrival
the visitors were entertained at a round of social engagements and
afforded the opportunity to break themselves in with inconsequential
games against ad hoc sides before settling down to the serious part of
the programme.

191

Much of the blame for the failure to play up to expectations in Australia in 1951/52 was attributed at the time to the itinerary which permitted only one first-class game, against then lowly Queensland, before the Test Match series commenced. Long train journeys throughout the length and breadth of India were tiring. In 1948/49 two days of continuous travel from Lahore in Pakistan preceded the start of the game against the powerful West Zone at Poona. Not surprisingly the Indian batsmen benefitted from below-form fielding and led by 200 runs before Clyde Walcott and Ken Rickard saved the game.

It was indeed hard luck if a key member of the party sustained injury. The choice lay between sending home for a replacement, who might not arrive for another two to three weeks, by which time the invalid could have recovered, or drafting into the side an inferior player more readily available on the spot. In 1948/49 the Jamaican, George Mudie, sailed half-way to India as a replacement before he learned that his presence was not required and he had to turn back. It couldn't happen today.

In addition to the ease of travelling from one country to another, air travel has made possible more compact and complex itineraries within a region. Hosts and tourists criss-cross the Caribbean or Australia for matches, often in different codes, arranged on consecutive days at venues situated hundreds of miles apart. Old-time players who criticise their successors for being injury-prone or liable to lapses in form do not take sufficiently into consideration the intensity of competition.

Traditionally the West Indies tour England more frequently than anywhere else. The gaps between the first eight tours were considerable — 1900, 1906, 1923, 1928, 1933, 1939, 1950, 1957 and 1963. Careers could blossom and fade between visits, and the longest intervals are explained only partially by the intervention of world wars. Since then, however, the world has contracted and the tours, including those in three Prudential Cup summers, have become more rapid — 1966, 1969, 1973, 1975, 1976, 1979, 1980, 1983, 1984.

The first Indian team did not come to the Caribbean until 1953, the first Australians in 1955, the first Pakistanis in 1958 and the first New Zealanders in 1972. The latter two did not return until another nineteen and thirteen years respectively had passed. Nevertheless, over the last two decades there has been almost, if not quite, one tour a year. There are few international celebrities that West Indian spectators have not had the chance to see at first-hand.

Cricket has changed by more than the floodlights and circles on the pitch for some one-day contests. The players even look different. Since the initial impact of the new wave of fast bowlers in the mid-1970s the majority of batsmen have worn helmet-protection, though the outstanding few, like Viv Richards, refuse to have this line of defence. Helmets and padding have given fieldsmen the confidence to creep in closer. Whatever the aesthetic merits, and the point is argued strongly on either side, helmets testify to the pressure of the combat at the crease.

The number of first-class matches on tour has been reduced. Until recently West Indian teams in England had a programme of at least a month of two three-day games each week before the first Test Match. Now the tour starts a couple of weeks later and includes three limited-over representative matches and another one or two one-day games against the counties with at the most only two or three first-class fixtures. The itinerary has been cut down also in Australia and in India, and in the Caribbean, where in the early days each territory had two games against the tourists.

It is no longer possible for an outsider to work himself into the Test Match team with a series of good performances, as Wesley Hall achieved in India in 1958/59. The first eleven is known from the start of the tour and replacements receive their chance only in the event of injury or lost form. Because there is now no 'safety net' of following county or state games in which to make restitution, every player is under greater pressure to succeed in Test Matches, each one of which can become a test of confidence.

The complexion of cricket, if not its face, has been changed by sponsorship. The major limited-overs competitions have captured the imagination of the public communications media and a large section of the public. Yet they are not accorded the first-class status given to many more minor games of lesser interest. The match-winning exploits of Viv Richards, Collis King and Joel Garner in the final of the Prudential Cup in 1979, though among the most thrilling in any international competition, are not recorded in their first-class career statistics.

Commercial investment has brought cricket to many areas from which direct participation was once absent. Sponsorship has provided the only significant regional competition. Without the Shell Shield, the Leeward and Windward Islands may well not have gained such swift attention and confidence. Youth tours and sponsored coaching schemes encourage the rising generation. The night-time knockabouts in pyjama-suits and the enhanced excellence of Test Match perform-ance, especially fielding, are different sides of the same coin.

Attention to the other end of the age scale is equally important. In the past retired cricketers could do little to remain in the game except, as with George Francis at Pickwick, to serve as groundsmen. Administrators and managers were drawn substantially from the same exclusive social classes as the captains. There were no career umpires, and coaching opportunities were restricted to colleges/schools and to commercial enterprises. It is little wonder that the majority of cricketers leaving the Caribbean as league professionals made their lives overseas.

The coaching programme of the 1960s bore fruit in the next decade. The increased frequency in the making and receiving of tours has raised the number of openings for managers/assistant managers, drawn now from wider social strata, and coaches. Personal example and communication have been always the main ingredients in passing on cricket wisdom, but, in the nature of things, such matters rely on meeting the right mentors at the right time. Now the lessons of experience are directed to the next generation in a less haphazard manner.

Glossary

allrounder a player who merits selection as both a batsman and a bowler. The term is used frequently also to describe a player who owes his inclusion in the team to a combination of batting and bowling skills.

amateurs players who usually, on account of their affluence and social standing, could afford to play cricket without direct payment. In the pioneer days amateurs often were selected in preference to professionals, irrespective of relative ability, if they could meet their own travel, accommodation and subsistence costs. Captains were chosen from the amateurs because of their financial independence and their social and educational standards and style of living.

batsman-wicketkeeper chosen primarily as a batsman but is also a competent wicketkeeper.

bodyline a variation of leg theory in which the ball was delivered at great pace in line with the batsman's body and rising sharply. The intention was to force the batsman, defending himself with the bat against potential physical injury, into lofting a catch.

bouncer/bumper a delivery pitched short, fast and rising sharply towards the batsman.

carrying the bat achievement of an opening batsman in batting without losing his wicket throughout an innings in which the other ten batsmen have been dismissed. The term is used incorrectly of a batsman other than an opener who is undefeated at the end of the innings.

chinaman the left-arm bowler's offbreak to a right-handed batsman.

club competition anything from a village knock-about for casual enjoyment to keen contests only just below first-class level. In the West Indies, where until recently there has been less international and regional competition, the leading players retain their club associations for longer than in England, and in some territories club matches are regarded popularly as first-class.

covered pitch the pitch is now covered at the end of the day and if play is suspended for rain. Consequently its character is affected less than hitherto by the elements. Previously a sticky wicket/pitch, affected by rain and subsequently drying under the sun, was extremely helpful to spin bowlers, causing wickets to fall rapidly. In such conditions fortunes could fluctuate substantially during a match, and batsmen were required to master greater defensive skills.

extras known also as 'sundries', runs added to the score but not scored by the batsmen, and comprise byes, leg-byes, wides and no-balls.

first-class cricket matches of three or more days' duration officially adjudged first-class and, at the time of writing, in the West Indies consists of matches played by teams representing Barbados, Guyana, Jamaica, Trinidad & Tobago, the Windward Islands and the Leeward Islands either for the Shell Shield or against other opponents adjudged first-class, the final of the inter-county tournament for the Jones Cup in Guyana, and the Beaumont Cup match in Trinidad & Tobago.

follow on the side batting first and leading by a stipulated margin may ask the side batting second to follow their innings and bat again. The margin required has varied from time to time.

full tour in which games are played against all, or the majority of, first-class teams in the host country/region with a programme of Test Matches at each major venue. The greater present facility for air travel and condensed schedules has led to more abbreviated tours with fewer Test Matches, a reduced number of other first-class games, and extra limited-overs fixtures.

googly known also as the 'bosey', delivery bowled out of the back of the right hand with an apparently leg-break action which on pitching spins as an off-break.

green pitch/wicket well-covered with grass, contains much moisture early in the day, pitch helping the quicker bowlers to obtain extra life and lift and assisting in the bowling of cutters. Such pitches are found most often in England.

hat-trick bowler's achievement in taking three wickets with consecutive deliveries in the same match.

league cricket here primarily competition below first-class standard but often involving first-class players. It is very competitive, each team plays the others at least once during the season, and matches are generally scheduled for completion in one day.

leg theory tactics of pitching consistently on or just outside the leg-stump with most of the fieldsmen on the leg-side. It is designed to limit the batsman's scope for playing attacking strokes.

limited overs competition known also as 'one-day cricket', now played extensively by otherwise first-class sides, usually on a 'knock-out' basis. This code of cricket has evolved its own techniques and practices, restrictions on bowling and fielding, and, not being subject to first-class control, has experimented with innovations such as coloured clothing and floodlights.

M.C.C. (Marylebone Cricket Club) founded in 1787 and based at Lord's, for many years the game's administrative and legislative authority. Earlier in this century the Club took over from independent patrons the responsibility for organising England's overseas tours. Consequently the team was des-

ignated 'M.C.C.' for all games except Test Matches.

middle-order batting those batsmen coming in after the opening partnership and first-wicket down and before the specialist bowlers and wicket-keeper.

new ball used at the start of each innings or after a stipulated number of overs. It aids the faster bowlers because the shine causes it to swing more in the air and, being harder, it comes off the pitch at greater pace.

oval name of several cricket grounds including those at Bridgetown, Port of Spain and Adelaide. The term 'The Oval' (without qualification) is used generally to refer to the ground in South London where the first Test Match in England was played in 1880. Here it is referred to usually as the 'London Oval.'

over the wicket method of bowling in which the bowler faces the wicket in delivery releasing the ball with the arm nearer to the stumps.

patron socially prominent and authorative person in the early days of the game's development who took the lead in establishing the team's character by involvement in its financing, selection, encouraging younger talent and arranging fixtures, whether within a locality or for a touring team. Subsequently these responsibilities have been taken over by committees and organisations.

professionals engaged initially to instruct 'gentlemen' in the game, to bowl at them for practice, and, then, to play for the team. They came from the less well-off who could not afford to take time away from work to play cricket unless they were recompensed by payment. The distinction became obsolete in the early 1960s, since when all cricketers at the higher levels of competition have been paid.

quick bowlers seek to obtain wickets by beating the batsman primarily by speed of delivery, by change of pace, or by using the seam to cut or swing the ball.

Rand rebels established players attracted by high payment to participate in an alternative 'representative' competition in South Africa, which had been isolated from accepted international cricket. These players were banned from conventional cricket either for a limited period or, in the West Indies, for life.

representative cricket competition in which the players are the official representatives of their country, region or similar entity. It describes also the highest level of competition not sanctioned as a Test Match. Thus, the series between the West Indies and England in 1925/26 was representative and that four years later was described similarly at the time but has been classified subsequently as Test Match.

round the wicket method of bowling in which the ball is released with the arm furthest from the stumps and with the bowler's back to them.

rubber series of three to six Test Matches contested by the same two teams. The West Indies compete against England and against Australia for the Wisden Trophy and the Frank Worrell Trophy respectively.

slow bowlers seek to obtain wickets by beating the batsman primarily by spin, by deceiving him in the flight of the ball, and by variations of length in delivery. The ball is spun by either wrist or finger action.

tail the lower batting positions, specialist bowlers and wicketkeeper, who are not expected to bat for long or to score many runs.

test matches the highest level of international competition and contested today usually over five days. The teams enjoying Test Match status are Australia, England, India, New Zealand, the West Indies, Pakistan and Sri Lanka. South Africa, a former Test Match country, has been banned from accepted competition because of their racially exclusive policy.

wicketkeeper-batsman chosen primarily as a wicketkeeper but also has significant batting skill.

Wisden cricket's authorative publication established in 1864 and respected as the cricketers' 'bible'. It contains the laws of the game, reports of all first-class matches and other principal competitions played throughout the world in the preceding twelve months, extensive records, obituaries, book reviews and articles of topical interest.

World Cup known sometimes as the 'Prudential Cup' after its initial sponsors, a limited-overs competition contested every four years by all the major Test Match teams and the leading non-Test country. It was played in England in 1975, 1979 and 1983, and is scheduled to take place in India/Pakistan in 1987. There is no comparable first-class competition.

World Series Cricket international matches conducted in competition to conventional Test Matches, and operating some different playing practices, initiated by Kerry Packer, an Australian television magnate, contracting many of the world's leading players at the end of 1977. These games were not recognised as official and the contracted players were not selected for traditional Test Matches. The breach was healed in early 1979. World Series Cricket made a particularly strong impact in the West Indies, Australia and Pakistan.

Index

198